Real Healing,
Real Awakening

*A Comprehensive Guide to Overcoming Suffering and
Expanding Your Consciousness*

PHIL GOLDING

BALBOA.
PRESS

A DIVISION OF HAY HOUSE

Poems by Phil Golding

Balboa Press books may be ordered through booksellers or by contacting:

Balboa Press
A Division of Hay House
1663 Liberty Drive
Bloomington, IN 47403
www.balboapress.com.au
1-(877) 407-4847

ISBN: 978-1-4525-0689-0 (sc)
ISBN: 978-1-4525-0690-6 (e)

Certain images were purchased from
The Big Box of Art from Hemera Technologies

Printed in the United States of America

Balboa Press rev. date: 11/09/2012

The following images in Diagrams 1,3,4,7,8,10 and Table 5 were purchased from The Big Box of Art from Hemera Technologies."

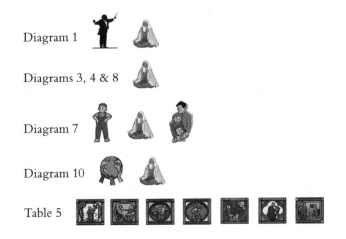

Diagram 1

Diagrams 3, 4 & 8

Diagram 7

Diagram 10

Table 5

All other images are the work of Phil Golding.

This work is dedicated to spreading peace and self realisation to all as a part of the work of guiding humanity toward being one harmonious family

ACKNOWLEDGMENTS

As I do with all my writing, I thank everyone who has crossed my path in life because you are the rich source of experience that has enabled me to learn about life and to place my experience into book form. Thanks in particular to all my clients and students who have given me the opportunity to transform my life experience into practical knowledge.

As a part of the evolution of this book, I thank Silvana Nagyl and Leonie Clarke for your help with editing. Thanks to Balboa Press for being patient and supportive.

I especially thank my wife, Osha, for sticking by me and supporting me in many ways throughout these long projects.

CONTENTS

EXERCISES

TABLES

DIAGRAMS

POEMS

APPENDIX

THE HEALER

I sit down opposite her.
Her penetrating, yet compassionate eyes
envelop me in an aura of acceptance.
Her gentle questions probe my vulnerable emotions
as they look for an escape but find no excuse.

She presents me with no agenda,
no assumptions that misread me,
only space carefully prepared for me to fill,
which my insecure self can't help but pour into.
She merges with me, and yet does not lose herself.
We are strangely one yet I'm freer than I have ever been.

I find myself revealed and brace for judgement,
but find only the calm smile of one who can identify and understand.
It washes over me like a soothing balm on my open wounds.
I suddenly laugh at the pain as though it is no longer mine.

I willingly open myself to her now.
We are partners in this dark journey of self-discovery
that has the promise of a fountain-head of Light divine.
That mysterious source of wonder, desire and dread.
She is the bearer of this Light, the revealer of the real.

It is my fourth visit to this place of solace.
She tells me that it's time to do some healing
as she prepares to guide me again into my awakening heart.
The fear of facing myself briefly confronts me as I pause at the heart's door
but is easily overcome by my longing for the touch of Soul.

AUTHOR'S NOTE

Those of you who have read my first book, "Five Steps to Freedom", will notice that it bears some similarities to Real Healing, Real Awakening, which is indeed true. Both books share the same initial template, a smaller booklet that I wrote for my clients, and therefore some sections are quite similar. So for you, this book will contain some revision. However, you will also notice that this book is far more comprehensive. Real Healing, Real Awakening delves deeper into philosophy and spirituality, and also contains a more fundamental message, and therefore, in many ways, a more powerful message. This book is designed to expand your consciousness further, and to deliver you to an important stage of personal development, where fear is no longer your enemy, but your servant. My poem, "Ode to Fear", on page 140, speaks of this mystery. By the time you reach the end of this book, and in particular, if you read it in the way that I suggest in the introduction, the answer to this mystery will be revealed to you, along with the immense power and potential that it contains. May your journey in this life unlock the chains that restrict your Soul and set your spirit free!

INTRODUCTION

Do you want to be free of fear, confusion and suffering? Do you want to gain peace of mind, fulfilment and self-empowerment? Do you want to be able to give something positive back to this world as a part of expressing your unique potential?

This book is designed to help you achieve these goals and to make a real difference to your life. It will do this by fundamentally changing the way you see yourself and the world around you. This change will both awaken and realign your consciousness to where it is in harmony with the Universal Laws of Consciousness. The Universal Laws of Consciousness determine the healing and enlightening of the human mind and its governing Soul. This healing and awakening will only occur, however, provided the information in this book is **studied**, **practiced** and **applied** the way that it is intended. The three highlighted words in the last sentence are chosen carefully and have significant meaning.

Studying this book means reading it several times whilst contemplating the subject matter. It means highlighting in the book what you don't understand at first, so that you can return to this material and examine it more deeply. It means taking note of what particularly applies to you and highlighting this. It means writing out the important concepts in your own words in your journal to help you assimilate the information and also draw forth your own intuitive knowing. It means seeking out those who are experienced on the path of self-realisation, even the author of this book, so that you can discuss the subject matter in order to deepen your understanding and clear up any confusions that inevitably arise.

Be aware that you are trying to access fourth dimensional information (personal experience) from a two dimensional medium. This requires a particular approach, which I will explore with you more deeply further on in the introduction.

The word, **practicing**, means doing the various exercises that are laid out in this book conscientiously and repeatedly so that you build within your consciousness a level of competency in the art of healing and awakening. You may want to seek out the assistance of a mentor and or counselling practitioner who is personally experienced in emotional healing and the process of self-awareness.

Applying this book to your life means putting what you learn, as you progress in your studies and practise, to your everyday affairs. When you think differently for long enough, you will then feel, perceive and act differently. When you act differently persistently enough, your world will change, because all those around you will respond differently to you, to varying degrees, due to your different actions. Be aware though, because you are still learning and growing, your actions will not always lead to the desired outcomes. This must be accepted as a natural part of the learning process and seen as a rich source of further learning while you seek a better understanding, using the material in this book.

In other words, you will do what is required to master this subject as with any form of study.

As with the exercises that are placed within this book, there are other aids to help you take this material into your conscious-awareness (see definition on page 147) such as summaries at the end of each chapter, tables and diagrams, clarity boxes and affirmations. These can be used as quick reference guides when it comes to reviewing the material. In addition to this is an index section at the back of the book.

As an extension of what you can learn from this book, I have also offered references for further reading, so watch out for the little reference numbers within the text and the footnotes. For your convenience (and mine), I have made extensive use of the free internet encyclopaedia, Wikipedia. This will give you a quick and reliable reference guide that, unlike other sites that come and go, will remain in place for perhaps generations. Other excellent features of Wikipedia are the fact that its accuracy is being constantly monitored and updated and also each article has many further links and references attached to it.

As you read this book, you will quickly be made aware that it offers a working framework on the nature of the human mind and the process of consciousness expansion. This framework is not meant to be dogmatised. In other words, it is not meant to be taken as the final word. Frameworks/concepts/theories are like vehicles. They are meant to take you a certain distance along a particular journey. The journey in question here is the journey to enlightenment, or in more basic terms, the journey out of suffering and into peace and harmony.

We are all progressing toward an ultimate truth, a natural law that is a foundation in the fabric of the cosmos. This is the truth of Unconditional Love. Aided by an appropriate framework, our capacity to comprehend this truth increases as we venture along this path. A basic framework that is useful at the beginning of a journey to enlightenment would not be so useful, say, two thirds the way along that journey. The new framework would need to be more sophisticated so that it represents an appropriate next step on that journey of real understanding. If the framework is not advanced enough (or not within the field of endeavour of the student), it will lose the interest of the student. If the framework is too advanced, it can lead to confusion, anxiety, a sense of inadequacy and could also attract disbelief. The usefulness of a framework therefore, is determined by its accurate reflection of ultimate truth, that are the Universal Laws of Consciousness, and the appropriate level of sophistication for the individual accessing the information. Again, this is normal for any course of study. This book offers a framework that is designed to take you to a point of healing and awakening where you have gained the ability to face and overcome any challenge that may cross your path.

In Buddhism, this point along the path of healing and awakening is regarded as an essential and significant stage to enlightenment. It constitutes a fundamental shift in your consciousness where your higher nature has taken definite control over your lower nature. Here you have entered into a level of consciousness where you are intuitively aware of, and living in accord with, the higher laws of consciousness.

In other words, you are able, in large measure, to know how to arrive at the right course of action in any given situation that is for the highest good of all. Within this knowing is also the knowing of how to take the best care of yourself. You have become skilfully self-responsible.

Those of us who have reached this significant stage of consciousness are not yet perfect. We still make mistakes. We still lose our way at times, but we are aware enough to sense when this lapse in consciousness is occurring and we are ready to face our mistakes. All experience in life, no matter what that is, for us is an opportunity to learn more about ourself and to expand our consciousness even further. We have not fully completed our journey to ultimate enlightenment, but we have genuinely become a part of the solution for this world, instead of being a part of the problem. We are amongst the new wave of consciousness that is leading humanity forward to being one harmonious community, however long that may take. We are able to do this simply by being ourself, by being a representative of the Universal Law of Unconditional Love in our own humble way. Together we constitute the new hope for humanity. Does this inspire you?

This book is based on the truth of Unconditional Love and the Wisdom that is contained within its power. For this reason, you will notice that the word "Love" is written with a capital letter when it is referred to in its ultimate potential as the Universal Life-Force, and in lower case when it is referred to as a general and variable expression of human desire. Some other significant words will be capitalised for the same reason.

As you read this book, you will also encounter some curious uses of the English language. I will often use the word *ourself* instead of *ourselves*. Ourself is of course a plural joined to a singular. I use this invented term, and other similar terms, throughout the book to reinforce the common experience of *our* collective humanity—*self*. Real Healing, Real Awakening is describing and exploring a journey of consciousness expansion that encompasses all humanity. Everyone, at some point on their way of this greatest of journeys, will become aware of this fact. I am talking about the evolution of consciousness that applies to every individual and also humanity as a whole. This implies that there is more to experience than this one limited, physical life. This statement may not yet make sense to you at this time, due to the limits of your own conceptual framework. In time it will, as you make your own way along this journey. I am writing therefore, about something that we all share, whether we are consciously aware of it or not.

For the same reason, I extensively use the term *we* instead of *you* or *I* or *his* or *her* or *them* or *they*. Another reason I have chosen to use such inclusive terms is that I want to include myself in this journey with you. I want you to know that I am walking with you on this journey. I am not some detached expert. I have lived and I am living this journey with you. What I have written has come from my own hard won experience. Bear this in mind when you read this book. Each paragraph is not just a theory, it is lived experience. The two dimensional words on the page in front of you contain living four dimensional experiences of great depth and meaning. In order to enter into this four dimensional richness, you must open your heart to what is written and then experience attempting to put it into action. Before you can do this, you must first open your heart to your own humanity with acceptance and compassion, no matter what you find.

"But I don't know how to do this", you may be saying to yourself. "All of this is a bit beyond me, and a bit scary for that matter."

Don't worry, the book will guide you and offer you the necessary stepping stones. All that is needed is your desire to be free and a solid commitment to pursue the ideal of Love as a healing and awakening force in your life. Love is right with you, like your closest companion. You may not know this yet. You may not be able to feel it yet, but you will, so long as you don't give up. You are on a quest to find your true Self, beyond what you can perhaps imagine right now. Just know that what you will inevitably find is beautiful beyond description, no matter what, in your present state of confusion, you think you are at this moment. The treasure of all treasures awaits you and it has your name on it.

CHAPTER ONE

GETTING STARTED

THE DOORWAY TO LOVE AND FULFILMENT

All feelings or emotions can be traced back to two sources, Love and fear. All feelings that are beneficial, life enhancing and healing come from Love. All emotions that are detrimental, destructive and painful come from fear. Everything we think, feel, say, and do in our journey through life is in some way an experience of these two opposing states of consciousness. The human experience of life is a constant pursuit of Love and fulfilment and the fear and pain of not being able to experience Love and fulfilment. As a demonstration of what I mean, read through the questions below and see how many you relate to.

- Do you struggle with sad and painful emotions?
- Do you worry a lot or suffer from anxiety?
- Do you have trouble letting go of hurts and regrets?
- Are you experiencing grief without knowing how to move on?
- Are you haunted by past trauma, afraid of the emotions that stalk your mind?
- Are you often burdened by guilt and shame?
- Do you experience yourself being frequently frustrated and angry?
- Do you feel cut off from others as though you don't fit in?

- Do you push your loved ones away, even when you long for their love?
- Do you feel as though you are not in control of your life, as though others are pulling your strings or have authority over you?
- Do you feel as though life is passing you by without a hope of catching up?
- Do you feel as though you have failed in your life and feel helpless and hopeless as a result?
- Do you feel trapped in a loveless relationship?
- Do you doubt if a fulfilling relationship will ever be yours to experience?
- Do you despair at all the suffering in this world, unable to find a meaning to such apparent chaos?
- Do you wish to live a meaningful life that may be of benefit to others, but don't really know where to begin?
- Do you want to really take charge of your life, to create a life that reflects your potential, your dreams, but find that you seem to make little progress?
- Do you want to reach into the heights of self-mastery but find yourself thwarted by your human limitations time and time again?
- Do you want to really experience Unconditional Love, as the giver and the receiver?

It is quite normal to identify with most of these questions, if not all of them, particularly if your consciousness is ready to expand. You have a strange knowing that there is more to life than all this drama that you can't seem free yourself from. The challenges of human life confront us all. Deep down we all basically want the same thing—Love and fulfilment. All too often though, fear and confusion invade our life, or we just get taken over with day-to-day survival. Don't despair, all this human stuff is the very doorway to your greater self, that greater reality that you intuitively sense.

There is a way to break free of these limitations. There is a way to overcome fear and suffering. In this day and age there are many teachers giving this important message from the basis of their own **personal experience**. In many different styles and flavours they are offering you a way to achieve this Holy Grail of Love and fulfilment. If you step back far enough you may be able to see that the same basic message is being communicated from these many different sources. This reveals a common truth. Personal experience is like that. It gives us new and more powerful ways to experience and demonstrate the same truth. After all, what works, works.

This knowledge, this truth, has also persisted throughout the ages of human history in many different cultures. It has been lost many times, only to re-emerge in another place and time, as though it has a life of its own. This knowledge is often called **"perennial wisdom"**.[1]

It is through the personal experience of this perennial wisdom that practitioners in the field of personal development and self-realisation, such as myself, come to know the answers to overcoming fear and suffering. Through this process, the doorway to real Love and fulfilment is revealed.

PERENNIAL WISDOM

We live in a wonderful age where we have access to so much recorded information that human beings have stored down through the ages. This information has revealed the teachings, and often the life examples, of great thinkers and sages in many different cultural settings throughout history.

What these guiding lights of humanity have revealed to us are the natural laws that govern the way things are. One science that is particularly ancient and has reached great heights is the study of the human mind and consciousness. These laws of consciousness have been termed *perennial* wisdom, because it is wisdom that endures unaltered through time. These laws or principles of consciousness are fundamental in their nature. This means that they apply to every human being.

When these fundamental laws of consciousness are understood enough and consistently applied to the way we think, feel and act, we naturally enter into a journey of emotional healing and increasing mental clarity as years of accumulated confusion unravel

---

[1] http://en.wikipedia.org/wiki/Perennial_Philosophy

and fall away. As a result, an increasing conscious-awareness of our potential as human beings arises. Rather than just cope with the life that we don't want, conscious-awareness and the right knowledge awakens within us the ability to create the life that we do want.

There are two of these fundamental laws of consciousness that underpin and empower all genuine wisdom teachings. These laws are:

1. **The Law of Unconditional Love.**
2. **The Law of Total Personal Responsibility.**

These two laws are linked inseparably together like yin and yang, or the two wings of the one bird, which I saw so eloquently put somewhere in a Buddhist text, the source I have since forgotten. This essential link is revealed when you consider that to be skilled in the law of Total Personal Responsibility is to have the wisdom to know how to Love Unconditionally under any circumstance. Here you have intelligent Love in action—a Love that enables you to honour all without compromising yourself. Such Wisdom can only be attained by firstly being the willing and dedicated student of these great principles and secondly through the depth of experience. In essence, this is the approach of ancient Chinese Taoism, and the root of any philosophical or spiritual/religious path that facilitates individual positive change and peaceful relations between people.

In Buddhism, these two fundamental laws are described in the first two steps of the "Noble Eightfold Path".[2] These two steps are known as the wisdom steps, and the rest of the steps of the Eightfold Path are about our journey of gaining that wisdom. The first step on the Eightfold Path is "Right View", which is ultimately Unconditional Love. The second is "Right Intent", which is Total Personal Responsibility.

In Christianity, the first law is: "Love the Lord thy God with all thy heart and with all thy Soul and with all thy strength and with all thy mind; and thy neighbour as thy self".[3] God is

---

[2] http://en.wikipedia.org/wiki/Noble_Eightfold_Path
[3] The Bible, International Standard Version (2008). Luke 10.27.

regarded as pure Unconditional Love. This law, therefore, urges us to devote ourself totally to Unconditional Love. Jesus then placed a second stage to this ultimate law; "Do unto others as you would have them do unto you"[4]—a clear statement of personal responsibility, and an excellent way to assess the right thing to do in any given situation.

FEELINGS AND EMOTIONS

When looking within, it helps to place emotions and feelings in different categories. Using this framework, emotions are said to flow from a lower, more vulnerable level of the mind. Emotions reveal our human needs, our fears and our pain. Feelings, on the other hand, flow from a higher self. Feelings reveal the highest potential of conscious-awareness. The highest feeling is Unconditional Love. Flowing from Unconditional Love are qualities such as joy and compassion.

It is hard to separate the words "feeling" and "emotion" in everyday language, as they are used interchangeably. As a concept though, it is useful to use them in this way for the sake of aiding clarity.

Feelings and emotions are designed by nature to inform us of the quality of our thinking. By paying attention to our feelings and emotions we can tell whether or not our mind is in tune with the natural laws of consciousness. This awareness is absolutely important for gaining command over our mind. If we are blind to the workings of our mind, we are then blind to the causes of our suffering.

It is very important that you learn to *feel* the difference between feeling and emotion. This is because the feelings associated with Unconditional Love are what you need to live your life by. It is from this higher level of your consciousness that you will find the capability to look after your emotional vulnerability.

Most of us let our emotions run our lives, which is like putting a young child in charge of our lives. Little wonder we get into such a mess. Feeling is like an all-wise and loving parent. Emotions are the child that needs to be cared for by that parent.

---

[4]   The Bible, International Standard Version (1984). Mathew 7.12.

Of course, learning to be the wise parent who looks after this "inner-child" is what this journey of life is all about. Much more will be said on this topic throughout this book.

PERSONAL EXPERIENCE

There are still sections in the more Western "orthodox" schools of science that remain sceptical about the ultimate power of Unconditional Love. There is a tendency to believe that evidence can only be impersonally gathered through statistical analysis in a laboratory, but the real world does not exist in a laboratory. The heart or consciousness can't be confined to a laboratory. Those in my field of Transpersonal Psychology regard life as the laboratory, although we still value orthodox scientific research. In addition though, we see our own life as the experiment, and ourself as the experimental subject. We first apply these principles of personal change to ourselves, because if we can't put this Wisdom to work in our own lives, how can we expect others to do the same, and how can we possibly know what it is really like? We endeavour to be less the out-of-touch expert and more the living example.

This knowledge therefore, can only be truly understood by personally opening your heart to a direct experience of it by endeavouring to put it into action. In this way, the knowledge is no longer just empty theory. Instead, with persistence, and if we are willing to step beyond the boundaries of our known self, we are able to *embody* the knowledge as we are applying it to our lives. In other words, it becomes a part of who we are and in the process, we are essentially transformed by the experience. Ultimately Life itself becomes our master teacher and our whole relationship with Life, including our inner-self, is inseparable to this process of learning. This is why it is so hard to teach perennial wisdom in a structured setting, such as a university.

Often we are able to experience the sensation of not just learning this knowledge, but in a deeper sense, awakening to it. We are able to gain an awareness that the centre of our own consciousness is where the source of this undying knowledge, this perennial wisdom, can be found. We discover another, more profound, more powerful dimension to ourself.

MY OWN JOURNEY

In 1984, at the age of 24, I discovered a way to break free of my own limitations. My life up to that point in time did not reflect my potential.

I had a difficult childhood for various reasons, such as having a sensitive character, experiencing the brunt of an angry and troubled brother and having parents who, even though they were good people, were not able to give me the protection and nurturing that I needed during this vulnerable time. These childhood difficulties and the conditioning that it gave me, contributed to chronic depression in my teenage and early adult years. As a result, I dropped out of high school and then college. I felt unloved and unworthy.

The depression further complicated my life by restricting my ability to make wise decisions on my own behalf, or I avoided making decisions altogether. I was stuck and afraid. I was also burdened with self-destructive thoughts and emotions and seriously considered suicide.

The chronic depression drove me into my first tentative steps to seek help. I began my healing and awakening process by attending self-help groups, based on the 12 step program of Alcoholics Anonymous. Someone close to me was recovering from alcoholism and was introduced to A.A. I attended an open A.A. meetings with her and when I saw the summery of the 12 step program laid out on a banner hanging at the front of the hall, it immediately made sense to me. It took me about another six months before I finally went to my own self-help group, but from there I never looked back. I was a regularly member of these and similar groups, coincidentally, for the next twelve years, as well as some counselling. Through these avenues of healing I was awakened to perennial wisdom in the form of this 12 Step Program for personal change. As I learned to put these principles for personal change to work, my life began to improve accordingly. I didn't reach out for as much help as I could have, such as regular counselling, but I kept steadily growing nonetheless, due to my commitment to the group work and to personal growth in general.

Even though I soon learned to function well, whenever I took on a major new challenge, my chronic depression would be triggered once again. Finally, after eight years of personal growth work that helped me in many areas of my life, I decided to spend some dedicated time focusing on my depression and nothing else. Using all that I had learned, I surprised even myself by finally breaking the back of my depression in just a few weeks. The final key for me was a deep enough level of self-acceptance, which is Unconditional Love that is applied to myself in the spirit of Self-Responsibility (the two Laws of Consciousness working in harmony).

I have experienced moments of depression at times since then, but I now know why it occurs and how to rise above it. Depression can no longer take hold of me. You could now say that I am immune to this chronic disorder. Of course I could have overcome my depression a lot sooner if I knew at 24 what I know now, but this was not the case. Besides, my experience has been my greatest teacher where becoming a Psychotherapist is concerned. It has helped me learn that every problem can be turned into an opportunity.

As I continued to work on myself, exploring existentialism, enlightenment through Eastern philosophy, and also alchemy through the works of Carl Jung, my natural interest in psychology began to blossom. Before I knew psychotherapy was to be my career, I was already well versed in the subject. My own higher consciousness knew this was my calling well before my more human mind was aware of it.

By the time I finished university as a mature aged student, I was ready to start my own practice as a psychotherapist. To help with this process, I poured all that I knew out on paper in the form of a book on psycho-spiritual philosophy. I then felt I needed to boil all that down to a concise set of principles, which seemed to intuitively flow from my higher consciousness. The result is what I simply call the **"5 Step Process"**. Over the years, I have continued to put this process into practice in my own life by continuing to develop myself, by helping others in my professional work through counselling and life coaching, and in my relationship with my wife and my two stepchildren. It has more than proven its effectiveness.

What I have laid out for you in this book is a powerful and effective process for emotional healing, wisdom and empowerment. This book is a manual on the Laws of Consciousness—a workable strategy for personal change.

COMMITMENT IS THE KEY—NEVER GIVE UP!

Where serious emotional difficulties such as depression, anxiety, addictions, anger, trauma, ongoing relationship issues and the like are concerned, there needs to be a commitment to long-term counselling/therapy or some sort of focused personal development work. In-depth therapy and group work in particular are very important. Such a commitment should be taken very seriously if we expect to get results. Long-term emotional difficulties rarely respond to "quick-fix" treatments. There may be some quick initial results, but the relief is often temporary, because the process did not reach the required depth.

If we have an expectation that the "cure" should be quick, we may assume the process is not working if this doesn't happen. Because of this our doubts and anxiety may interfere with our commitment to healing. We may jump from one therapist, self-help group or philosophy to the next without giving any of them the required time and commitment needed to work. Worse still, we may just lose hope and give up, only to remain a prisoner of our mental confusion and emotional pain.

Instead of looking for the illusive cure, it is more empowering to approach emotional recovery as a change of lifestyle. This new lifestyle must be one of ongoing self-care rather than self-neglect, regardless of our circumstances.

For me it is like gardening. The soil of my mind gathered a lot of weeds during my formative years. I have done my best the remove these weeds but their roots go very deep and their remnants are hard to find. If I neglect my garden for too long, these weeds can take hold once again. Furthermore, it is not just the weeds from my own garden that I have to watch out for. Unwanted seeds are always blowing in from outside. The work of tending the garden of my mind must be an ongoing process if I expect to get the most out of life.

The mind is the most essential part of our human nature, and yet it is the most neglected. If our mind is out of balance, so is the rest of our life. Learning how to look after our mind, and then making this form of self-care a matter of routine in our life, is essential for a happy and fulfilled life. The laws of Unconditional Love and Personal Responsibility must be persistently put into action, even if your ability to do this is very shaky at first, which is more often the case. A determined commitment to yourself to never give up is essential in order to make the most of any help you are seeking from anywhere else. Perfection is not necessary, but commitment and persistence is.

Such a healing journey is never smooth sailing. Human life will always have its difficulties, even in normal circumstances. It is unrealistic to think otherwise. A life of happiness and fulfilment is *not* about no longer having challenges to deal with. Rather, it is about learning and practicing the skills to enable you to confidently meet those challenges and learn even more in the process. The commitment to self-care, which can also be called mind-management, applies to anyone who wishes to succeed in life, no matter what level of personal development an individual may be starting on. Being self-responsible enough to learn the skills of ongoing mind-management is essential for a well balanced and successful life.

I have everything I need within me and around me to take care of myself and change my life. It is a matter of searching for it until I find it!

The following passage outlines what you need to give yourself a head start on your journey of healing and awakening.

WHAT YOU NEED TO GET A HEAD START

Just having someone to talk to who is detached but caring, accepting, and objective is therapy in itself. However, if deep healing and sustained peace of mind is your goal, emotional recovery also needs a pro-active approach. Therefore, an active strategy for tackling your negative thought-patterns and clearing

REAL HEALING, REAL AWAKENING

your stuck emotions is essential. Such a strategy enables you to gain awareness of those negative thought-patterns and then learn how to replace them with ones that work for you. It also helps you to learn how to take care of and heal your emotional pain. Such a strategy is often called a process, a program or a path. I use my "5 Step Process", which underpins all my counselling and personal development work. I will introduce this process in the next chapter.

It is also important to note that the 5 Step Process is designed to embrace and enhance any other healing or philosophical path that you may be on. The power of this process is in highlighting the Laws of Consciousness (the essential active elements) that effect positive change in our life. The rest is about how to put them into practice. I am not claiming to have discovered some new magical technique, further mystified by giving it a highly scientific name. All effective processes for change work because they are based on the two essential Laws of Consciousness that I described earlier and will highlight again shortly.

This book purposefully has a lot of depth, because it is meant to make a real difference to your life. For it to truly make a difference to your life, it must be studied like a manual; not read once like a novel and then put on the shelf. What I have written here is lived experience. For a full understanding, it will require time and a willingness to put these principles into practice daily. The more you put these teachings into practice, the more you will come to understand them.

In so doing, you will learn self-awareness and emotional processing skills. As your mind-healing and mind-maintenance skills increase, so too will your ability to effectively manage your everyday life. Below is a set of suggestions designed to give you a head start on your journey to healing, clarity and creating a bright future for yourself. Please take it seriously. Doing so may save you a lot of wasted time and unnecessary suffering.

1. Laws of Consciousness
Recognise the fundamental laws of consciousness that heal and develop the mind. Also, be aware of the infinite depth of these principles. You can sincerely study and practice them all your life without exhausting their potential to further expand your

11

consciousness. Every step closer to understanding and living these principles is a life happier and more fulfilled.

1. Unconditional Love.
2. Total Personal Responsibility.

As I pointed out in my personal story, your first responsibility is to give yourself Unconditional Love. It is very hard to give real Love to others in a sustainable way if you don't first give it to yourself. Your life starts and ends with you. It is your total personal responsibility to learn how to Love yourself unconditionally. In the process of sincerely walking this path of healing and awakening, the secrets to true Love and fulfilment will be revealed to you. I will cover this in more depth in the following chapters.

2. Find an Effective Process

It is essential to find a process, program or path that enables you to understand and put into practice these Laws of Consciousness. Such a process should be non-dogmatic and facilitate your personal healing, freedom and empowerment and above all, have the two fundamental Laws of Consciousness as their foundation.

3. Counselling/Therapy/Life Coaching

Not being able to solve our problems on our own or within our immediate family circle does not mean we have failed in some way. To solve our problems, particularly emotional ones, we often need to find a new perspective on the situation and on what we believe about it.

What prevents us from seeking counselling or similar help is often our lack of self-worth, which leads to certain fears such as shame and mistrust. Shame is a very uncomfortable emotion to feel and we cope with this by covering it up with pride. Pride says we have to pretend we are OK when we know that we are really hurting and lost inside. We are afraid to be seen as "not normal". Pride stops us reaching out and getting the care that we need.

Another common trap is fixating on changing others in order to be happy, resulting in conflict and resentment. When we take this approach, someone else will always have power over our happiness.

Allowing ourselves to stay trapped in negative emotions and self-defeating beliefs is very damaging to our wellbeing. It is literally toxic to our mind and body. Our lack of self-worth, and the suffering that it causes, is something that we have learned over time. It is not a natural part of who we are. It is not a part of our genetics, for example. It is a confusion in the mind that can be healed with self-awareness and persistent self-care.

Find a practitioner or mentor or both to help you achieve your goals. It is an advantage to receive help from guides who have walked this journey themselves. Such people are more likely to know what they are talking about and can offer a real example of how to get to where you want to be. Such people are also more likely to deeply understand what you are feeling.

We are all limited by our personal experiences and beliefs. We all need help to move beyond these limitations in order to access our potential. Every athlete who wants to reach a high standard needs a coach. We need to interact with someone who is trained in mental/emotional "fitness" to give us a helping hand and a new perspective on our life. Being genuinely happy in a sustainable way is a skill, and this skill needs to be learned in order to gain the fulfilment we are looking for. Such practitioners are also facilitators. In other words, they will help you realise your own potential. Everyone would benefit from working with a personal counsellor/life-coach, and most highly successful people do just that.

In Table 1 on page 14 are some useful questions to ask a practitioner to help you determine whether he or she is right for you.

Table 1: Finding an Appropriate Therapist

✓ Do you believe Unconditional Love is the key to my healing?

✓ Do you work directly with emotions in a way that will help me honour them, clear them and take care of them?

✓ Can you help me develop the skills to consciously take care of myself and to keep growing in conscious-awareness and self-love?

✓ Can you help me to develop these skills so that I can continue to raise my consciousness to higher states of awareness such as acceptance, personal responsibility, self-empowerment, peace of mind, forgiveness of myself and others, wise personal boundaries that reflect loving kindness toward myself and all others?

✓ Can you help me find a community of conscious people devoted to self-awareness with whom I can develop a healthy support network and ongoing friendship?

✓ Can you help me in these matters in a way that honours my individuality, my freedom to think for myself and my freedom to find my own way without having dogma or doctrine imposed on me?

✓ Do you consider your own life to be a journey of self-realisation where your therapy skills are directly connected to your own personal growth experience?

4. Self-Awareness Groups

Fear traps us into self-defeating beliefs. For example, when we believe we can't trust anyone. I sometimes hear the statement, "I don't trust anyone I don't know." How then are we going to get to know anyone new? How are we going to learn anything new? We also want people to be perfect in some way that suits our own particular comfort zones before we trust them.

Such fears can only be genuinely overcome by learning to trust *ourselves* to know how to work with any new situation. We can always think of instances when people have hurt us, but when we think of these instances we don't take the next step and look at how we got ourselves into these situations in the first place. It is not what happens to us, it is how we deal with it that determines the quality of our experiences.

Finding a self-awareness group in which to participate, that is dedicated to healing and awakening, enables us to be in a group of like-minded people who are making the effort to accept themselves and care for themselves. We hear how they are putting the principles of personal care and self-improvement to work in their lives. We hear about their pain, their struggles and their successes.

When we make the effort to regularly attend such a group, we quickly realise that we are not so different after all. We discover that the other group members' stories are very similar to our own. We also gain more perspective on our own lives as we share experiences with one another.

We are not perfect, and neither are the other group members, but in this atmosphere of personal responsibility and acceptance, we soon feel more comfortable about ourselves as we experience the acceptance from others in the group. We also increase our own ability to be accepting and tolerant of others. As our trust grows, we give ourselves the opportunity to be a part of a community of people who truly know how to care about us, because they are making the effort to care about themselves. Our life grows richer and more fulfilling as a result.

Such a group is not there for us to emotionally hide in. It is not there to prop up our fears and insecurities. It does, however, provide and safe and nurturing environment for us to learn to accept ourselves and work toward overcoming our limitations.

Participating in such a group on a weekly, or at least regular, basis is one of the best ways of finding self-acceptance and developing the life-skills that you are looking for. When this is combined with personal counselling/therapy/life coaching, your process will be that much more empowered. When my clients take this approach to their healing journey, their success is guaranteed.

On the following page are a few guidelines on what is an appropriate group.

Table 2: Finding an Appropriate Group

An appropriate group is:

✓ Skilfully facilitated so that everyone is cared for and gets an equal chance to share.

✓ Skilfully facilitated so your personal freedom and your ability to think and feel for yourself is protected.

✓ Focused on a positive and proactive process, program or way of personal change more so than a particular personality.

✓ A place where emotional and physical safety is carefully facilitated.

✓ Light on your budget and does not pressure you into increasingly expensive courses.

✓ A group that shares responsibility and facilitates opportunities for group members to grow into mentoring and leadership/service roles if they so desire.

✓ Facilitated in a way that skilfully manages potential conflict.

✓ Moderate in its views and accepting and honouring of the wider community in its diversity.

✓ Is transparent in the way that it runs its affairs.

5. Your Commitment to Yourself

Without a *never-give-up* commitment to yourself, you have very little to work with. No matter how much others may try to help you, if you are not willing to help yourself, little will be achieved. Even if your old conditioning (the weeds in the garden of your mind) causes you to believe that you have nothing to offer and that you don't have what it takes to learn, don't believe it. Everyone has the power within them, especially you. Give it a chance. You will be amazed. Never give up on yourself, no matter how many disappointments confront you, and Life will never give up on you either. The key to a happy and fulfilled life is in *you*. No one else has it. Your commitment is the doorway that allows the power of Life/Love to enter your heart and transform you.

CHAPTER ONE SUMMARY

1. Set your intention to live your life according to the Laws of Consciousness and they are:

   a) UNCONDITIONAL LOVE
   b) TOTAL PERSONAL RESPONSIBILITY

2. These laws or principles of consciousness apply to every human being.
3. Perennial Wisdom (the Laws of Consciousness) can only be truly understood by personally opening one's heart to a direct experience of it by endeavouring to put it into action. Only then can we hope to be transformed by the experience.
4. Emotions are said to flow from a lower, more vulnerable level of the mind, while feelings, on the other hand, flow from a higher self.
5. Emotions reveal our human needs, our fears and our pain. Feelings reveal the highest potential of conscious-awareness. The highest feeling is Unconditional Love.
6. Feelings and emotions are designed by nature to inform us of the quality of our thinking.
7. Feelings associated with Unconditional Love are what you need to live your life by. It is from this higher level of your consciousness that you will find the capability to look after your emotional vulnerability.
8. Find an effective process that is based on those laws.
9. Find an experienced guide who has "been there and done that".
10. Find other people who are walking the same journey of healing and growing.
11. Amongst these groups you can find friends you can relate to and who understand what you are going through.
12. Never give up on yourself. Your commitment is the key to your success.

✓ **Get with the Power**
✓ **Find a Path**
✓ **Find a Guide**
✓ **Find some Comrades**
✓ *NEVER GIVE UP!*

CHAPTER TWO

STEP 1:
TOTAL ACCEPTANCE
PART ONE

A BRIEF INTRODUCTION TO STEP 1

Total Acceptance (Unconditional Love)
Without self-acceptance we cannot heal or grow. At first we think
that our emotional pain is caused by not being accepted by others,
until we come to realise that our pain is pointing to the many
ways in which we don't accept ourselves. A lack of self-acceptance
on a fundamental level is the root cause of emotional vulnerability
and suffering.

Every human being has fears and insecurities and gets
confused. Every human being also has a direct connection to the
Universal Life-Force of Love and Wisdom that is our Higher-Self.
This direct connection to the Life-Force is found within one's
own heart, or centre of being. We are therefore a human being
learning to be our Higher-Self. When we are truly committed to
learning what it takes to be our Higher-Self, the doorway to our
true potential is revealed. We learn to be the Higher-Self by being
the compassionate carer of our own human-self as best we can
each day. We can heal our own wounded and confused mind even
as we are learning and growing. With this growing ability to care
for our own human-self, we are increasingly in a better position
to care for others. We are also in a better position to accept and
work with any challenges that we may face in life.

BARBARA AND BRYAN'S STORY

Let us start by having a look into the lives of a couple named Barbara and Bryan. Barbara and Bryan are an average sort of couple who are trying to get ahead in the world with a sense of meaning, purpose and connectedness. They are fictional characters but they could be any one of us. They have been created from my own experiences as well as the experiences of my many clients over the years of my professional work as a psychotherapist and group leader.

Their story is not only about their relationship, but more importantly about their own personal journeys. The story begins with Barbara . . .

Bryan and I had an argument last night. For some reason he forgot about our dinner date and came home late from work after having had too much to drink. Bryan has been going to counselling and participating in a personal development program for a year now. His lapse in progress took me by surprise and I reacted badly.

I was looking forward to our special night out. We make a point of spending quality time alone together now that we are doing our best to look after ourselves and our relationship. When Bryan didn't arrive home on time I began to worry. I tried to phone but he was not in the office and his mobile was switched off. By the time two hours had gone by I was convinced he had been in a car accident or something. I was about to start calling hospitals or the police when he finally came home. It was obvious he had been out drinking. My concern instantly turned to anger.

I launched into him with a barrage of "how could you?; you should know better; is this how much you care about us?! . . ." and so on. In my anger I didn't think to ask what was going on for him. Bryan reacted with the "get off my back" routine and we just went around and round getting nowhere constructive. We eventually retreated to opposite ends of the house without resolving anything.

This morning I felt raw and betrayed and my old feelings of depression were tugging at me. The feelings of betrayal and the emerging depression were like allied forces doing battle for control of my head. Fortunately there was a third force vying for control, and that was my conscious-awareness.

I started on my own personal development journey about a year or so before Bryan got on his own path. As a result, I have become very aware of my old self-destructive ways. I knew that there must be a reason for Bryan's slip-up, but my old issues around drunkenness were doing their best to drag me back to the ways I used to think and react.

When I was a child, my dad abused alcohol and frequently stayed out to all hours. He and mum would frequently argue about it. I remember hiding in my bedroom when things got too heated. I would put my pillow over my head sometimes so I couldn't hear. At other times I would listen while praying that it would stop. Eventually they had had enough of each other and at the age of fourteen, I watched my family fall apart.

Until recently, depression had been my long-term companion. Through counselling I came to realise, that due to all the ongoing negativity and blaming that went on in my home as a child, I developed a sense of self-condemnation whenever I supposedly failed at something. The way I treated Bryan last night and behaved in front of the children was triggering that same sense of failure. Not only was I beating Bryan up, I was doing a good job of beating myself up.

By the time we were up and getting ourselves off to work, there was still a three way battle in my head. I did my best to keep to myself and responded minimally to Bryan in fear of blurting out the wrong thing. I could see Bryan was doing his best to get a grip also. He made a point of apologising and facing up to his part of last night's debacle. Even though I didn't really acknowledge him that well, his honesty helped me to feel a lot better. It gave me some reassurance that we can sort things out tonight.

Fortunately I work part-time and so had a few hours this afternoon to get my head straight.

At these times, what pops into my head is "back to basics." The first step to straightening my head out is self-acceptance. I am human. Like Bryan, I am going to make mistakes now and then. Neither of us had the greatest start to life. We both have our fair share of baggage.

The moment I arrived back home from work I picked up my self-help books. I chose the book that I use as a quick reference to the principles of self-care and self-healing. The book really helped to remind me that I am the guardian of my own life and as that guardian I must be responsible for the way I treat myself. I could feel my heart slowly open again as I worked through an exercise on accepting and forgiving myself. With the help of the exercise I poured out my confusion and pain in my journal. As I explored my emotions, old memories, that were connected to the pain, began to surface and I found myself back in my childhood where all my self-defeating mind-programs started. The way I see it now is that this child that I once was, who is still alive in my memories, belongs to me. I am my own parent now. I am now the adult and my memories are my domain. They are in my control. My mind belongs to me.

I stop writing while I imagine myself going back in time to my childhood, as the adult I am now, in order to take care of the child I was then. I use the hurts of last night to find where the pain is still alive in my memories. Waves of emotion well up in me as I consciously connect to that pain—sadness, helplessness, and anger. I do my best to stay open and compassionate to it, which is not easy because the pain is triggering a lot of negative thinking. I struggle to stay above the negative self-talk that is coming from the pain. These self-attacking thoughts used to be what dragged me down. I get a better perspective on it by writing it down while reminding myself that I am worthy no matter what. Through this process I am able to have a good hard look at the unreality of the negativity. I am able to strengthen my clarity and see it for the confusion that it is. I recognise that what it says about me is not true. The self-attacking thoughts soon dissipate, allowing me to drop into a softer, more self-nurturing space. My growing compassion for myself deepens now and I feel the loving warmth of my self-acceptance, my Higher-Self, flowing into me. More tears come, but they are tears of healing. I am back in my heart now, wrapped up in my inner-sanctuary.

This process works really well for me because the feelings are so real. I can literally feel the love I am giving to my child-self, which is now my vulnerable humanness. All I needed when I was a child was someone who could accept me as I was—someone who could give me lots of hugs and acknowledgment and have compassion for how I was feeling. I can now be that for myself. When I do, it is much easier to face my issues because I can feel okay about myself even when I make a mistake. Self-condemnation and pride then doesn't get in the way so much.

I do some more writing about the new relationship I am creating with the child me that is in my memories. I imagine my adult-self hanging out with my child-self. We are doing projects together while also just being silly and having fun.

I then move on to sorting out what I actually know about last night from what my fear-based imagination was inventing. I get myself in a better headspace to work through things with Bryan tonight.

It hasn't always been that easy. At first I needed my counsellor to help me get through my anger and self-condemnation so that I could release my pent-up emotions and allow myself to be nurtured. Over time I have learned to work through this process for myself. I can really feel how I have created new programs in my mind that are self-caring rather than self-destructive. Because I really do care about myself now, I still see my counsellor for "maintenance" sessions once in a while and regularly go to groups. I want to keep growing because I have experienced the benefits.

There is one other motivation that really keeps me on track and that is wanting my children to have my good programs and not be struggling later in life with their version of the baggage that I have had to deal with. They will still have their issues. We are not perfect parents and we can't always shield them from life. I know, though, that they have had a better start than I had. Every good thing I do for my mind benefits all those around me. I know I have to do it for myself first though. That is where is starts and finishes—my journey.

WHERE OUR CONFUSION BEGINS

Self-acceptance is the doorway to healing our emotional pain and destructive thoughts. Self-acceptance awakens our potential to take charge of our life. The opposite of self-acceptance is negative self-judgment or self-condemnation. Self-condemnation, more than anything else, blocks us in our efforts to heal and grow.

In my personal and professional experience, I have found that all destructive thoughts stem from one fundamental belief, or rather *misbelieve (mistaken belief)*, that is forged in our mind when we were a vulnerable and defenceless child. This misbelief is:

⃠ I am unworthy because I am human.

Beliefs are thought-patterns that have become habit and often slip below our awareness. As a child, in particular, we are unaware that we are forming such beliefs. We are simply trying to survive as we instinctively seek love and happiness. By the time we grow into adulthood, these deeply ingrained beliefs determine the way we perceive everything that happens to us.

By the term "human" I am meaning "not perfect". For a child in particular, the standard of perfect behaviour is measured by others. To further create confusion in the child's mind, there are invariably many different versions of what this perfect standard is, depending on who is handing out the discipline. This standard can even change from moment to moment with one individual disciplinarian, depending on his or her changing moods and parenting skills.

These multifarious and often irrational standards that a child is supposed to somehow live up to are laced with the fears, insecurities, and resulting confusions of the disciplinarian. This confusion inevitably distorts the quality of love that is given to the child.

When we are children, this deep misbelief that we are unworthy for simply being human becomes embedded into our minds, because love is repeatedly withdrawn from us for being childish. As children, we are placed in a profound dilemma. Being children means that we have little capacity to control our natural childish cravings and emotions. We simply can't help ourselves. We are doomed to fail when we are expected to be "good little adults" by well-meaning but confused carers, or carers who are plainly abusive.

We may also have had a sensitive or intense character as a child, which can compound the situation and put more demands on the skill of the parent.

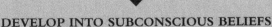

Clarity Box 2:1

REPEATED CHILDHOOD EXPERIENCES
⬇
DEVELOP INTO SUBCONSCIOUS BELIEFS
⬇
THAT CONTROL MY EVERYDAY PERCEPTIONS

As powerless, vulnerable children we are so dependent on our carers that we are compelled to conform to their confusion no matter how impossible this may be to achieve. In the face of this dilemma, we feel so powerless and unworthy. The more often a particular statement is repeated to us when we are children, the more likely we are to be influenced by it. As a result, we are inclined to believe negative judgments about ourself, even though in our hearts it doesn't feel right. Even a rebellious or strongly spirited child is still going to be deeply affected by such experiences.

Of course all children need guidance and discipline. This is how they learn to take control of their own emotions and needs. All discipline, however robust it may need to be at times, must be patient, loving and compassionate, otherwise it contains elements of destructiveness.

For most of us, this is where the confusion starts, and we then pass it down the line from generation to generation.

When we were children, we may not have had any other example of care to relate to, so we grew to regard this confusion as a normal way to think. It became our standard. Due of this "normalizing", as well as the vulnerability of our mind as a child, these self-destructive judgments become imbedded into our subconscious mind. This repeated information then creates negative belief-systems that control the way we think and react to life. The result is our *negative social conditioning*.

Clarity Box 2:2

REPEATED CHILDHOOD EXPERIENCES

DEVELOP INTO SUBCONSCIOUS BELIEFS

THAT CONTROL MY EVERYDAY PERCEPTIONS

=

SOCIAL CONDITIONING

Negative conditioning can be evident as early as two years old and it keeps on being created all through childhood if the child's environment and standard of care doesn't significantly improve. These distorted beliefs then create programmed, or habitual, ways of reacting to life's circumstances that can be very self-defeating. These programmed self-defeating reactions then create ongoing difficulties throughout our life, such as conflict in our relationships, when conflict wouldn't be present otherwise.

An example of this distortion of perception is when we take offense at an innocent remark made to us by someone who had no intention of causing harm. We think we are being attacked. We think we are being condemned, but all that has occurred is an old belief-system, created by repeated experiences of being condemned in the past, has been triggered. The trigger can be as simple as a familiar phrase or gesture. In reality, without being aware of it, our own mind is thrown into a time–warp. We unconsciously think the present situation is the same as the past and react in a way that is inappropriate for that present situation.

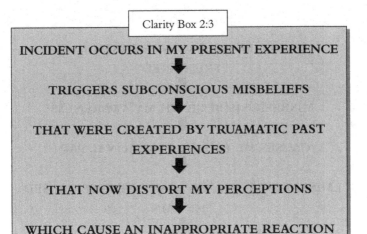

Clarity Box 2:3

INCIDENT OCCURS IN MY PRESENT EXPERIENCE
⬇
TRIGGERS SUBCONSCIOUS MISBELIEFS
⬇
THAT WERE CREATED BY TRUAMATIC PAST EXPERIENCES
⬇
THAT NOW DISTORT MY PERCEPTIONS
⬇
WHICH CAUSE AN INAPPROPRIATE REACTION

At times people do treat us badly and we do need to take some sort of action to protect our wellbeing. Due to these distorted perceptions, however, we may feel powerless to act or we may over-react.

This means that our very perceptions of reality become distorted early in childhood. Due to these misbeliefs, we then continue to create a distorted reality for ourself throughout our life until we become aware of these self-defeating beliefs and change them.

As adults, we often think that the words and actions of others are causing our emotional pain, as it did in childhood. This is not the case however. To be an adult means we have the capacity to be self-responsible—to take command of our own thoughts and emotions, whereas a child only has limited access to this ability. Unlike children, adults are predominantly at the mercy of their own ingrained conditioning. As adults, it is our own self-condemnation emerging out of our negative conditioning that makes us vulnerable to the judgments of others. From this position of vulnerability and confusion, our survival instincts may then be inclined to judge and attack as a form of defence, oblivious of the fact that the perceived danger may be an imaginary one. The words or actions of another person may be perfectly innocent. Even if the other acted unkindly, we tend to react in a way that makes the situation worse.

Clarity Box 2:4

MISBELIEF (SELF-CONDEMNATION) IS TRIGGERED

MISBELIEF IS BENEATH MY AWARENESS

CAUSES ME TO FEEL EMOTIONAL PAIN

I MISTAKENLY ASSUME SOMEONE ELSE CAUSED THE PAIN

LASH OUT AT PERSON I ASSUME CAUSED THE PAIN

MY OWN UNCONSCIOUS CONFUSION IS THE CAUSE OF THE PAIN AND MY INAPPROPRIATE REACTION

What is really driving our pain is our own mind telling us we are unworthy of Love. As children, we were dependent on getting love/acceptance/approval from other people in order to feel loved. When we didn't get it, we felt abandoned. As an adult, when we react, our unconscious childhood belief that we have not measured up enough to get love has been triggered. We may only feel this as anger toward the other person, but underneath this anger is the wounded and confused child within us believing he/she is unworthy of Love. When we blindly react, without knowing it, we are attacking our own self with our own misbelief.

In comparison, when we have a healthy self-esteem, we can shield ourself from the unfair judgments of others, as well as our own negative self-talk. This inner-strength is created by choosing to accept and believe we are worthy even when we make human mistakes.

Clarity Box 2:5

STRONG CONVICTION IN MY ESSENTIAL WORTHINESS
⬇
CREATES HEALTHY SELF-ESTEEM
⬇
OVERRIDES SELF-CONDEMNATION
⬇
SHIELDS ME FROM OUTSIDE CONDEMNATION
⬇
LEADS TO APPROPRIATE ACTION

This is the crux of Unconditional Love where our own mind's foundation of self-esteem is concerned. Our worthiness must be regarded as absolute, because it is! In order to heal the confusion that has taken over our mind, our belief in our fundamental worthiness must become an unshakable conviction. Our worthiness is *not* in the hands of other human beings, regardless of what anyone has, or may think, say or do. Not even our parents have authority over our worthiness. The only qualification we need for this fundamental worthiness is to *exist*. **That's it!** As adults, despite what our ingrained confusion may tell us, we have the ultimate authority over our own self-esteem. Other human beings have the power over our worthiness only when we give it to them, and we only do that when we are confused about the truth of ourself. Unconditional Love is UNCONDITIONAL. There are no shades of grey. The only doubts that exist are to be found in our own human confusion. We are all on a journey toward a full conscious-awareness of this essential fact.

It is worth repeating that other human beings do not own our Love any more than they can own the light that shines on us from the sun, or the air that we breathe. Love is the Universal Life-Force that is the core of our being. Love is Life itself. That is why it is unconditional. It has nothing to do with the human mind. It is a universal, all encompassing life-force that is everything.

Nothing can take that away from us. We can never be outside Life and therefore we can never be outside Love. All that is happening is that we are getting caught in our own confusion, which, through the power of our own conscious-awareness, we can undo to reveal the Love that we are always in. This is not some hocus-pocus mystical belief. This is a scientific fact that is at the core of real healing and awakening. It is a fact that can be repeatedly put to the test and repeatedly proven, which it has been all through the ages of human history. I am also suggesting that this is the driving force behind our human desire to evolve.

Of course, undoing the confusion that besieges our mind is the challenge. Despite being caught in this confusion, we have the capacity of consciousness that gives us the power of reasoning to know what *feels* right, and to trust that feeling. Understanding the nature of emotions and feelings is, therefore, vital to developing conscious-awareness. This Universal Life-Force of Unconditional Love *is* our Higher-Self. It is the bench mark that our feelings are set to (see "Feelings and Emotions" on page 5). If our thoughts are out of alignment with Unconditional Love, we feel pain in the form of negative human emotion. If our thoughts are in tune with Unconditional Love, we feel joy, the Unconditional Love that is our Higher-Self.

Clarity Box 2:6

UNIVERSAL LIFE-FORCE OF LOVE AND WISDOM IS THE CORE OF MY BEING

THIS IS THE BENCH MARK MY FEELINGS ARE SET TO

IF MY THOUGHTS ARE NOT LOVE, THERE IS PAIN

IF MY THOUGHTS ARE LOVE, THERE IS JOY

THIS IS MY INTERNAL GUIDANCE SYSTEM

Considering how simple and beautiful this internal guidance system is, it is amazing how we manage to get so confused. But we do, due to our vulnerability as a child and the confusion this experience sets up in our mind.

Self-condemnation cuts us off from Love because it closes our heart off from our own self, and ultimately our Higher-Self. If it wasn't for self-condemnation, the acute vulnerabilities we feel in adulthood would not be there in the first place. Without this prior self-condemnation, the unfair judgment of another would have little impact. We would simply know that the person speaking harshly to us is perhaps having a bad day and is obviously confused. We would know that we don't deserve to be spoken to that way, no matter what mistake we may have made. We would decide for ourself who we are and what we are worth and that would be in accordance to the truth that we are one with the Universal Life-Force, Unconditional Love in other words. This is what it means to know yourself as a "child of God". As a result, we would easily let the other's confusion go.

❤ *My ultimate worthiness is beyond question, no matter how human I am; no matter what other people may think, say, or do.*

PRIDE AND DENIAL

What is called false-pride is another symptom of self-condemnation. For example, this is what causes us to deny our part in a conflict and to use blame and similar strategies to cover our vulnerability. False-pride creates in us the need to be right and to see the other as wrong in an unrealistic black and white way of perceiving. We need to feel bigger and better because, deep down, we actually feel less than those around us.

Often we know when we are indulging in a game of denying reality, but our fear of being judged as unworthy gets the better of us. Our fight-or-flight instincts take over in reaction to our fear and our heart becomes closed. We often feel utterly powerless to change this self-defeating way of coping, and we are often reluctant to change, due to the false sense of security and power pride gives us. Usually we are not aware of the underlying dynamic of self-condemnation that creates pride. This lack of awareness only adds to the seemingly endless confusion.

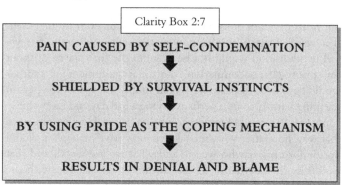

Clarity Box 2:7

PAIN CAUSED BY SELF-CONDEMNATION
⬇
SHIELDED BY SURVIVAL INSTINCTS
⬇
BY USING PRIDE AS THE COPING MECHANISM
⬇
RESULTS IN DENIAL AND BLAME

UNHEALTHY DEPENDENCY ON OTHERS

It is quite normal to assume that our only hope of escape from this nexus of self-condemnation is to find someone who is willing to Love us unconditionally, even when we are unable or unwilling to return that same quality of Love. This of course is an unrealistic expectation that leads to inevitable conflict and disillusionment. There is no "perfect" someone out there for us. We can only ever end up with an imperfect human being like ourself. As a result, in desperation we try to "renovate" our loved one in order to get what we want. We become locked in a struggle to control and change other people, places and, things in order to feel loved.

The other side of this dynamic is compromising our values and wellbeing in order to hang onto a relationship at all cost. This is driven by the same lack of self-worth, but through a personality that looks for love by pleasing others at one's own expense.

In reality, relationships succeed, and personal fulfilment is achieved, not so much because other people love us, but because we possess a healthy form of self-Love. This healthy self-Love provides us with an inner-peace and openness that makes forming loving and healthy relationships with others a natural outcome.

It is a self-Love that respects and protects our core values and personal wellbeing.

> *When I give myself Unconditional Love, I naturally open my heart to the Life-Force of Love. I can then overflow this real Love on to others while caring for myself.*

SELF-ACCEPTANCE IS SELF-CARE

After recognising that there is a problem with the way we treat ourself and others and with the way we approach life in general, acceptance is the first step in taking action to do something about it. This first step of acceptance is applied on many levels. Accepting our right to be human in the form of self-acceptance is an essential part of Step 1. Self-acceptance opens the door to Love and Healing

The following contemplation exercise may help you better comprehend the nature of self-acceptance / Unconditional Love. (Fill in the blanks with the right gender for you to make it more personal.)

EXERCISE 1
AWAKENING TO LOVE

Imagine yourself as a newborn baby lying on a bed with you as your adult self looking down at this delicate, vulnerable and precious being. Now as you are looking down at this beautiful little being, can you say in your heart that there is anything about your baby that is unworthy of Love? Can your baby do anything that makes it truly unworthy of Love? For instance, ... may frequently wake you up during the night by crying . . . . may also dirty . . . . nappy a number of times per day. Neither of these experiences are very pleasant to have to deal with as the carer of this baby. Is your baby still worthy of Unconditional Love even when . . . . acts this way? Some people actually get angry at this unconscious behaviour of a new born baby. Is the problem with the baby or the carer?

Now your child is one-year-old and crawling around, getting into whatever . . . . can reach. Sometimes this little toddler is difficult at meal times, and can still keep you up at night. Your toddler is just doing what a toddler does. Is there anything about . . . . that is unworthy of Unconditional Love?

Now your toddler is a delightful two-year-old and becoming a real handful . . . . is now walking and therefore getting into more things. There is a lot of boundary testing going on as your toddler exercises . . . . awakening self-will in fits of defiance. This little one is also starting to talk in the cute way that toddlers do. Is there anything about this child that is undeserving of Unconditional Love? Would anyone be justified in getting angry at and judging this toddler if . . . . accidentally knocked over and broke that prized porcelain jug that you got for your wedding? Again, this child is just doing what a two-year-old does. If the carer gets angry at the child, where does the problem lie—the carer or the child?

Now your child is five, very active and talking fluently. Even though . . . . is still quite the bundle of love, there is already some negative conditioning evident in this child's mind. You are already having a tussle with your child's newly forming ego. And yet even now this five-year-old is just doing what a five-year-old does. Where does the responsibility for the child's social conditioning lie—with the child or the child's carers? Has the child conditioned his or herself? Again, is there anything unworthy about this five-year-old child? Is the child still worthy of Unconditional Love, a child who is still so vulnerable and dependent on the quality of care that . . . . receives?

And now you are watching yourself as a ten-year-old, playing with friends and going to school. Your child freely interacts with the rest of the family, a unique personality clearly emerging . . . . is full of hopes and dreams for the future and yet still vulnerable and dependent. There is often conflict with brothers and sisters as your ten-year-old competes for love and approval. Negative conditioning is clearly visible. Deep behaviour patterns have been well established. Still this ten-year-old is just doing what a ten-year-old does. Is this growing child still worthy of Unconditional Love? If a carer withdraws their love from this child, where does the problem lie?

Now you are watching yourself as a fifteen-year-old, well into puberty and the new social scene. Your adolescent self is spending less time with family and instead seeking peer approval in . . . . own social group, sometimes in defiance of parental guidance. This leads to frequent conflict . . . . is now experiencing the first forays into dating and relationships with its inevitable excitement and at times crushing disappointment. Your adolescent self is often moody and even behaves a bit oddly as . . . . searches for an independent identity. Childhood conditioning is now deeply entrenched and overlaid onto this youth's natural character. Again, your adolescent self is just doing the best that . . . . can. Should your adolescent self be judged for that? Should guidance come with condemnation or Unconditional Love?

How would it have been if you were given Unconditional Love all through your childhood? How would it have been if you felt safe to share your deepest fears, emotions, joys and dreams with your parents all through your childhood and received nothing but loving guidance, caring, wise discipline and encouragement that never made you wrong as a person? Isn't this what we deserve as children, no matter how many mistakes we made or how confused we may have become at times? How can a child be held responsible for . . . . own upbringing? Surely the responsibility lies with the carer.

Even as an adult this same rule applies. Even having to firmly say no to a person's confused and misguided behaviour can be done without withdrawing Unconditional Love.

When you look inside yourself now, you are looking at and feeling this child, a child that is still looking for, longing for that unconditional loving acceptance. You can find this child in your most vulnerable emotions. You are now the adult and this "inner-child" now belongs to you. Your carers did the best they could. Their job is now over. Now it is up to you. How have you been treating your child-self? How would it be if you lovingly accepted yourself unconditionally in a real heartfelt responsible way, instead of judging yourself and mistreating yourself whenever you make a human mistake, or don't supposedly measure up?

Even as an adult we are just doing the best we can. Mistakes are a natural part of being human. This deep form of self-acceptance enables our ego to wake up from its blind judging and blaming and instead consciously embrace and care for this human-self of ours. With self-care, healing and growth are inevitable, along with maturity and wisdom. It is through self-acceptance that we can increasingly awaken our consciousness into higher states where it unites with Unconditional Love and therefore the power to heal the deepest fears and confusions.

🖤 *I accept my right to be human.*

As hard as it may at first seem, it is easier, more effective and more empowering to change ourself rather than try to change someone else. We have no real power to control the hearts of others, but we can learn to skilfully manage ourself. This self-change must come in the form of self-care. It is a conscious loving and caring relationship with our own humanness. We are not changing ourself to please others or just to conform. We are learning to make positive and empowered decisions on our own behalf, decisions that lead to self-respect and therefore respect from others.

As was stated in Chapter One, there is a strong tendency in many societies to feel ashamed when we cannot psychologically function according to the "norms" of a particular society. Everybody suffers emotional crises from time to time, but when this crisis becomes prolonged for one reason or another, there is a perception that we are unworthy because of it. We think we have somehow failed. We cannot control another's misguided perceptions, but we can do something about our own.

We are like a priceless one-of-a-kind car that has broken down. It would not make sense to regard this car as not worthy of repair. When this priceless car breaks down, it is then a matter of objectively and carefully taking it apart in order to find and correct the problem. It would be only logical to want to give this car ongoing maintenance, care and attention. We human beings tend to resist taking care of ourselves, as though we shouldn't need it. We think such maintenance is an imposition on our lifestyle. It is little wonder we end up emotionally breaking down. Our body/mind is our vehicle for our entire life. Human beings are like highly complex and delicate machines that need constant care and attention.

Often we *do* try to care for ourself, but we have not learned how to do this effectively. In particular I am talking about taking care of our emotional life. For too many of us, appreciating and looking after our human emotions is a mystery. The usual way we seem to treat our emotions is to shut them down, or shove them onto somebody else. When we are not doing that, we often use our emotions as an excuse to beat our own selves up.

You are hardly going to be motivated to tend the garden of your mind if you are ashamed of what is growing there. This garden may be full of weeds. It may not reflect what you prefer to see about yourself. Nevertheless, this garden is yours to tend. This garden is waiting for someone to come along and nurture it, to sort the good plants from the ones that don't belong there. It does not matter if you are not a very good gardener to begin with. What is important is that you care and that you keep doing the work. The rest flows naturally from this.

Rather than being a liability, when understood and effectively integrated into our conscious-awareness, our emotional life is a source of great wisdom and inner-strength. Before we can take advantage of this potential inner-strength however, because of long-term self-neglect as well as the difficulties we experienced in childhood, we usually need to do some serious healing work first.

❤️ *I have what it takes to heal my confusion and truly care for my own wellbeing.*

OPENING THE DOOR TO LOVE AND HEALING

There is often a backlog of emotional pain waiting to be cleared once we are willing to open our heart to our own humanness. The build-up of this pain results in emotional states such as depression, anger, fear, guilt, shame, anxiety and stress etc. This emotional build-up, if allowed to continue unchecked, can lead to various physical health issues, substance abuse, addictions, relationship conflict or breakdown, child abuse, thoughts of suicide and other such serious consequences. In my experience, help is initially needed to safely release this emotional pressure and to learn how to take effective care of our emotional self on an ongoing basis.

Be aware also that this pain can take time to reach the surface, and it usually comes through in stages. Post-traumatic stress is an example of this delayed emotional release. Actively seeking to heal and grow on an ongoing basis can greatly reduce the time this healing takes and can also reduce the impact on your life and relationships.

Deep emotional wounds take time to heal, so don't be fooled into thinking that you should be over it in a few weeks or even months. Concentrate on learning how to care for your emotional pain with self-acceptance, patience and increasing clarity, rather than wanting to just "get rid of it". Wanting to just get rid of the pain usually leads to ineffective healing and further crises later on. Your emotions are an essential part of who you are. Caring for your emotions properly ensures that they will work for you and not against you.

For example, when you feel anger, your mind is calling your attention to something that it perceives is violating your boundaries. What the mind does not know at first is whether this violation is something real from a present situation or an emotion-charged memory that has been triggered from the past. Anger is simply a call to your conscious-awareness to pay attention and check out the situation. Having learned about self-care and self-awareness, you can then tune into this emotion without jumping to conclusions. You can stay open to the emotion and observe it and in so doing, gain insight into what is really causing it. Most of the time the emotional pain is caused by our own confusion. When we blindly blame others for the way we think, and therefore feel, we lose any chance of gaining insight into the real cause. As a result, we remain powerless over our negative emotions.

Emotions are designed to enable your adult conscious-awareness to stay in touch with your human-self and also with the world around you. It is a form of "energy touch" or "energy in motion"—emotion.

Self-care is therefore essential to our wellbeing. It is the very foundation of our entire life. Truly accepting our humanness—accepting that we are still worthy even while we are being human, is essential for being motivated toward self-care. We are unlikely to be motivated toward this healthy self-care while we are busy condemning ourself. We can hardly have a healthy relationship with someone we resent. We won't have a chance to know them and appreciate them unless we accept them as they are. This is what facilitates genuine intimacy. We must grow to know ourself intimately if we expect to be able to look after ourself.

Self-care is about having an active, loving relationship with ourself, particularly if we need to change some deeply ingrained self-defeating habits. On the following page, Exercise 2: "Be Your Own Loving Guardian" and Table 3: "Caring for Your Human-Self Check List", will give you direction on what you need to do to take care of yourself. I suggest you make a copy of Table 3 and place it somewhere prominent, or in your journal perhaps. Read it through regularly as you read this book and do your best to apply it to your life each day.

I accept myself as I am and I am dedicated to the principles of Love and Wisdom. With this powerful guidance I can effectively take care of my own life.

EXERCISE 2
BE YOUR OWN LOVING GUARDIAN

Make good use of your journal while doing the exercise. Writing down your thoughts greatly increases the effectiveness of the process. See "5 Keys to Caring for Yourself" on page 122.

Read the exercise through first before you start in order to gain a good feel for the process. Also, make good use of appendix 1 and 2 at the back of this book to help you identify and work with your emotions.

1) What this exercise is about is being the wise, loving parent to your own fragile, vulnerable, confused, and often frightened human-self. It is realising that love is something that we can access internally. We are always within the embrace of Universal Love and we access this love at any time through actively and responsibly caring for ourselves.

2) Today, right this moment, make a rock solid commitment to treat yourself and speak to yourself only with loving kindness, compassion, forgiveness, and acceptance.

3) Keep a little notebook in your pocket or your handbag that you can use to write down your self-rejecting thoughts as you become aware of them.

4) When you catch yourself thinking this way, in that moment or later on that day or evening when you can make time, focus on that thought and feel into what it does to you. Write down what you discover.

5) When you are aware of this state of self-rejection, imagine this human-self that you are putting down is you when you were a vulnerable child just wanting to be loved.

6) Be open to whatever emotions that may be released during this process. Do your best to let them flow. Acknowledging your own pain works the same as when someone else important to you acknowledges your pain. This will help you feel safer to let it out. Let it flow and trust that the emotional release will pass naturally and have a chance to heal in the process. Much of this pent up emotion comes

from childhood. You were so small and powerless then. It is normal to feel this vulnerability again as the emotions are coming through. This can be uncomfortable at first. Remember that you are an adult now with conscious-awareness. Know that your intentions to care for yourself will help heal this pain.

7) Imagine yourself as that child and think of how you would want to be treated and explore this in your journal. Just let this come in any way it comes. After exploring this, write a note to your adult-self telling your adult-self how you want to be treated.

8) As your adult-self, spend time contemplating the significance of your relationship with your vulnerable human-self, this emotionally wounded child within you. Contemplate the reality of your responsibility toward yourself and the consequences of not taking loving care of yourself.

9) Realise that you did the best you could in the past with the awareness that you had. This also applies to your efforts now. Forgive yourself for your human mistakes and realise that you now have an opportunity to treat yourself differently, and to work toward healing the wounds of the past. Forgiving yourself is an important step toward living this new way of life. Spend some time writing in your journal about what is coming through for you about this.

10) Contemplate ways to mentor yourself and care for yourself, considering what your inner-child has communicated to you.

11) Let your feelings guide you as you explore this new way of caring for yourself. To help you recognise what is for your highest good, consider these new ways of caring for yourself in the long term. Would it be sustainable? Would it enhance your life in the short, medium and long-term?

12) Don't be concerned about finding the perfect answers. It is all a journey of trial and error. Any step toward genuinely caring for yourself is going to improve your life. Be free

and open to learn from each attempt to act more lovingly toward yourself.

13) Write out on a card or in your pocket book your new positive intentions toward yourself and refer to it regularly in order to keep your conscious-awareness active (refer to point 2 of this exercise).

14) You can even program your mobile phone to give you this message every couple of hours. Regular reminders are essential for reprogramming the old conditioning.

15) When you catch yourself again in a state of self-rejection, you have these new strategies to fall back on. When you refer to these new positive intentions in that moment, you will have more clarity of the consequences of self-rejection. You will also have more clarity around how to treat yourself with loving kindness in that moment.

16) Continue to put this exercise into practice on a daily basis. Try to see this as your new lifestyle, not some unrealistic quick fix. Recognise that when this is your new lifestyle, you will naturally continue to heal and grow. Happiness and fulfilment are inevitable.

17) In order to empower your healing and personal growth, explore ways that you can reach out for help and support. This is also caring for yourself. Refer to "Five Keys to Caring for Yourself" on page 122.

Table 3: Caring for Your Human-Self Check List

✓ Am I accepting my right to be human and do I see my confusion and mistakes as an opportunity to know myself better and to take better care of myself?

✓ Do I provide plenty of space in my life to take care of my vulnerable emotional human-self?

✓ Am I taking responsibility to care for my own needs?

✓ Do I really have compassion for my human-self?

✓ Do I impose unrealistic standards or expectations on myself and/or others, causing me to experience stress and conflict?

✓ In what ways can I reorganise my life so I have the time and space to heal my emotions and confusions and strengthen my consciousness-awareness?

✓ Am I willing to make this commitment to care for myself an ongoing and essential part of my lifestyle for the sake of my happiness and wellbeing?

✓ Can I see that adjusting my lifestyle in this way will help me achieve what I want, rather than be a waste of time?

✓ Am I judging and blaming others for not fulfilling my needs instead of standing on my own two feet?

✓ Am I aware of my genuine needs? Do I truly listen to what my emotions/feelings are telling me? Am I indulging my neediness (fears, insecurities, self-pity, addictions) rather than facing them and overcoming them?

✓ Do I have a healthy support network? Am I willing to make the effort to establish one? Am I expecting one person to meet all my needs?

✓ Am I actively learning what it takes to constructively communicate with others?

✓ Am I actively learning what it takes to conduct a healthy relationship?

✓ Do I have joy, play, recreation in my life?

✓ Do I appreciate the beautiful, simple things around me like nature, for example?

✓ Do I allow my mind to be filled with negative thoughts that cause me pain, or do I concentrate on gratitude to ensure my mind is at peace even in the face of difficulty?

✓ Do I take time to appreciate those around me?

✓ Am I aware that my humanness is my total responsibility to compassionately care for? Am I truly committed to do whatever it takes to learn how to care for myself and therefore my future?

✓ Can I see that accepting full responsibility to care for my own mind, including reaching out for help, is my foundation for a successful life?

CONTEMPLATING UNCONDITIONAL LOVE

Because of its absolute quality, the idea of living one's life based on the principle of Unconditional Love can be very confronting. We may scoff at such an idea, regarding it as just plain fantasy. We may feel that it would be wonderful to live that way but regard it as unrealistic. We may even feel guilty or sad for not living up to this ideal because we think we "should", but at the same time think we're not good enough.

Unconditional Love becomes more reachable when we regard our commitment to loving unconditionally as a *sincere intention*. In other words, we intend to Love ourself and others unconditionally, knowing full well that achieving such a high ideal is a journey that is unlikely to be completed in this life. Even so, we can honour the ultimate truth of the principle of Unconditional Love and make it our guiding Light, while also accepting our humanness. We can see that learning about life through each experience of this journey is perfectly okay and normal for gaining maturity. We can see that any step along the road toward Unconditional Love will bring more harmony into our lives and advance our conscious-awareness in the process. Our sincere intention, our willingness to never stop learning, pulls us forward through each of life's experiences toward literally *becoming* the ideal of Unconditional Love. In so doing, we call on Life (another word for Higher-Self / Higher Power / Universal Life-Force / God etc) itself to become our teacher.

This Master of all teachers, the Universal Life-Force of Unconditional Love, is at the very core of our heart and consciousness and is with us in our every step, our every thought and feeling, our every breath. As we learn to face ourself with acceptance and open our heart to what we find and work with it, we are in fact accepting the role of being the representative of Unconditional Love to our own human-self and even to the world around us. Even in our faulting, uncertain steps toward self-awareness, we are invoking this Universal Life-Force of Love into our being. It is like plugging into an electricity supply. The force is unseen but always there ready to power us up. The effects of plugging into the Universal Life-Force may not be so obvious due to the initial inadequacy of our ability to open to it, but it has its ongoing effect on us none-the-less. The more we can open our heart to our own human-self from the standpoint of the two supreme Laws of Consciousness, Unconditional Love and Total Personal Responsibility, the more we can let the Universal power of Love be the foundation of our conscious-awareness.

Through my sincere intention to be Unconditional Love, I align my conscious-awareness to the Universal Life-Force of Love, and with this ultimate power I first heal and empower myself.

On page 56, Exercise 3 is designed to help you explore a deeper understanding of Unconditional Love / healthy self-care.

On page 273, Exercise 10 is designed to help you process and heal your painful emotions and confusions.

ACCEPTANCE AND THE KEY TO CONSCIOUSNESS

There is an old truism that goes, **"what we resist will persist"**. This aligns to what Buddha taught when he gave the world his "Four Noble Truths" which are as follows:

1. **The reality of suffering**
2. **The nature of suffering**
3. **The answer to overcoming suffering**
4. **The path of overcoming suffering—The Noble Eightfold Path**

The first teaching, "The reality of suffering" refers to the fact that everything in the physical world that is dependent on physical properties is impermanent. For example, your body will grow old and die, if it does not die before that through misadventure or disease. You will inevitably lose all your loved ones, whether they leave you or they die. Most of your material possessions that you may own throughout your life will wear out and have to be replaced. Those that don't wear out, such as diamonds or gold, you will have to leave behind when you die anyway—that's if they don't get stolen before that. Even your identity—who you think you are—will change many times over the course of your lifetime, sometimes quiet dramatically. There is nothing in this physical world that is not shifting, changing, dying or being born, and physical pain is an inevitable part of these experiences of physical life. Everything is in a state of flux. In other words; everything is impermanent.

The insecurities that impermanence causes in the human mind must be dealt with. We must accept and work with the fact that human beings get confused and outright deluded. We place too many expectations on each other in a futile attempt to avoid the insecurity caused by impermanence. Conflict is the inevitable result. Unless you are Buddha or some other enlightened master, that means you too.

Due to this fear and confusion, we think we are being threatened or attacked, when most of the time we are not. In reality, we are thinking that we *might* be threatened or attacked and try to act first to protect ourself from what we think other people are thinking, or what we think they might do. As are result, we threaten and attack others based on what we think they are thinking. If you think all this is very confusing, you are right!

All these misperceptions, however, are just our own fear-based imagination running off—our negative conditioning spinning out of control. The same goes for the meaning we place on events, big and small, that conclude that we are being threatened or attacked. At least ninety percent of all this drama is being played out in our imagination. The most tragic thing is that we then base our actions on these imaginary conclusions. This is the cause of all the injustice in the world today and in every preceding age. The world is over-run and literally run by our unrestrained egos, turbo charged with fear-based imaginations. These delusions continually trigger fight-or-flight instinctual reactions that pull us down into an "every man for himself" state of mind.

Sound depressing? It shouldn't be. These are just plain facts. These are simply the conditions of this world. This is the reality of suffering. The reason that Buddha pointed them out is because we spend a huge amount of effort in our lifetime being frightened of, denying or getting angry over the reality of life as a human being and this is where the problem lies. Our resistance to the facts of life points to the second teaching, "The nature of suffering". We feel frightened, powerless and angry. We are in conflict with reality.

As the story goes, Buddha began his life on top of the social heap with abundant material wealth and princely status, largely shielded from the suffering that humanity generally experiences. When he was confronted with poverty, old age and death he was shaken to the core. This experience awoke in him deep compassion and a burning desire to solve this dilemma of life. He wasn't moved to solve the situation by building better roads and housing. He could see that this was just a band-aide. He wanted to get to the very core of the issue. He was intent on solving the very nature of suffering in the human mind itself.

He first looked for the answers to suffering by becoming a renunciant, which meant that he left behind all his worldly possessions, even the clothes on his back, and joined a band of holy men who practiced strenuous forms of yoga in an attempt to reach enlightenment.

After a number of years, he became a very high yogi, but he still hadn't reached his goal. This just made him even more determined, and while fasting and meditating for a long period, he had a profound revelation. He realised that earlier in his life he was trapped by his attachments to his wealth and privilege. He also realised that he was equally trapped by his rejection of his worldly life. Everything suddenly made sense to him. He could see that the human mind suffers because it becomes trapped in a nexus of attachment/clinging/greed on the one hand and aversion/hate/rejection on the other. He saw that this dynamic covered all areas of human affairs. We try to possess and consume what brings us comfort and call this love, and run away from, or be in conflict with, what may cause pain and discomfort and call this bad and thus hate it. He realised that the human mind becomes lost in confusion as a result. He saw that the mind further causes its own suffering by projecting this confusion onto all that is experienced until the confusion appears to be reality and reality itself seems unreal. Buddha realised the nature of suffering.

The cause of our suffering that I gave at the beginning of this chapter, regarding ourself as unworthy because we are human, ties right in here. The self-condemning belief that we are unworthy because we are human creates within us a feeling of emptiness and a sense of separation from the Universal Life-Force of Unconditional Love. It is a belief that flows from a mind that does not know the true nature of itself. Perceiving itself to be separated from the Life-Force, our conscious-awareness becomes mere ego and tries to survive by seeking fulfilment from the impermanent and confused physical world and the inevitable result is being trapped in the nexus of attachment and aversion.

Buddha realised that the answer was to pull his conscious-awareness free of all this attachment and aversion and instead rest in the still silence in between as the detached observer of himself and life. In this still silence he found himself at one with the supreme consciousness of the Universal Life-Force that is behind and within all things. His awareness and spiritual training was so powerful at this stage of his journey that this revelation was enough to place his mind in perfect alignment with Universal Consciousness and thus render his mind impervious to all suffering. In other words, he became enlightened, free. In the process, he realised the true nature of himself. He fully awakened to the fact that he was not his vulnerable, mortal human-self but his indestructible Higher-Self. As this Higher-Self, he realised that he simply could not be threatened in any way by the physical world. His human mind, with its attachments and aversions, no longer had an effect on him. The answer to overcoming suffering was therefore revealed to him.

The fourth teaching is about how he went about teaching these truths all those years ago. The 5 Step Process is a simplified version of this type of teaching.

Jesus revealed that he understood the deeper meaning of impermanence as well when he said, "build your house on rock, not on shifting sand."[5] Your "house" meaning your mind that you live in. By "rock" he meant the permanent laws of consciousness, Unconditional Love and Total Personal Responsibility. By "shifting sand" he meant the impermanent physical world.

The beautiful statement in the Bible that says, "Be still and know that I am God,"[6] speaks of this inner-stillness that Buddha, as well as Christ, literally became.

This brings us back to, "what you resist will persist". You can expand this a little by saying that if you resist, get upset over and argue against the reality that appears in front of you, you will suffer. It is like arguing with the tide or the weather. It is ultimately futile. The tide is going to come in whether you agree with it or not. The sun will shine or it will rain. You have no control over it. You just have to work with it. Suffering, therefore, is regarded as a mental condition that is self-induced due to confusion about the nature of reality.

Physical pain is not suffering as such. A pain in the leg, for example, is just that—a pain in the leg. The suffering is caused by not accepting and working constructively with the pain in the leg. Added to the pain in the leg, therefore, is fear and anger, for example. The natural grief surrounding the loss of a loved one is not suffering. Not accepting that your loved one is gone and believing that you can't live without that person is the cause of the suffering. Even facing death is not suffering, because to the Higher-Self, death has no real meaning. The passing away of the physical body is just another experience on its journey of ever expanding consciousness.

Of course the ego is in conflict with this because it can't relate to itself beyond the physical body/mind and what it can possess with that physical body/mind. Peace cannot be found in the ego. It can only be found in the conscious-awareness of the Higher-Self through the practise of acceptance.

The various conditions in which we live simply make up our environment. It is what we think about our environment, the

---

[5]   The Bible, International Standard Version (1984). Matthew 7:24-27.

[6]   The Bible, King James Version. Cambridge Edition. Psalm 46.

meanings we place on it and as a result, what we feel about it and do with it that determines our suffering or our peace of mind. It also determines whether we act destructively or constructively.

The answer is in understanding that on the level of the human fear-based mind, we know nothing about the reality of things. Our pain and fear confirms this. Only on the level of conscious-awareness can we hope to see true reality with any real clarity. Only when we let go of the aversions and attachments that blind us to the reality of what is around us, and even to the nature of our own mind-states, do we start to slip out of the nexus of or our confused habitual unconscious mental programs. Only then can we transcend into a state of conscious-awareness. Only at this level of consciousness does true insight come that leads to real solutions, such as working to improve the way we communicate with a loved one, for example.

Your relationship with the world at large once again points to your relationship with your own mind. Are you *being* the mind that is lost in its confusions, or are you working toward *being* conscious-awareness that is endeavouring to rise above and take care of the mind, using the tried and proven principles of Unconditional Love and Total Personal Responsibility? Are you accepting full responsibility to Love yourself unconditionally and in so doing, setting yourself free from your futile struggle with the world, as well as those immediately around you? Are you recognising the true nature of yourself?

The key that frees you from suffering in within YOU.

I bring peace to my mind by accepting life as it is and working positively with it.

See Table 4. on the following page for a break down on the cause of suffering and how to overcome it.

Table 4: The Cause of Suffering and its Solution

- ✓ We get confused because we start out as vulnerable children, who are emotionally and physically dependent on confused people and our physical environment. This dynamic is repeated over many lifetimes.
- ✓ This confusion blinds us to the reality of who we are, because we are led to mistakenly think that we are a mere mortal body/mind and that we can only get Love from other people and material things.
- ✓ Who we really are is consciousness that is eternal and one with the Universal Life-Force of Unconditional Love and Wisdom.
- ✓ Because of our confusion, we think that in order to be worthy and to experience Love, we must wait for, convince or forcefully make other people love us. Our potential of consciousness is reduced to mere ego.
- ✓ Because we think that Love is outside of us, we endlessly chase after and try to possess what makes us feel good and run away from or hate and fight what does not make us feel good.
- ✓ Trying to play out this ego game of aversion or attachment only leads to suffering and a lack of awareness and/or denial of our true Self.
- ✓ True Love remains elusive because the ego is created out of confusion and can only create more confusion.
- ✓ Our ultimate worthiness is, in reality, without question.
- ✓ Other human beings do not have ultimate control over our worthiness.
- ✓ Our worthiness and our mind as a whole is totally within the control of ourself as consciousness-awareness.

✓ We realize the true nature of suffering by stepping out of aversion and attachment and into the inner-stillness of a detached observer, where we gain conscious-awareness of the impermanent nature of attachment and aversion, and therefore the mind and its ego.

✓ As this detached observer, we overcome suffering by accepting total personal responsibility to Love ourself unconditionally and thus awaken within us the power of conscious-awareness, our first experience of the permanent, true nature of ourself.

CHAPTER TWO SUMMARY

1. The opposite of self-acceptance is self-condemnation, which says we are unworthy because we are human. This is the root of all destructive thought—suffering.

2. Repeated thoughts develop into subconscious beliefs that control our everyday perceptions.

3. A misbelief is any belief that contradicts Unconditional Love.

4. As children we are powerless, vulnerable and dependent on our carers.

5. As vulnerable children we are compelled to believe what our carers repeatedly tell us or demonstrate to us, even when it is not true.

6. What we learn to believe as children becomes our social conditioning.

7. Misbeliefs distort our perceptions of reality, which can cause us to act/react inappropriately throughout our life.

8. When we blindly act out our negative conditioning, without knowing it we are attacking our own self with our own misbeliefs.

9. Self-condemnation, whether conscious or unconscious, leaves us vulnerable to the negative judgments and actions of others.

10. Self-condemnation, whether conscious or unconscious, can lead us to mistake innocent actions of others for something malicious.

11. Self-condemnation, whether conscious or unconscious, leads to selfishness—an unhealthy dependency on others and material things.

12. Self-acceptance opens the door of our mind to Love and healing.

13. Self-acceptance is a healthy form of self-love.

14. We are worthy of Unconditional Love always. We always have been worthy of this Love and we always will be, no matter what mistakes we make, no matter what anyone else says to us or does to us or thinks about us.

15. Love is the Universal Life-Force that is freely available to everyone unconditionally.

16. All we have to do to qualify for this Love is to exist.

17. This Universal Life-Force of Unconditional Love is the very core of our being, our Higher-Self. It is the benchmark that our feelings are set to.

18. If our thoughts are out of alignment with Unconditional Love, we feel pain in the form of human emotion. If our thoughts are in tune with Unconditional Love, we feel joy, the Unconditional Love that is our Higher-Self—our higher feelings.

19. We can't control how others love us, but we can take charge of how we love and care for ourself.

20. This self-care then creates better relationships with others.

21. It is easier to face and overcome our fears and insecurities when we accept our right to be human.

22. Misbeliefs of self-condemnation can create a build-up of emotional pain that can lead to destructive behaviour.

23. This back-log of emotional pain needs to be released with care and skilful guidance.

24. Emotions and feelings exist to tell your adult conscious-awareness vital information about the state of your mind, and what is going on around you.

25. To effectively manage your life, you must learn to tune in to your emotions and feelings and understand what they are telling you.

26. Self-care is about having a genuinely loving relationship with yourself.

27. Start by setting a sincere intention to be that Loving Guardian to your own human-self and be willing to learn as you go.

28. Buddha taught us that we suffer because we are not accepting this impermanent world as it is, and that we don't know the true nature of ourself, which is pure conscious-awareness that is not threatened by anything.

29. Buddha taught that when we suffer we are caught in the nexus of chasing after and trying to consume what brings us comfort and call this love, and running away from, hating and fighting what does not bring us comfort.

30. Buddha taught that stepping out of this endless ego game of attachment and aversion and into the inner-stillness of acceptance of what is, enables us to connect our consciousness directly to the Universal Life-Force of Unconditional Love (Universal Consciousness).

31. By accepting total personal responsibility to Love ourself unconditionally, we can awaken to our oneness with Love itself.

✓ **Your emotions/feelings are a vital source of information.**

✓ **Believe in your absolute worthiness of Unconditional Love.**

✓ **Be the Loving Guardian of your own human-self.**

✓ **If you want others to love you, love yourself.**

✓ ***NEVER GIVE UP!***

EXERCISE 3
CONTEMPLATING SELF-ACCEPTANCE /
UNCONDITIONAL LOVE

As you work with this exercise, be aware that there are no definitive answers here. This is simply an exercise designed to gain awareness of your attitudes regarding Unconditional Love and to get you started on the journey of expanding your awareness. Your thoughts on this subject are naturally going to evolve over time.

Read through the whole exercise first to get a feel for the purpose and process of the questions.

1. My thoughts on Unconditional Love
   a) Spend some time exploring in your journal your attitudes concerning Unconditional Love.
   b) Perhaps you can start by jotting down random dot points as thoughts come to you.
   c) You can then return to some of these points that are more important to you and explore them more deeply.
   d) Some questions that may get you thinking are:
      • Do you believe Unconditional Love is real?
      • Do you believe it is possible to love unconditionally?
      • How would you describe Unconditional Love?

2. What sort of Love have I received?
   a) Think back over your childhood and contemplate the type of Love you received as a child.
   b) How unconditional was this love?
   c) If the love was conditional, what form did this take? What were the conditions? In other words, what did you have to do to earn that love? For what reasons was the love withdrawn?
   d) Also think about what you know of your parents' childhoods and how they were loved.
   e) Can you see some correlations between how they were loved and how they loved you?

f) Think about the love that you have received from significant people in your life such as siblings, extended family members, and past and present partners.

g) Does it correlate to the type of love that you received as a child? What ways is it the same? In what ways is it different?

h) Write down what comes to mind with each question.

3. How have I Loved others?

a) Think about the ways in which you, yourself, have shown love to others. Do your best to be honest while being forgiving of yourself. See this as an exercise in simply getting to know yourself so that you can begin to work with what you have. Every day is a new starting point on your journey of life. Remember the importance of self-acceptance. Remember that everyone else in your life is human like you. We are all struggling to comprehend what real Love is about. Now you have an opportunity to deepen your awareness of the dynamics around your experiences of love in preparation for making more appropriate choices for the sake of your own wellbeing. You have an opportunity to work toward breaking some old negative family patterns. This is also an exercise in identifying what has worked well in your life and reinforce that. We can learn from the past in order to make the most of the future.

b) It helps to choose specific people to focus on, such as mother, father, siblings, extended family members and past and present partners.

c) Write down your thoughts.

4. How have I Loved myself?

a) Think about how you have treated yourself over the years, including the decisions you have made.

b) Have these decisions honoured you?

c) Have you allowed others to treat you unkindly?

d) Have you compromised yourself too much to please others? This is different to the normal sacrifices that we make for family, and particularly our children. Problems occur when we lose ourselves in our relationships to the point of no longer having a life of our own. You are in there somewhere, but most people that you know, especially your family, may be surprised to see the real you. Perhaps it is about time they did.

Children often grow up thinking a parent (especially the mother) doesn't have a personality of his or her own. They think that their parent does not have feelings and needs that also deserve to be nurtured. They can carry this attitude into adulthood toward their parents and also toward themselves.

Being taken for granted like this happens because we don't set healthy life-style boundaries. We have given all of ourself to our children or partner—lived our life through our children or partner, in other words—instead of pursuing our own interests, our own unique life. Often we think it is selfish to have our own life as a mother or father, but in reality this is a form of self-neglect and we actually set an unhealthy example by living this way. We may be teaching our children to be either over-giving to the point of burnout, or selfishly unaware of the needs of others, depending on their particular character. We may be allowing our partner to control too many aspects of our life, while perhaps resenting this at the same time. Finding the right balance between serving our family and responsibly caring for our own human-self is essential.

Contemplate this question, therefore. Perhaps there are some insights to be found here.

e) Have you been taking loving care of yourself—your body, your feelings, your mind, your spiritual life?

f) What are some ways you can take better care of yourself now? Use Table 3 on page 43 as a guide.

g) Write down your thoughts around this theme of self-care.

STEP 1:
TOTAL ACCEPTANCE
PART TWO
KNOW THYSELF

It is a fact that so often the person that we least know is ourself. It is little wonder we have such difficulty knowing how to take care of our own minds. In order to transform our lives, we must become like a loving parent or guardian to our own vulnerable humanness. The potential that enables us to become this guardian of ourself is within our conscious-awareness. Conscious-awareness is above, or in other words, transcends, the habit bound conditioning of our human mind and our limited primal instincts. Only from the higher perspective of conscious-awareness do we find the ability to gain awareness of the different levels, or dimensions, of our potential as a human being and beyond. This is essential to overcoming our fear and confusion and for building new and effective life-skills.

In this chapter, I will lay out a basic framework to help you understand and, over time, gain a feel for these different dimensions of yourself. If you are new to looking into yourself in this way then the idea of this multi-layered self may be a little confusing at first. As you read further into the book, however, it will make more sense to you. Windows will open in your mind and, over the coming weeks and months, you will have the opportunity to see yourself with far greater awareness.

💚*Observing myself with self-acceptance awakens my conscious-awareness, and it is here that I gain the ability to take charge of my life.*

LOVE IS THE ONLY REALITY

When introducing my clients and students to the idea of loving oneself, the obvious question that comes back is **HOW?** How can someone who does not Love themselves suddenly *start* Loving themselves? The key is to regard real Love as a supreme Life-Force that flows through every human being, giving us life and consciousness. This ultimate potential is available to us all the time, but it is our consciousness that controls how fully we are open to experiencing and utilising this flow. If our consciousness is not awake and taking active care of our lower human mind, then the flow of this ultimate source of Light/Life/Love is restricted.

I say Light/Life/Love to give these three words the same ultimate meaning. These words have been used in certain wisdom teachings down the ages to give greater meaning to the Universal Life-Force. Lately, quantum physics has literally shed more "light" on this subject by revealing that the very foundation of all matter is quantum light. This is what atoms consist of. This is the fundamental building block of everything. This means that you and I are ultimately made of the same stuff as every other thing on this planet, including the planet itself, as well as the greater universe. Further still, physicists have discovered that this quantum light may have a form of consciousness that responds to our thoughts, to our intentions[789]. This is something that spiritual masters have always known. The spiritual masters go further by stating that the essential quality of consciousness is Love. This is

---

[7]   McTaggart L. (2003). *The Field: Quantum Physics Explained.* Harper Paper Backs. London.

[8]   Feyman R. P. (1988). *The Strange Theory of Light and Matter.* Princeton University Press. New Jersey.

[9]   Arntz W. & Chasse B. (2006). *What the "Bleep" Do We Know!?—Down the Rabbit Hole Quantum.* 20th Century Fox. DVD.

how the Universal Life-Force can be experienced through the heightened sensitivity of the human consciousness, or what is often called the Soul.

It is a universal force that anyone can consciously draw on when they set their mind to do so.

Loving yourself is, therefore, a matter of setting a sincere, committed intention to be the representative of Unconditional Love to your human-self as best you can every day.

This also includes being willing and ready to learn all you can about Unconditional Love, from every experience of attempting to be the representative of this Love. In this way, Light/Life/Love literally becomes your teacher in this challenging and yet marvellous journey of awakening to Love.

This is the crux of the spiritual path, and the way to stay consistently grounded and centred on that path. There is often a strong temptation to chase after the spiritual experiences as a process of avoiding facing the challenges of opening our heart to our human-self for the purpose of healing it and mastering it. We are trying to avoid our pain and confusion, hoping that some higher-power will take it all away, while all along that power is within us. In the process of avoiding facing ourself, we also avoid growing up, like the teenager who wants all that adults have without accepting the responsibility of what it takes to achieve it. Being on this earth in a physical body is like going to a spiritual gym for a good work out. We are building spiritual muscle, whether we know it or not. The act of consciously embracing our vulnerable human-self is the very thing that enables us to realise ourselves as Love—as a direct extension of the Life-Force itself.

The illusion that Love/Life-Force is something that is outside us is so deeply imbedded into our human psyche. This is a confusion that constantly confronts us and beguiles us on the way to becoming consciously aware and genuinely self-empowered. It is the natural result of many lifetimes of thinking we are the sum total of this body and its mind that is so dependent on this world. We are not conscious of the true nature of ourself.

To help you better understand what I mean, imagine you are a quantum fish swimming in an ocean of quantum Light. Your body is made of this Light that is set on a denser vibration, so you can experience life on another dimension as a separate entity, a physical body, in other words. This is similar to when water freezes. You can have a block of ice floating in a body of water. The ice has become seemingly separate from the water due to the different vibratory rate of its atoms.

Because you have what appears to be a separate body, you also develop an individual mind and in the process, you lose awareness of your original quantum state. You are now like a quantum fish swimming in this ocean of quantum Light. In this state you quickly become confused, because you are not yet conscious of who or what you *really* are within this new denser dimension. This separateness frightens you and you think you are vulnerable and alone. This confusion in your mind then becomes like a bubble that surrounds your as yet, unawakened consciousness, preventing you from experiencing yourself as indestructible quantum Light, the Universal Life-Force of Love, which is what you really are. Your consciousness has become trapped in this bubble of mental confusion. Your body gets enough of this Life-Force to keep it going for a while, but you can't feel it on the more subtle levels. The mind bubble formed when you were a very small child, without you even knowing it, and any real direct awareness of this Light/Life/Love became lost to you. Instead, you came to believe that Love, the ultimate quality of this Life-Force, can only be accessed through other fish. You are therefore always getting this Love second hand as it flows through the minds of other fish, becoming distorted and diluted along the way. You even try to get this Love from places and things, even conceptual things like your personal image and status.

You think you are getting Love from these things, but in reality, when these material things, including the other fish, please you, your heart opens a little more and you receive an inflow from the Universal Life-Force that is already within you. All the while, the Love is coming through you directly from the Life-Force without you realising it. In your confusion though, you think it is coming from outside of you.

Trying to get Love from material things, including other people, is always fraught with suffering because, as Buddha pointed out, every material thing is unstable. If you lean on it too hard, you will end up falling over. You could save yourself from this suffering by realising that you are **IN LOVE** all the time! You are not just in Love, you **ARE LOVE**, and you can literally *be* this Love by choosing to be so every day as best you can. As this fish living in this physical form, you are in the unique position of being able to relate to this ocean of Light/Life/Love as well as being the ocean itself.

I know I am probably stretching you here beyond what you can comprehend at this time. If you can keep your mind open to these concepts and let them filter into your consciousness in their own time, it will make sense to you at some point along your journey and you will be amazed at this new vision of yourself and your true relationship with Life itself.

If you choose to live your life from the perspective of *being* Love as best you can each day from now on, you *will* experience yourself gradually being transformed as your awareness/potential awakens. You *will* come to have ample Love for yourself and a consistent overflow of this Love to share with others, rather than competing for it as though Love is a limited resource. As a result, you *will* also attract more Love to you. This is the real secret to success and fulfilment.

By doing my best to be Love every day, especially to my own vulnerable human-self,
I open the door of my heart directly to the
Universal Life-Force of Love.

As we negotiate our way through life while trying to expand our consciousness, this process of transformation may not look or feel the way your ego thinks it should. Your ego may have a set of vague ideas about what should come to you in order to free you from your suffering. These ideas are usually about gaining material comfort, including that dreamed of relationship that never troubles you. The difficulty here is that the ego is constructed out of confusion about the reality of things. Ego is a slave to fear. Ego does not see itself as the source or author of its experience, positive or negative. It instead sees itself as a child pleading with certain outside forces to give it what it wants. It is like a student who wants a university degree, along with all its benefits, without doing the work to achieve it.

Even though the reality of your journey of transformation from powerless child to empowered conscious-aware adult may not be what you always expect, it will nonetheless be what it needs to be in order to deliver you to a more expanded state of consciousness, which is the whole point in being here. It is therefore essential that you trust what Life presents to you every day as something that is for your highest good. If you accept it, work with it, and see it as a way to be more aware and accepting of yourself, you will be moving forward efficiently and effectively. The Universal Life-Force is the core of your higher-consciousness and it is aware of what you need to evolve far beyond your ego's limited comprehension. Life is always good because Life is Love. If you embrace it, it can then embrace you. Suffering is the product of a confused human mind having a free will that is disconnected from conscious-awareness and therefore the natural laws of consciousness.

Gaining material comfort is simply a product of living skilfully through conscious-awareness. You will realise that Love is the real treasure, and the treasure is right there in your own heart, with you always. The more you experience this reality within your heart, the insatiable need for more and more material things to fill up your emptiness falls away. A more balanced, sustainable approach to life naturally emerges from this deep conscious connection to the Life-Force of Love.

All that is permanent or real, in other words, is Light/Life/Love. The rest is created by the confused ego. To switch on the power to transform your life, it is essential to become the representative of this ultimate Love to your own hurt and confused human-self. It does not matter how unskilful you are at first. Setting a sincere and determined intention to *be* this Love is the key to becoming one with it. This is the way to break down the ego barriers that blind and constrict the mind so that you can access the unlimited potential that the Universal Life-Force offers you. This is how to awaken your own conscious-awareness.

It is important to understand that you must *act* as the representative of Unconditional Love before this Love can be experienced, because it is the action of being Love that draws Love through you. Consistent action must come first. It is the same as looking after a young child. That child is not going to look after your needs. You are there to take care of the child, and when you do, Love flows into the experience. When a confused parent expects the child to supply the Love, the parent will naturally get disappointed and even angry. The connection to Universal Love will be lost. In this case, the child is your own human-self, who is incapable of supplying the Love. Only you as conscious-awareness can do this.

You are also free to relate to this supreme Life-Force of Love in any way you choose. This ultimate Love, this Supreme Consciousness, connects to you within your own unique heart/mind/imagination, because it is already the essential core of who you are. You may relate to this ultimate Love from a religious perspective. You may look to the new wave of spirituality that is emerging today. You may see it in the beauty of nature or find great meaning in philosophy. Whatever path you choose at any given time, the essential factor is always Unconditional Love. In addition to this, you are in a separate physical body that you must individually manage, so Total Personal Responsibility is also a must. You are like a car out on the road. There are natural laws that govern the harmonious flow of all this human traffic. It is simply about working from a basis of reality in order to reconnect to reality.

Clarity Box 3:1

UNIVERSAL LIFE-FORCE OF UNCONDITIONAL LOVE

SINCERE INTENTION TO BE LOVE EACH DAY AS BEST I CAN, ESPECIALLY TO MY OWN HUMAN-SELF

INVOKES INFLOW OF LIFE-FORCE OF LOVE

THAT EMPOWERS MY CONSCIOUS-AWARENESS

THAT ENABLES ME TO SEE ABOVE AND THROUGH EGO CONFUSION

MY VULNERABLE HUMANNESS FINDS SANCTUARY AND HEALING WITHIN THE LOVING ACCEPTANCE AND INCREASING CLARITY OF MY CONSCIOUS-AWARENESS

To switch the Light on, you have to *be* the Light and keep doing your best to be the Light until enough of your mind's confusion has been washed away to reveal the truth of Light/Life/Love, the truth of yourself. Every sincere attempt to be this Love, no matter how unskilful, will help to further awaken you to reality.

This may seem to be just some obscure theory to you. What so many others who have trod this road before us have discovered through such a process, however, is a potential within themselves that they never before knew they had. They discovered the power to transform their own lives and a whole lot more.

I often hear people express, with a cynical attitude, that this level of consciousness is not real, that there are no real examples of such a thing. Scratch underneath the surface, they say, and you will find a fake with a fancy façade. I suggest that often we don't want to see because we don't want to face ourself, due to our own self-condemnation. This is one of the tricks our ego plays. Our ego looks for the faults in others in an attempt to avoid taking responsibility for our own. Real living examples of Unconditional Love are everywhere and in all walks of life. I could fill this entire book up with examples, but I won't because I want you to find some for yourself. All these positive and compassionate people are still human in their own ways, but they are sufficiently awake to be able to give significantly more Love than they need to take from the world around them. Some have done and are doing great things for all to see. Most are quietly working behind the scenes, unnoticed except by those who are touched by their ability to Love unconditionally.

To help you find such people, I have given you some examples of the qualities of Unconditional Love to look for. See Appendix 4 on page 369.

THE MULTI-DIMENSIONAL SELF

What awakened people also discover is that there are different levels of the mind. It is hard at first to perceive these different dimensions within ourself when we are not used to looking inwards. Like any subject of study, however, the more you look, the more you see and the more you also feel. It is time to no longer be a stranger to yourself.

There are three main dimensions to the mind and its consciousness that can be readily experienced:

- The first dimension of mind is our more primal or primitive level of humanness that is more about habit, instinct and mere survival, which is nonetheless very powerful in its own way. The active controller in this survival level of mind is regarded as the ego, which is like the manager of our mind who is trying to access our potential and get ahead. Ego is the potential of consciousness that is not yet awake. Ego is consciousness that is held captive by the primal survival self and its powers are used in a very limited, fear-based way.

- The second dimension of mind is consciousness-awareness, which is our ability to observe our more primal self from a higher level of awareness. Conscious-awareness is the open door to our potential. Living from this level of mind ensures that we can adapt, grow and manage our affairs with increasing ability. Genuine Unconditional Love and Wisdom is first experienced at this level.

- The third dimension is the ideal self or Higher-Self that contains our ultimate potential—the power of Unconditional Love and Wisdom that has the capacity to transform our lives. This is where we literally are Light/Life/Love.

With this greater understanding, you can be in a better position to build your identity as the loving guardian of your human-self and its ego. This will help to unlock the mystery of how to heal and grow from your own source of personal power.

I will now describe these different dimensions of self in more detail.

EGO / SURVIVAL MIND / HUMAN-SELF

The ego reacts out of FEAR. I also call it the "survival mind" due to it being in the position of struggling to survive against the elements of the world. Even when the ego gets to the top of the heap, due to a dominant will and/or material success, fear is still the motivating force behind all it does.

When we are living from the survival mind, our limited primal instincts are more in charge. This pulls us down into a more short-sighted, dog-eat-dog type of approach to life with little comprehension of long-term consequences. This, in turn, hampers our heartfelt connection to our loved ones, the world at large, or to our own wellbeing. The survival mind is basically equipped to deal with short-term emergencies where "fight-or-flight" is necessary. The only tools it has to work with are *fleeing, dominating and suppressing.* Values on this level of being are more akin to "survival of the fittest".

When our ego is controlling our lives, we tend to allow our decisions to be based on what we fear. As a result we tend to build protective walls around ourself and see the world in a negative light. We live in the restricted boundaries of these limited perceptions. For example, we may have a fear of being criticised. In order to protect ourself from feeling this fear, we isolate ourself and become a "prisoner" to this fear. This same fear may cause us to lash out at others or try to escape at any cost from the situation that triggers the fear. We survive, but we certainly don't live in the full sense of the word.

To further compound the obvious limitations of this lower self, the distortions and illusions of our childhood conditioning or programming are overlaid and interwoven into this fear-based reactive type of functioning. This lower survival level of consciousness is unable to see beyond conditioning and assumes it is true reality. It has little ability to objectively examine a potentially difficult situation on its own merits. Rather, we end up blindly reacting in old habitual ways that are dictated by our base instincts and social conditioning. This is all very well if the conditioning is useful and positive. When the conditioning is too negative and destructive, however, the ego is unable to cope or find any real answers to its suffering. As a result, the mind soon gets pulled down into the limited fight-or-flight mode of operation where stress, sadness, conflict, and disappointment become the experience. Frequent poor health and fatigue is often a further consequence.

Often this lower level of functioning is referred to as being unconscious rather than conscious, due to its blind, habitual and often self-defeating nature. Our fear-based survival mind tends to be stuck in the past and therefore remains out of touch with the realities of the present moment.

The ego tends to live life seeking approval from others and takes on roles for the sake of this approval and for material security. It is always dependent on something external in order to feel secure and complete, even with positive conditioning, but never fully achieves its aim, because of the false reality it creates. In other words, it is always caught in the nexus of aversion and attachment. Underneath the ego's façade is always some level of fear and insecurity.

Clarity Box 3:2

BASE INSTINCTS

+

FOCUS OF MERE SURVIVAL

+

CHILDHOOD/SOCIAL CONDITIONING

+

POTENTIAL FOR CONSCIOUSNESS

=

EGO

This primal self does have a good side. It takes over many of the automatic processes of the mind that we don't want to have to always think about, such as our ability to read and write, or drive a car, or ride a bike and so on. It is designed to serve and support our higher consciousness, the ultimate source of potential in our life. It is not equipped to be in charge of our life.

For simplicity, let us call this more basic and often confused and fear-based survival mind the *ego*. See Diagram 1 on the following page.

Diagram 1. The Development of the Ego Personality

Past Memories and Conditioning

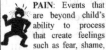

PAIN: Events that are beyond child's ability to process that create feelings such as fear, shame, abandonment, rejection etc. Such events evolve into negative conditioning.

EGO IDENTITY CONFUSION Who am I beyond my ego role-playing?

JOY: Events that child experiences as affirming self-worth, a positive ego identity and emotional security in general. Such events evolve into positive conditioning.

Despair, Demanding, Tantrums, Hopelessness, Avoidance etc.

Command, Flexibility, Nurturing, Adventurous etc.

Highly developed instinctual / habitual defence / offence strategies to protect emotional vulnerability.

Ability to be present in the moment using conscious communication, cooperation and emotional processing due to being connected to higher consciousness.

Survival Protector-Self

Higher-Self

Sum of all these parts can be called the *Ego*

Here I am. Where's my future?!

◄ **PERSONA:** What one wants the world to see.

Emotional Baggage boxed up and made to look like we are the innocent victim with no part in the conflicts that are perpetuated in our life. The shadow self that takes over in moments of insecurity and vulnerability, such as after the honeymoon period of a relationship is over.

HIGHER-SELF: Our conscience, intuition, better judgement. Often taken for granted and neglected in favour of short-term gratification and control games.

HIGHER-SELF

The Higher-Self represents our ideal self from where we can access our highest potential. It is from this level of our being that we directly assess the Universal Life-Force of Unconditional Love. It is where we are all directly plugged into Life itself.

The Higher-Self is described as super-consciousness, due to its mysterious ability to transform our lives beyond the limited reasoning of the ego. It can be seen as our God-Self or Divinity. Some people call it Christ Consciousness while others call it Buddha Nature or simply the Higher Power. There are many names given to the Higher-Self, depending on creed and culture, but I believe that we are all referring to the one universal source of supreme consciousness that is the very source of Life in the human mind and Soul. True Saints or Masters operate at this supreme level of consciousness. In regards to consciousness, the Higher-Self is where we are all heading. It is our own unique version of our ultimate potential as an evolving human being.

Even though we are on the journey of consciously becoming this Higher-Self, our Higher-Self already exists as our own personal connection with the Universal Life-Force or God. It is like our spiritual template or blueprint. It is like our own ultimate inner-Guru. The greatest desire of a true Guru (a spiritual master who you have chosen as your personal teacher) is to help you become as great, or even greater than, his or herself. A wonderful quality of a true Guru or high Spiritual Guide is that they not only see the depths of your humanness but they also see your highest potential, even when you cannot.

The Higher-Self responds and operates from Unconditional Love. It remains above and unaffected by any distorted conditioning of our ego. It has the power to embrace the woundedness and confusion that accumulates in our vulnerable human mind and actually heal it. This higher consciousness also has the power to override the basic instincts of our primal-self when it is for our highest good, or for the highest good of others, such as with spontaneous acts of heroism.

Our Higher-Self always knows what is the highest path to take that has the greatest long-term benefit, not only for ourself, but for everyone concerned. Rather than isolating us and building cold walls of fear and mistrust, like the survival mind of the ego does, our Higher-Self creates healing, harmony, openness and connection. This higher consciousness can do this while at the same time providing us with a deeper and more stable sense of security and emotional wellbeing.

When we can connect to this divine dimension of consciousness, qualities such as compassion, courage, insight, joy, serenity and genuine intimacy can be experienced. The Higher-Self can see Life as it is and knows the greater purpose behind what we see.

The Higher-Self enables us to grow and evolve. In fact, it is the driving force that pushes us along our evolutionary path. It is also the source of good health and vitality. When we are living our life through this higher consciousness, it is commonly described as "following our heart."

You already access this sublime state of super-consciousness during the most exquisite moments of your life, such as being in awe of a beautiful scene in nature, a spontaneous act of courage, being "in the zone" while engaging in sport or the performing arts, selflessly pulling together with others in a crisis, or the bliss of experiencing your own child being born, and so on. It is also the power behind one's ability to accept, work with and emotionally rise above adversity.

Clarity Box 3:3

OPEN HEART OF CONSCIOUS-AWARENESS

+

SUPREME LIFE-FORCE OF LOVE/WISDOM

=

HIGHER-SELF

THE TRANSFORMATION OF EGO TO CONSCIOUS-AWARENESS

We all experience these higher and lower dimensions of our consciousness to varying degrees. This is not right or wrong, we are simply experiencing our evolving human nature.

We have the ability to take charge of our mind and empower our personal development. By waking up our conscious-awareness, we can observe what our confused ego is doing to us and learn how to choose a different path. It is obvious from which side of our consciousness we would rather operate.

Western medical science regards the human being as a body with a brain that produces a mind. Consciousness is regarded as a product of the mind and therefore dependent on the body/mind. Such a perspective limits the ways in which we can perceive our potential. It confines our consciousness to being mere ego, a slave to the primal drives and mental confusions of the human mind and body.

Drawing on the various wisdom teachings of past ages, modern research is discovering increasing evidence that consciousness is independent and transcendent of the body/mind. During deep brain surgery, for example, the patient is required to be rendered clinically dead for an extended period of time. To perform this difficult operation, the patient is placed on life-support, the body temperature is kept extremely low, and the blood is completely drained from the brain. According to medical science, the patient cannot be in any way consciously aware. Where scientific research is concerned, this is an environment where the variables are known and controlled. Despite this, it has been frequently scientifically recorded that such patients have been powerfully conscious in a way that was independent of the body. These transcendent states of consciousness were ordered and rational to the point of being super aware. During these episodes, these patients were usually in a state of calm serenity and even bliss. The patients were in fact having what is called a "near death experience" of which there is now a vast amount of research.[10]

In reality, we are a body within a mind that is within this powerful, unlimited consciousness that is powered by, and is a direct extension of, the Universal Life-Force. Our consciousness contains our real potential and our real identity. Consciousness has a potential that extends beyond the limits of the body/mind.

[10] Atwater P. M. H. (2007). *The Big Book of Near-Death Experiences: The Ultimate Guide to What Happens When We Die.* Hampton Roads Publishing.

It is our awakened consciousness that has the power to reorder the mind and even influence the body. See diagram 7 on page 80.

Our ego is like the manager of our mind and therefore our life. As the manager of our life, it has the potential for consciousness-awareness. I say "potential" because until we wake up to our real *power of conscious choice*, our ego is all too often blindly driven by our lower fear-based survival instincts and our distorted childhood conditioning. This is what gives the ego a bad name. The ego is not yet truly conscious until this power of choice is understood and activated. Ego is the servant of fear.

Ego/Consciousness therefore gains its power and motivation from the differing qualities of the survival-self (human-self) and Higher-Self. When motivated by the lower survival-self, the ego is controlled by positive or negative conditioning and has a limited capacity to think for itself. Ego is truly awakened and transformed into conscious-awareness only when it is able to let go to and serve the greater power and the higher principles of the Higher-Self. We become conscious that we are consciousness, in other words, and not merely a mortal body with a mind that is dependent on the body. We are therefore in a position to consciously manage our lives, guided by the ultimate laws of consciousness—Unconditional Love and Total Personal Responsibility. With this greater power working through us, we are able to discern how best to live in any given moment, regardless of old conditioning.

This journey into conscious-awareness often does not begin until the ego runs up against a crisis from which it finds itself powerless to escape. We are then forced to look beyond how we previously perceived life. Due to the ingrained nature of the conditioning of our survival-self, this transition from blind ego to aware consciousness is usually gradual and often faltering.

Therefore, let us refer to this aspect of our mind as *ego* if it is unawakened to its power of choice, and *conscious-awareness* if that choice-realisation has occurred.

See Diagram 2. on page 76 for a further summary of the different levels of the mind and consciousness.

Clarity Box 3:4

HIGHER–SELF

+

HUMAN POTENTIAL FOR CONSCIOUSNESS

=

CONSCIOUS AWARENESS

Diagram 2. Mind Flow Chart

HIGHER SELF

- Highest, unlimited potential.
- Ideal Self.
- Superconscious.
- Unconditional Love, Wisdom, Power and be wise.
- Responds from Love.
- Limitless growth, evolution.
- Power to heal and integrate human-self.
- Intuition, insight, inspiration.
- Eternally in the now.
- Always adaptable.
- Empowers consciousness with awareness.

Human-self or body/mind or survival mind—consisting of:

- **Instincts** - common to all—basically unchangeable—survival orientated. Limited to safety, comfort, and fight or flight.
- **Character** - unique to individual—mostly unchangeable, can be subject to limited refinement—character being a combination of Will, Thinking, and Feeling.
- **Conditioning / Programming** - emotional needs of the human-self, often symbolised as **Inner-child**.
   - Unconscious, Subconscious.
   - Fear-based reactions.

LOWER SELF

AWARENESS
- Serving Higher-Self.
- Loving Guardian of Human-Self.
- Conscious processing to balance mind and body.

CONSCIOUSNESS, MANAGER
- Controlled by Human-Self.
- Unaware of being controlled by Human-Self.
- Predominately survival strategies

EGO

Ego must be transformed into the Aware Conscious Manager serving the Higher-Self so that the input from the human-self can be appropriately processed. Rather than dominating consciousness for the sake of limited survival, the mechanisms of the human-self must serve and be subordinate to Conscious-Awareness. When this optimum alignment is in place, continual growth and maturing of conscious self-mastery can occur.

- Conditioning / Programming is defended by instincts that regard it as truth and resists change from outside of self or even from own Conscious-Awareness.

- Conditioning / Programming - learned from social interaction mostly from years 0 to 10. Habit bound but can be modified or extensively reprogrammed. Bound to the past, constructed from past experience and perception. Can be positive or negative.

- Automatic reactions to routine situations or situations perceived as familiar.

BEING THE MANAGER OF OUR LIFE

It is normal, once we have awakened to our power of choice, to switch back and forth between ego and conscious–awareness, depending on whether we are succumbing to our fears or openly choosing to face them. Throughout our life we are naturally experiencing this anyway, but often with little awareness.

When living from ego, learning from our mistakes and life's many challenges is going to be very limited. Because of self-condemnation and pride, our life is likely to be a confusing struggle. Even our successes are often at the expense of other areas of our life and those around us. For example, success in business achieved at the expense of family life or the environment.

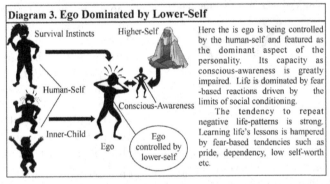

Diagram 3. Ego Dominated by Lower-Self

Survival Instincts — Higher-Self — Human-Self — Conscious-Awareness — Inner-Child — Ego — Ego controlled by lower-self

Here the is ego is being controlled by the human-self and featured as the dominant aspect of the personality. Its capacity as conscious-awareness is greatly impaired. Life is dominated by fear-based reactions driven by the limits of social conditioning.

The tendency to repeat negative life-patterns is strong. Learning life's lessons is hampered by fear-based tendencies such as pride, dependency, low self-worth etc.

In contrast, when we are living from a consciousness that is aligned to our Higher-Self, we are able to more effectively heal and grow. Our life tends to be more harmonious and balanced, even in the face of life's challenges. We can approach life in a more positive and constructive manner.

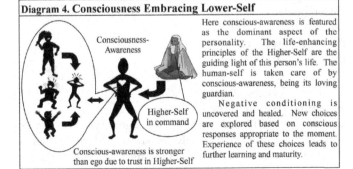

Diagram 4. Consciousness Embracing Lower-Self

Consciousness-Awareness — Higher-Self in command

Conscious-awareness is stronger than ego due to trust in Higher-Self

Here conscious-awareness is featured as the dominant aspect of the personality. The life-enhancing principles of the Higher-Self are the guiding light of this person's life. The human-self is taken care of by conscious-awareness, being its loving guardian.

Negative conditioning is uncovered and healed. New choices are explored based on conscious responses appropriate to the moment. Experience of these choices leads to further learning and maturity.

Conscious-awareness always resides in the present moment, unlike the ego, which gets lost in the past and habit-bound conditioning. Conscious-awareness has the ability to see the whole picture. We can review our past, sense our potential and plan our future. This is why it is the manager of our human life. Ego has the potential for this, but is continually being overpowered by its confusion as it becomes lost in its fears and misbeliefs. Conscious-awareness, the awakened ego, can stay above this due to the power it gains from the Higher-Self.

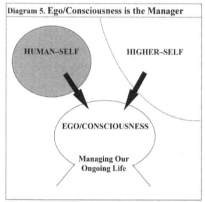

One of the main roles of consciousness is its free will, its power to choose. It stands between the seemingly opposing forces of the ego and Higher-Self, who are vying for control of our human-self. See diagrams 3, 4, 5 & 6.

In order to live the life that we want, it is therefore essential that we consciously endeavour to dedicate our life to the better guidance of the Higher-Self, rather than fall prey to the fears and confusions of the ego. Following the principles of Unconditional Love and Personal Responsibility is the surest way to stay aligned to the Higher-Self.

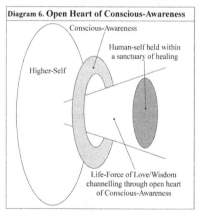

The Higher-Self is the real power in our life. Because ego is still largely unaware of this greater power, it thinks of itself as the power, but it is really unconsciously drawing from the power of the Higher-Self while at the same time being in the grip of the survival-self. Often we intuitively know this, but because of the shame-pride dynamic, we live in denial.

Conscious-awareness, being awake, learns how to let go to the Higher-self and becomes like an open doorway to it. This is what is meant by opening the heart. With the Unconditional Love and Wisdom of the Higher-Self at its disposal, conscious-awareness is able to create a whole new relationship with the human-self. We can become the human-self's loving guardian and offer a sanctuary of compassion, acceptance and wisdom to it in the form of the Higher-Self, the higher principles that we endeavour to live each day.

Within this sanctuary of self-acceptance, our human-self can find nurturing, healing, guidance and security.

For more perspective on this framework, see Diagram 8 on page 88.

MORE ABOUT THE HIGHER-SELF

I want to go deeper here into the nature of the Higher-Self and reality itself. This is to further build up an effective framework that will enable you to see yourself and the world from a whole new perspective. This framework is also designed to resonate with your deepest intuition, even though it may be hard to grasp at first, and may be a little confronting. This is not for the purpose of aimless philosophising. This is for the purpose of empowering your ability to heal, to awaken to a greater reality, and to create a life that is fulfilling—that reflects your potential.

All these different levels of being that I have described so far in this chapter are simply different aspects of yourself that are in the process of continual evolution and consciousness expansion. The human-self/survival-self and its ego is evolving or integrating into conscious-awareness, which can also be regarded as Soul or Buddha Nature etcetera. Conscious-awareness is, in turn, evolving into the Higher-Self or God-Self—our ultimate potential.

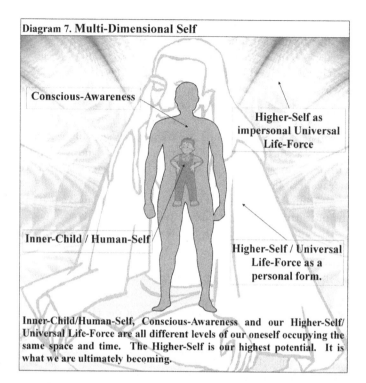

Diagram 7. Multi-Dimensional Self

Conscious-Awareness

Higher-Self as impersonal Universal Life-Force

Inner-Child / Human-Self

Higher-Self / Universal Life-Force as a personal form.

Inner-Child/Human-Self, Conscious-Awareness and our Higher-Self/ Universal Life-Force are all different levels of our oneself occupying the same space and time. The Higher-Self is our highest potential. It is what we are ultimately becoming.

These different levels of ourself occupy the one space in the here and now. In other words, they are not separate in any real sense. They are more like different octaves on a musical scale. The higher the note, the higher the consciousness—the physical body and its primal instincts being at the lowest end of the scale, and the Higher-Self at the upper end of the scale. See Diagram 7, "The Multi-dimensional Self" above.

The Higher-Self can be regarded as the Universal Life-Force that has formed itself into an individual consciousness. Why? In order to know itself, is the answer that most commonly emerges in response to that question. How can you know something, be conscious of it, in other words, if you are totally one with it? There has to be some form of perceived separation. It can then be further speculated that this "separation" had to become even more profound in order to create the most powerful degree of consciousness. To achieve that aim, the Higher-Self then repeats the process by throwing out an aspect of itself in the form of the Soul. The Soul is then set on a journey into the darkest depths of the physical dimension where the illusion of separation is most profound. All the while, ourself as Soul, is no more separate from our Higher-Self than a thought is from the thinker. This thought, this Soul, is very special though. It is designed to experience itself as having its own separate consciousness with its own free will so that it can experience itself in its own right.

At the beginning of its long journey into the physical world, the Soul is like a new born babe with no experience. Not surprisingly it soon gets itself lost in the physical world experience and becomes very confused about the true nature of itself, hence its initial identity as a human mind and its ego. Refer to my quantum fish analogy on page 62.

This does not tell the whole story though. Another quality of the Higher-Self, apart from Love and Wisdom, is its ability to create. This ability is also reflected in the Soul. We are all creators actively creating with varying degrees of awareness as to the nature of the power that we have at our disposal. Most of us don't realise what we are creating most of the time. For example, all our misbeliefs about love and communication go toward creating all the relationships that we experience. Little wonder we get ourself in such a muddle.

Our Higher-Self, therefore, and the Universal Life Force as a whole, are not separate from us. Even when the Higher-Self is perceived as an impersonal Universal Force of ultimate consciousness, it is just as much a part of ourself as it is a part of everything else. It is in fact the essential Self—the very core of our being.

We feel the Higher-Self at first like a homing device, calling us ever forward to where we know not, other than to more than what we are. This calling is felt as some sort of instinctual urge toward self-betterment on any level. As the Soul evolves over the expanse of time, it inevitably becomes more aware of the nature of this inner-beacon, this inner-Light of ultimate consciousness, its true Self. This is why we call the Higher-Self the inner-Master or God-Self. This is why it is said that God is found within our own heart.

We can consciously connect with this Universal Life-Force through our human mind via the experience of living the principles of Unconditional Love and Wisdom. Furthermore, this connection can be uniquely personal to ourself, because our mind is unique. No two minds perceive the same experience in the same way.

The ultimate consciousness of the Universal Life-Force is able to relate to you and I in any form that *we* like, and yet it is still itself and cannot be anything other. What *is* essential in regards to identifying the authenticity of that ultimate force is Unconditional Love and Total Personal Responsibility. This is the ultimate permanent nature of the Life-Force that cannot be mistaken for something else, no matter what personal form our mind may choose to clothe it in so that we can better relate to it.

It matters not, therefore, whether your current image of your Higher-Self looks like some classic Buddha or Christ or your own personal creation, even yourself as an older, wiser being, which can be quite useful. The ultimate qualities, perfect in their transcendent beauty, are what counts.

The Higher-Self is what we are each ultimately becoming. It is our ultimate potential and yet it is also self-created. The reality of the true nature of ourself has this circular oneness about it that is incredibly challenging for our rational mind to comprehend. How can we be the Higher-Self and be becoming the Higher-Self at the same time? In fact our rational mind will simply burn itself out if it seriously attempts to try to understand. As if to protect itself, the rational mind therefore tends to reject such ideas outright. We can only reach a comprehension of this oneness on a higher intuitive level, which is a more inclusive feeling type of intelligence. This intuitive knowing is accessed by opening our heart to Life as it is, and to the Life in our own self by embracing our humanness as its responsible loving guardian. In the process of trying to be this, we increasingly connect to this higher knowing through various types of what are called "peak experiences"[11], where our consciousness briefly expands more than its normal

---

[11]   Maslow. A. H. (1998) *Towards a Psychology of Being*. 3rd edition. Wiley.

state (See "Higher-Self" on page 72). Meditation is a way of deliberately cultivating such higher states of consciousness.

We are all slowly but surely evolving toward being Unconditional Love and Wisdom and being able to consciously create in line with this reality. The Higher-Self is the living force that transforms our mind and therefore our life.

Here I have only touched on the subject of the evolution of our consciousness and what this means for us in our everyday life. In Chapter 6, "Reincarnation, Karma and Enlightenment", I will explore this subject much more comprehensively as a part of Step 2, Total Personal Responsibility.

As a follow-on from Exercise 3 "Contemplating Unconditional Love", I want to offer you now an exercise that will help you develop your conscious connection with your Higher-Self. As this connection grows, so too will your ability to be the loving guardian to your human-self, which then naturally enhances your ability to realise your potential.

You will also find this exercise very useful when it comes to exploring the exercises that follow.

EXERCISE 4
HIGHER-SELF MEDITATION

a) A central feature of meditation is the breath. Focusing on the breath is used as a form of concentration, enabling you as conscious-awareness to pull free sufficiently enough from your human mind and bodily sensations in order to observe the mind and body from a higher perspective (Refer to pages 263 to 267 for more information on this subject).

b) Consciously embracing and utilizing the breath in this way also enables you, the meditator, to influence the energy flow of the mind and body. In this exercise you will be consciously setting up an energy pathway between your human-self, conscious-awareness, and your Higher-Self.

c) It does not matter what your skill level is when practising this meditation or whether you initially feel anything positive or not. Your skill level will evolve over time. At any level of skill, this practice will assuredly guide your awareness in more positive directions and add to the process of reprogramming your mind in a way that is of benefit to you.

d) Be aware that you are literally within the higher vibratory energy of your Higher-Self and also the ultimate ocean of Light that is the Universal Life-Force, and it is also within you. This is the reality. There is no real separation. The only seeming separation is caused by the limits of your growing conscious-awareness and the negative conditioning that still limits your mind. As I pointed out, don't let this discourage you.

e) The Universal Life-Force, your Higher-Self, is pure Unconditional Love, along with all the Wisdom and power that comes with it.

f) Imagine therefore, that you are now, and are always, within an ocean of radiant spiritual energy that is pure Unconditional Love. The blissful energy of your Higher-Self is even more intense and occupies a large space around you as well as the space within every cell in your body and especially represents a beautiful energy field within your heart.

g) This is your true Self, the real you. It is your real identity, even as you are becoming this greater Self. Do your best to identify as this great being, this wonderfully blissful Life-Force and see this greater power as the source of your breath. It is the Life energy within the breath. Every breath you take is you, your Higher-Self, embracing you, your human-self, with Love and compassion and all similar qualities.

h) Every breath you take, therefore, gently and lovingly lifts your conscious-awareness into the Light of Love, and in turn, gently and lovingly lifts your vulnerable human thoughts and emotions into this ultimate loving sanctuary of total forgiveness, acceptance, self-responsibility and peace.

i) Remember that you are a child of God. There is nothing you need to do to be worthy of this Love. It is yours freely with every breath. You are always alive, with or without your physical body. Therefore, you are already one with Light/Life/Love. This cannot change.

j) It is simply a matter of being aware of this reality anywhere, anytime, in the process of breathing. Make this your everyday reality, your normal state of being. Make every breath you take a gift of Love to yourself on every level.

k) Try to focus in this way for extended periods of time, say five to thirty minutes as often as you can. Don't be concerned if you lose concentration. As soon are you are aware again, simply refocus.

l) To empower this meditative process, continue to explore ways of relating to your Higher-Self. Don't be afraid to be free with your imagination. Be free to give this great Being any form that feels good to you, or no form at all. Just explore, observe, and feel. Rest within your Higher-Self and know that this great being (who is your ultimate Self) is also within you now. What are most important are the qualities of Love and the resultant feelings this image evokes within you. Your own mind is where you intimately connect with the ultimate spiritual reality. It is where you can enjoy your own personal relationship with your Higher-Self and beyond. There are no go-betweens. No one has authority over this most precious sanctuary but you.

m) Remember; do not be discouraged if you struggle to feel the Love from your Higher-Self. Do not be fooled into thinking that just because difficult times have come your way, your

Higher-Self has abandoned you. We must face life's challenges and your Higher-Self is right there with you to help you through. Know that the Love is always there, playing its part in your journey of healing and awakening. Your perceptions are the things that vary. Carry on this process regardless, because Love is always with you.

n) Furthermore, feel free to talk to your Higher-Self, and any other level of spirit that you are open to. You can call this prayer if you wish, but you don't have to. "Help me to help myself" is the best prayer of all. All prayer around this theme helps to strengthen your connection to, and your identification with, your Higher-Self. After all, your Higher-Self is what you are becoming, step-by-step. Your Higher-Self is your most faithful companion. This greatest of Love will never and can never abandon you, no matter what the circumstance. It is Life itself.

o) If you combine prayer with your conscious Life-Force-empowered breath, it will give even more power to your alignment with your Higher-Self.

p) Realise always that you are *not* appealing to some god to love you. The Love is already there. It is already yours. It is *unconditional*. It is your own confusion that you are overcoming. It is your own confusion that clouds your perceptions of the reality of Love. This makes it all very simple. You only have to concern yourself with your own mind, which is within your conscious-awareness always.

q) This process makes every breath a healing breath. Every breath can remind you that you have never been separate and you have never been without Love. In time, because you are *being* Love more and more, you will be more skillful in being aware of the Love that is all around you and within you. You will be able to inspire those around you to be the Love that they are. You will engage more with their heart and bring that to the surface. You will attract the best from people, rather than trigger their lower nature. When you change, the world changes with you!

SOCIAL CONDITIONING

Of course, social conditioning is not always negative. A positive and loving upbringing naturally facilitates greater access to our Higher-Self. This reveals itself in our everyday lives as being naturally positive and loving. In this case, our habits are more constructive than self-defeating, but can still lack the power of conscious-awareness when real challenges are faced.

There are many factors that influence our lives and many of these factors are beyond our control, such as the forces of nature, the environment we were born into, or even our natural born character. The inevitable social conditioning of our childhood can appear to be like another of these uncontrollable factors of our life, and indeed old habits can be hard to change.

Our childhood conditioning is a major determining factor in our lives, and for most people it is perhaps *the* major determining factor. It is with us twenty-four hours a day and can influence every aspect of our thinking, feeling, and action. It determines the quality of our attitudes, which determines the quality of our relationships and choices in general. The negative side to this conditioning is that it is the dominant cause of our fears and insecurities in adult life. Because this conditioning is so ingrained in us, we often assume we were born this way, as though it is a part of our character, but this is not so.

In an attempt to overcome the negative influences of this deep childhood conditioning, we are likely to try many things, such as moving to a new location, getting a new job, looking for a new relationship, going on a diet, taking medication and so on. Sometimes this is enough. Often it isn't. Often our negative conditioning continues to interfere with our life, creating the same problems, no matter what changes we make. If this is the case, some form of personality / mental / emotional breakdown can be the result, perhaps leading to antisocial and irrational behaviour, poor decision—making, substance abuse and so on.

Diagram 8. Summary of Different Levels of Human Nature

 Higher-Self represents our highest potential for Love, Wisdom and empowerment. It has the capacity to integrate and coordinate the personality into an effective and harmonious whole. It is the power to heal emotional wounds and enlighten the confused mind.

Ego / Consciousness
Awakening to the power of choice gives ego the ability to choose to identify with and let go to the Higher-Self. By choosing loving acceptance and personal responsibility, ego is transformed into consciousness-awareness, the carer of one's own body and mind—the human-self.

Base Instincts	Negative Childhood Conditioning creates the wounded inner-child, becoming part of the fear-based survival mind of the ego. Self-defeating habits that distort our perceptions and create negative life patterns.
Base instincts of the fear-based survival mind. Short-term survival strategies without true heart connection  with self or others. Habitual mind reactions. Not equipped to guide us toward a full and happy life.	**Positive Childhood Conditioning** creates the contented, joyful inner-child. Useful habits that create positive attitudes and life patterns. Also unconscious and limited until conscious-awareness develops.

There can be another, deeper factor that influences our lives that also falls under the category of social conditioning. Many people have a belief in reincarnation. In other words, our Soul (conscious–awareness) continues to evolve over a succession of many lifetimes, growing gradually in awareness and self-mastery as time marches on. An essential aspect of this phenomenon is an accumulation of confusion, gathered from life after life, that we all must face and inevitably overcome as a part of the evolution of our consciousness. There is much observable evidence to support this and reincarnation is indeed a strong part of many wisdom traditions throughout the ages, East and West.

As a psychotherapist, I have experienced and worked with people's past-life experiences and seen how some emotional and perceptual carryover from these experiences can influence a person's life, both positively and negatively. I have also experienced this personally while exploring the depths of my own mind and consciousness.

This only highlights the importance of social conditioning as a key factor in our lives. When all is considered, we are conditioned socially in every life, which contributes to the confusions or strengths that are carried forward into future lives. The job of the parent is to minimise the negative traits of the child and maximise the positive ones. When we reach adulthood, we are our own parent. We must work with what is in front of us and within us in the here and now. The laws of consciousness apply to every life, including the life we are living now. Now is the point of change. The past is only good for teaching us how to better work with now.

The degree of evolvement or experience of our Soul determines the level of conscious-awareness with which we start out at birth. This could explain why some people have natural talents that seem to be easily accessed, while others struggle to learn the same thing. It can also explain why some people have a natural emotional resilience under adversity, while others struggle to survive and crumble in the face the same challenges in life.

Real change to our conditioning is possible, but only if we can access the greater power of our Higher-Self whenever we need to. Accepting total responsibility to Love ourself unconditionally is the key, no matter what our experience may be on a Soul level.

See Chapter 6 for a more in depth exploration of this subject.

UNCONDITIONAL LOVE—THE POWER FOR HEALING AND AWAKENING

To accept someone as they are is to regard them as worthy of Love no matter what. This means that as a human being you are worthy of Unconditional Love always, no matter who you are, no matter what mistakes you have made, or what anyone has ever said about you or done to you. This is a vitally important statement and needs to be deeply contemplated on a regularly basis. It is the very depth of the first step of acceptance.

It is essential to keep repeating this point, because this is the hardest thing for so many of us who are stuck in suffering to really hear.

Rarely in our lives do we experience being loved unconditionally. The way we are loved as children greatly determines the way we learn to love ourself as well as others. This is the reality of human confusion and limitation. We cannot control the hearts of other people. We can, however, make a choice to be the one to Love ourself unconditionally. But here again we run up against our own human confusion and limitation. We have become habitually and blindly convinced that we should condemn ourself for our humanness, often in ways that we are not even aware of. We need to recognise that this form of negative judgment is an insidious form of violence that poisons our whole society.

Where acceptance is concerned, if we have strong negative self-worth and self-judgment issues, we find it hard to accept our right to be human. This is without even going to the next step of considering our worthiness of Unconditional Love.

As I mentioned earlier, many of us deny our self-condemnation by blaming others for our emotional pain. We cover our pain up with pride and self-righteousness. Nevertheless, the root of blame is non-acceptance of our own humanness and our essential worth as a human being. In other words, when we deny our own humanity, consciously or unconsciously, we are then naturally prone to deny the humanity in others.

Without the assistance of very aware carers, our childhood ego doesn't have the power to overcome and heal strong negative conditioning. It only has the limited survival instincts to help it. As a defense against condemnation from others, the ego only has those three rudimentary tools at its disposal—*fleeing, dominating and suppressing, or in other words, flight, fight and denial*.

For a young child, when facing a negative parent for instance, running away is not a good option, and displaying anger doesn't work very well either. Stuffing it down is usually the safer option. Therefore, what the human-self can't forget, it will try to deny, because holding condemnation in his/her consciousness is just too painful for the tender mind of a child. This defense strategy then tends to carry over into adulthood. Once in adulthood, using the first two survival tools of running away or bashing it down becomes easier. As a result of these ego defences, the mind gets caught in this strange dynamic where unconsciously it is run by self-condemning conditioning, but consciously it is either unaware of this reality or actively denying it. This mental defence system becomes an imposing barrier to facing and therefore healing our negative conditioning.

Our self-condemnation is often triggered at times of emotional vulnerability, which creates in us acute emotional pain. As a result, we become afraid of our own emotions. We do our best, therefore, to avoid looking into ourself. We keep ourself continually distracted so as not to feel this vulnerability.

For the same reason, we find it hard to consider that we have a grander side to our consciousness that is so beautiful and so powerful. We don't believe we are good enough or worthy enough.

As human beings, we are not perfect, due to the confusion embedded in our survival mind. However, we do have the potential for perfection, which is the natural state of the Higher-Self—hence our journey of ever expanding consciousness. As we grow through our personal development work, we are becoming more of our Higher-Self and less the limited ego. The greater qualities of the Higher-Self, therefore, become the ideals that we strive toward. **In my experience, Unconditional Love is the ultimate ideal. It is the most transformative ideal to consciously strive for. It is the journey toward living this ideal in our everyday life that facilitates inner-healing and personal growth—true wisdom and maturity.**

What makes this approach to healing and growth so powerful is that we don't have to wait around for someone else to love us. We can do it for ourself, because Love is our own Life-Force that is beyond the limitations of the human mind. Anyone can plug into it directly any time they want. All this connection to Life's ultimate gift needs is the desire for it, a reasonable set of guidelines (which there are many), and the determination to keep having a go.

♥ *I am my own loving guardian.*
I will never give up on myself.

Often I hear people remark; "Isn't all this talk about self-Love really just about being selfish. Surely we should concentrate on loving others."

I am not talking about selfishness. I am talking about personal responsibility. I am talking about establishing a level of healthy self-Love and fulfilment to where it should be. I am talking about returning to a healthy balance.

Instead, we have a society of people who are continually running on empty. When this is the case, we try to fill ourself up by taking from others, or from the environment in destructive ways. This taking, this unhealthy dependency, and endless materialism, causes us to lose touch with the important things in life. For instance, we think our children need more and more toys rather than the essential life-blood of Unconditional Love. As a result, we confuse our children so much that they become dependent on more and more material possessions without realising that it is Unconditional Love that they are really longing for. In the process, they don't learn how to Love themselves and instead stay selfishly dependent on others and on material things. In other words, self-neglect is actually the cause of selfishness! Responsible self-care is what leads to real fulfilment and selflessness.

I believe, and it has been my long and repeated experience, that if you consciously make an effort to accept your humanness and take care of it, like one should lovingly and wisely care for a child, you then naturally begin to open up to and experience higher states of consciousness such as compassion and creative motivation. If we don't, we risk living our life being blindly driven to destruction by the endless cravings of a confused ego, who is always like a vulnerable and needy child. At the very least, we don't reach our potential.

To be a human being is to have this higher consciousness of Unconditional Love naturally available to us. This Life-Force enables us to overcome all difficulties if we make the effort to learn how to open to it and if we then give it a chance to work its way into our life. It is within this higher side of our human nature that we find an ultimate meaning in life, and we are free to define that meaning for ourself. Countless individuals who have gone before us have found access to their Higher-Selves and they point the way for us to follow.

In most cases it takes some help and persistence to push through long held negative perceptions about yourself, perceptions that are simply not true. In the process though, you will discover a whole world of people who know what Love is about and who welcome the opportunity to give you a helping hand on your journey to being who you really are.

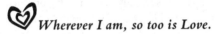 *Wherever I am, so too is Love.*

On page 97 is a visualisation meditation to help you to contemplate and experience being the loving guardian of your vulnerable human-self.

CHAPTER THREE SUMMARY

1. So often, the person that we least know is ourself.
2. In order to find the power to overcome our fear and confusion, we need to gain awareness of our potential as a human being.
3. Our potential is contained in our Higher-Self and accessed through our conscious-awareness.
4. Consciousness has the power to rise above the human mind's fears and confusions and observe them.
5. Real Love is a supreme Life-Force that is above and beyond the human mind—it is the ultimate quality of consciousness.
6. Love is a universal force that we can all consciously draw on once we become determined to do so.
7. As conscious-awareness, we can gain the power to take care of our human-self by choosing to identify with the Life-Force of Unconditional Love.
8. We identify with Unconditional Love by setting the intention to be Love's representative to our own human-self.
9. By working consistently to build this new identity, we tap into a potential that is beyond what we have known.
10. Through self-observation, we discover that there are three main dimensions to the mind and its consciousness that can be readily experienced.
11. These three dimensions are:

   • EGO / SURVIVAL-SELF / HUMAN-SELF: The first dimension of mind is our more primal or primitive level of humanness that is bound to habit, instinct and mere survival, which is very powerful in its own way. The active controller in this survival level of mind is regarded as the ego, which is like the manager of our mind who is trying to access our potential and get ahead. Ego is the potential of consciousness that is not yet awake. Ego is consciousness that is held captive by the primal survival self and its powers are used in a very limited fear-based way.

- CONSCIOUS-AWARENESS: The second dimension of mind is consciousness-awareness, which is our ability to observe our more primal self from a higher level of awareness. Conscious-awareness is the open door to our potential. Living from this level of mind ensures that we can adapt, grow and manage our affairs with increasing ability. Genuine Unconditional Love and Wisdom is first experienced at this level.

- HIGHER-SELF: The third is the ideal self or Higher-Self that contains our ultimate potential, the power of Unconditional Love and Wisdom that has the capacity to transform our lives. This is where we literally are Light/Life/Love.

12. Our survival-self or ego is rooted in fear.
13. Our ego can't see beyond its conditioning.
14. Our ego is prone to blindly reacting due to confused perceptions.
15. The ego is more unconscious than conscious.
16. Ego awakens into true consciousness when it realises its power of choice.
17. By choosing to serve the Higher-Self, as conscious-awareness we find the power to care for our human-self (ego/survival-self).
18. It is normal to be shifting back and forth from blind ego to conscious-awareness while we are growing in awareness.
19. Our Higher-Self has the power to embrace the woundedness and confusion within our mind and heal it.
20. The Higher-Self has the power to over-ride the basic instincts of our survival-self when it is for our highest good.
21. Our Higher-Self knows the right path to take in any situation.
22. Ultimate security is found within our Higher-Self.
23. Some qualities of our Higher-Self are: compassion, courage, insight, joy, serenity and genuine intimacy.
24. The Higher-Self is true reality and also the power behind personal development.

25. We access the power of our Higher-Self and experience its benefits by following the principles of Unconditional Love and Total Personal Responsibility as best we can each day.

26. By building our new identity based on the principles of the Higher-Self, our conscious-awareness builds a defence against the self-condemnation of our negative conditioning.

27. Making a deep, daily commitment to Love ourself unconditionally is the ultimate form of self-responsibility.

✓ **Your Higher-Self is the real source of Love and Fulfillment.**

✓ **Make the Higher-Self the source of your new identity as conscious-awareness.**

✓ **Be conscious-awareness, the representative of Love and Wisdom to your human-self.**

✓ *NEVER GIVE UP. SUCCESS IS INEVITABLE!*

EXERCISE 5
OPENING YOUR HEART TO
YOUR HUMAN-SELF

Visualisation Meditation

Here is an opportunity to contemplate being your conscious-awareness, who is reaching out to your vulnerable human-self, your wounded inner-child, with the power of love and compassion that is drawn from your Higher-Self.

Most of the work we need to do surrounding our inner-child is acceptance—loving, compassionate acceptance. To better relate to our wounded inner-child, it is important to build an image and a deep feeling for this small vulnerable self. It often helps to find a picture of yourself when you were a child and keep it out to remind you of how small and vulnerable you were back then.

Maybe you can put it beside a picture of yourself as you are now, to remind yourself that you are now an adult as well, who is now capable of taking care of that child. And further still, find a picture that reflects your Higher-Self to remind you of what you are becoming, your wonderful potential.

Find a quiet, private place where you can sit or lie comfortably, close your eyes and allow yourself to fully relax, breathing slowly and deeply.

After a few minutes, allow your breathing to find its own equilibrium in readiness for the visualisation meditation. Read the passage through in a slow, meditative way to help you be in touch with your feelings and to better visualise. Be free to pause at any time to feel into and explore what you may be experiencing. On the other hand, you may prefer to have someone slowly read it out to you, pausing at the end of each sentence, while you are meditating. Another way is to make your own meditation recording.

You will notice there are blank spaces within this passage. As with Exercise 1, take a pencil and fill these blank spaces with either "him" or "her" or he or she etc., depending on the gender of your inner-child.

Close your eyes and imagine that you are standing at the edge of a large and beautiful park. The park is covered in lush green grass, colourful gardens and many wonderful trees. The sun is shining and there is a light breeze that carries the scent of flowers. Take your time and allow the picture of this beautiful park to unfold before you. This park belongs to you. It is your own private space where you come to rest and contemplate. (It often helps, while keeping your eyes closed and focused inward, to describe this park to your friend as it is unfolding in your mind. Don't be afraid to actively use your imagination in this process, but let things be spontaneous at the same time).

In the centre of the park, some distance away, is a cluster of trees covered in purple-violet flowers that also cover the ground below. The sun is shining in a dappled pattern through the trees, creating a wonderful and mysterious energy of colour, fragrance, and shady comfort. You feel yourself drawn to this serene place within this beautiful park.

Now you are slowly walking toward this place within the park and as you draw nearer you notice a small child sitting under the trees, with . . . . head down. Even from this distance you can feel the sadness in this child. As you draw nearer you recognise this small sad child as your own wounded inner-child, and the emotions that you feel in your inner-child you recognise as your own trapped emotions that you have buried deep inside. You recall the difficult times of your childhood and young adult years as the heavy emotional echoes of those sad memories rise to the surface of your mind. This pain is now sitting there ahead of you in the form of your sad, wounded inner-child.

You hesitantly pause a little distance from your inner-child, not sure that you have what it takes to deal with this. You want to comfort . . . , but you are afraid of the intensity of your inner-child's emotions. You naturally don't want to feel this pain and you are perhaps a little confused as to what to do.

Your inner-child does not acknowledge you at first as you stand there wondering what to do with this sad energy. Now your child looks up but . . . . eyes are empty and disconnected from you, as though . . . . is almost wishing you would go away. You feel the sting of your wounded inner-child's rejection. You feel the discomfort of this, and despite wanting to reach out and do something, you feel powerless to help, and think about leaving because you really don't want to be in this pain any more. But then, deep down, you realise that leaving won't get rid of the pain either.

You know you have to stay and find a way to reach your wounded inner-child, who has . . . . head down once again as though you are not even there. You know you need to somehow find the strength to reach into and heal this pain and also find the wisdom to know how. To do this you know you have to reach into yourself to find your inner-source of Unconditional Love, your own Higher-Self.

What you have been taught regarding connecting to your own heart of compassion comes to mind. You close your eyes, focus inward and breathe in deeply. With the inbreaths you open your mind and heart to the gentle warmth of loving acceptance. You remember that as conscious-awareness you are the loving guardian of your vulnerable humanness and that you are always embraced and supported in this Universal Love. Your heart opens and softens a little more.

The moment you do this you feel a wonderful presence drawing near to you. You look up and see your Higher-Self standing there fully radiant, powerful, graceful, and strong. Light radiates from your Higher-Self, a light that you experience filling you with warm, loving feelings. You turn to your Higher-Self who lovingly embraces you. You find yourself enveloped in the energies of wisdom and compassion as though they are one with you. You feel the loving power of the Life-Force connect to you, at one with you, enveloping you as though you have finally come home—the home you have always longed for. The embrace from your Higher-Self is totally giving, totally unconditional. Within this wondrous energy you feel utterly free to be whoever you want to be, and do whatever you want to do, and feel you have the power to do so. You linger in this embrace, soaking up the loving energies as your Higher-Self remains fully present with you.

The word "heal" comes into your mind and you immediately think of your sad, wounded inner-child. As though attuned to your every thought, your Higher-Self releases the embrace so you can once again focus on your inner-child. You feel yourself drawn to gently sit down in front of . . . . When you do, you feel the Loving energy of your Higher-Self flowing through you, giving you the strength and knowing that you need.

You feel your heart opening up to your inner-child now. You feel less afraid of being vulnerable to this sadness. You spend a little time just sitting there with your inner-child, breathing . . . . into your heart of compassion, welcoming the pain and sadness into your heart, the Light of your own Higher-Self.

While doing this, you realise that your inner-child's rejection of you is just a fearful reaction to the rejection . . . . received in your past. Your inner-child is expecting non-acceptance from you. You can see right through this barrier of pain now to the innocent, soft, and gentle heart of your inner-child.

You let the barriers dissolve from your mind as you stay present with your inner-child and resolve to be there for . . . . now and for always. You are in no hurry. You child shyly gives you a glance that says . . . . it's okay for you to be there. You observe . . . . softening and relaxing a little now.

In time you reach out and gently stroke your inner-child's hand . . . . looks up, feeling the impact of the Love and acceptance that is now radiating from you. You keep your breath open and deep, accepting your child-self into your compassionate heart. Your inbreath is like opening your heart and drawing your child in. Your outbreath is like wrapping the loving warmth of your heart around your child.

You now take your inner-child's hands in your own and patiently look deeply into . . . . sad eyes, with your heart and mind fully open to . . . . now. You simply sit for a while, just being there, allowing your inner-child to feel you, feel your acceptance and your understanding. You send out a signal from your heart that you will be here for as long as your child needs you.

As you sit there with your child's hands in yours, you see life coming back into . . . . eyes. You now feel the need to say all those things to your inner-child that . . . . has always longed to hear. It is your opportunity now to care for this small vulnerable being, who so full of potential joy and ability. It is your opportunity to enable the Love of your Higher-Self to heal the wounds of the past. (Spend some time now speaking to your inner-child with Unconditional Love).

While you are speaking to your child, you can feel . . . . opening . . . . self to you. Suddenly . . . . falls into your arms and you spend time holding and stroking . . . , pouring your power of Love, healing, and rejuvenation into this little self. Your inner-child has finally come home.

You feel the oneness between you now, as with yourself and your Higher-Self. In fact you feel yourselves merging into one. You feel the power, compassion, Love, and vulnerability merging into the one that is you.

Sitting beneath the trees amongst the purple-violet flowers, green grass and soft sunlight, you find yourself alone and yet filled with a wonderful presence. You reflect on the newfound strength and compassion that is within you. The sadness has transformed into a soft warmth. You feel a deep acceptance of the vulnerabilities of your past, and feel the possibilities of future healing. You no longer feel so much fear of your vulnerable emotional human-self.

When you are ready to leave the park, know that this inner-sanctum will always be with you to revisit and deepen whenever you wish.

You can visit yourself in this way whenever you are feeling vulnerable. Remember that simply staying present with your vulnerable emotions, with your heart and mind open to acceptance and compassion, is enough to create the initial connection and healing.

You can also explore your inner-child's needs. Be the loving parent of your child. Interact with your child and find ways to play together and explore your child's natural potential—all those things you wished you could have done if you had the chance, along with someone loving and encouraging to do it with. These are your memories. They are yours to do with what you want. Your child now has you. Furthermore, don't just limit this exercise to your mind. Get up, take yourself out and have some fun!

CHAPTER FOUR

STEP 2
TOTAL PERSONAL RESPONSIBILITY

A BRIEF INTRODUCTION TO STEP TWO.

Total Personal Responsibility (Wisdom)

Personal responsibility is the total commitment to care for ourselves in the spirit of Unconditional Love. By identifying ourselves as beings of conscious-awareness, empowered by Unconditional Love, we have the power to stand apart from our wounded and confused human mind. With the heightened awareness that this detachment gives us, we gain the power to see through our confusion. Whenever we experience suffering and discontent, we have an opportunity to care for and heal our painful thoughts and emotions. As conscious-awareness, we have the ability to compassionately accept our humanness and to learn from our mistakes. Our pain is our responsibility. We are not victims. We accept total responsibility for everything we think, feel, say, and do. As conscious adults we have full authority over our own lives. No matter what circumstances we are in, no matter what others may do or say, we have a sanctuary within the Unconditional Love we give to ourselves. With this knowing, we can choose the best path to take that serves our highest good, whilst remaining compassionate to others. We can also care for ourselves by reaching out for help. Step 2 reveals to us the vital importance of this absolute commitment to care for ourselves, and how this commitment enables us to recognise how to genuinely care for others without compromising ourselves. This is wisdom.

BARBARA AND BRYAN'S STORY

Continuing the story with Bryan . . .

At the end of a particularly stressful day at work, I used to do what countless people do in this situation. I'd go to the pub and have a few too many to drink to drown my sorrows. Unfortunately this habit hasn't been fully overcome. The other day I had a bad argument with the boss, and down to the pub I went. As a consequence I arrived home to my family two hours late, having forgotten the plans I had made with Barbara to go out to dinner that night. Barbara got frustrated and snapped at me and I reacted by blowing my top. My day went from bad to worse.

Question: How did I deal with my feelings surrounding my argument with my boss?

Answer: I didn't. Actually, I abandoned myself. Instead of taking time out and getting in touch with my emotions, I actively tried to shut them down. It is like I got my inner-child and shoved him in the closet and locked the door. In other words, I not only abandoned myself, I abused myself as well. Who needs enemies?!

Because I closed the door on myself, I also closed the door on my higher intelligence. As a result, I let my shame and anger run the show by over-drinking and depriving myself of a pleasant night out with my wife. Was that my boss's fault? The answer is an emphatic NO. Was it my fault? I have finally learned that blaming is a pointless waste of time.

Today I am learning to take responsibility for my life by consciously caring for myself, and this episode constituted a temporary lapse in my progress, nothing more. Like I said, beating myself up about it is a waste of time, but of course I did it anyway.

The next morning I realised that I made a mess of things, but still felt confused and angry at myself, my boss, and still a bit angry at my wife. Nevertheless I am learning. At the back of my mind I heard those words, "I am okay, and caring for myself is my responsibility." And then I remembered that everyone else has to be okay too.

These words contradicted my state of self-condemnation, and my resentment and anger toward my boss, but I knew it was the truth. I knew that my confused mind was the thing that needed sorting out. Furthermore, I recognised that there was not much I could do about it right then, because I had to get to work and get on with my day. I also knew I had to admit my mistake to Barbara as a prelude to clearing the air between us.

I could feel my pride coming in with justifications as to why I didn't need to apologise. After all, Barbara's behaviour wasn't the best either. I have learned enough by now, however, to recognise when my mind is trying to delude itself. I can let my partner take care of her behaviour while I concentrate on doing something about mine. I can come to this conclusion because I am learning to see my life from a larger perspective. I have learned enough about blame and justification, which is just a form of denial, to know that I am actively throwing my life away by falling into the blame trap. I can't be self-empowerment if I am holding other people responsible for my behaviour.

Before walking out the door I said to Barbara, who had been avoiding me up to then, "Honey I stuffed up last night. I got hassled at work and didn't deal with it very well. I'm sorry for messing up the evening. When I get home tonight I need to spend some time alone to sort through how I'm feeling; then maybe we can talk about it."

In reply I got a "whatever," and a cold shoulder. Inside I could feel my anger level rise but I knew that it was my pride just wanting some absolution for my own feelings of guilt. In that moment I was determined to take back control of my mind and make a conscious choice to be loving toward my partner and not condemn her for whatever she was going through. After all, if I can have my stuff then so can she. I was again realising the importance of self-acceptance, and how it helps me to give her some space. Instead of opening my big mouth and saying something else I might regret, I kissed her on the cheek and left it at that.

I then made a point of apologising to the kids. I popped my head around the kitchen door as they were having breakfast and said, "Sorry about the ruckus last night kids. Your dad went off the rails a bit."

"Yeah, we noticed," My teenage son replied, testing me out with a sly grin on his face. Despite the grin I could feel his cynicism and see the anger.

I took a deep breath and did my best not to get defensive. Instead I kept with the humour and countered his comment with, "I just thought I'd give you an example of how to stuff up a perfectly good evening."

"Very funny," My son replied, appreciating the humour and looking more relaxed.

My eight-year-old daughter observed our bantering and I knew that in her own way she was picking up on my self-acceptance and best attempt at humility. I have experienced how this helps her to let go of such incidents and not have it play so much on her mind during the day. "Daddy's taking care of it. It is not about me," is the message her subconscious mind hopefully picked up. I made a mental note to check with them about it at the end of the day.

I know my kids are resilient, but they do need to know what is going on. I have learned how much they appreciate me being real without unloading too much on them or getting morbid about things. If they ask me more about such matters, I make a point of answering them matter-of-factly, like I'm talking directly to their higher knowing. I no longer assume that just because they are kids they won't understand or it is none of their business. This is their home too.

One of the things I regret most about my childhood is not being able to have real conversations with my father. He would rarely ever be open with me about his mistakes, about how he truly felt. People tend to think that you lose face with kids when you admit your mistakes or vulnerability to them, but I have since discovered that the opposite is the case. With mum, there would be big heavy sighs when she was stressed. She would also put herself down in front of us kids. I would often feel guilty when "burdening" her with my issues. As I understand it now, she didn't know how to care for her own emotions.

Kids have eyes and ears and a heightened ability to feel. They don't miss a thing. When I am authentic with them I know it gives them a sense of trust, and because I am doing my best to take responsibility for my own humanness, I am also being an example of real adulthood to them. I am showing them what it means to take care of one's own mind.

On my way to work, I decided to spend the day staying out of trouble and staying tuned into myself, listening to what was going on within me. I also took some reading material about the principles I am learning that help me improve myself. I read it during my break to prepare for the evening's self-reflection.

OUR CONFUSION ABOUT LOVE

So here you are, face-to-face with your own mind, the garden that is your total responsibility for your entire life. It is up to you to learn how to be a good gardener. Others can teach you and guide you, but they can't tend it for you. Some may promise to, but when their promises, however well-intentioned, fall short, as they inevitably will, you will still be none the wiser. To be the confident and skilful gardener, who is able to nurture the Life that is you and bring it to flower, you will need to get your own hands into the soil of your mind and become intimately familiar with it.

In order for Personal Responsibility to be a force for healing and growth in our life, it must be combined with Unconditional Love, the water of Life. In other words, to be healthy, well adjusted and positively motivated individuals, we must accept our Personal Responsibility to Love ourself Unconditionally.

Unfortunately, many of us have learned that being responsible and therefore disciplined means oppressing ourself with rigid and unrealistic standards that we can't possibly live up to. For example, when we were children, we may have been expected to get tasks that were new to us right the first time. We were often criticised or ridiculed instead of being encouraged to learn by trial and error, a much more realistic and healthy approach to learning. Now we think we have to be "perfect" to be worthy and we may be frightened to try new things for fear of being criticised if we make a mistake.

Even when we do manage to live up to these standards, they rarely bring us the happiness we are looking for, because they are not designed to meet our own unique needs in each moment. We end up living our life the way we "think" we should, rather than having a lifestyle that *feels* right in our heart, and we deny our better judgment to our detriment. Instead of consciously assessing the best approach according to each situation in the present moment, we are blindly acting out old childhood conditioning as though we have no other choice. We are still unconsciously running our life according to other people's confused expectations.

As a child, we may have also had a character that was sensitive or difficult to manage, which can compound the situation. In other words, children often display strong personality traits and emotional dispositions seemingly from birth. We are not necessarily a blank slate before we start. Nevertheless, the weight of responsibility is on parents to skill themselves up for the task of parenthood. It is the parent's challenge to constructively work with and reduce, or hopefully help their child overcome negative traits. It is also an opportunity for the parent to help the child reach his or her highest potential. Children are children. They cannot be expected to successfully parent themselves. Children do not have full access to their consciousness, which is why they are truly vulnerable.

As a child, we were largely powerless over our environment and our circumstances in life. Our choices were indeed very limited. We were naturally dependent on our carers for Love, resources, protection, and guidance. As children, when we lack a real emotionally intimate connection with our primary carers, over and above having our material needs provided for, we often grow up still feeling emotionally empty, needy and dependent. As a result, we attract to ourself unhealthy relationships and then we cling onto these destructive relationships by continually compromising ourself. This disconnection from our childhood carers can also cause us to go to the other extreme and be emotionally cut off and mistrustful. Often we are afraid of opening up to love for fear of not receiving it and getting hurt again. A third dynamic is becoming angrily controlling and dominating to our loved ones for fear of not getting the love that we want.

Like a child, we still think we can't get Love unless someone else gives it to us. Once we enter adulthood, this is no longer true. Unlike children, as adults, we have full access to our potential for conscious-awareness. This means we can consciously and deliberately tap directly into the Universal Life-Force of Love.

As adults, particularly where caring for children is concerned, we are supposed to give Love. If we don't already have a source of Love to give, where are we going to get it from? We can't expect to get all the Love we need from our partner. Where is our partner going to get all this Love from in order to give it to us? Our partner, and every other adult, is in the same dilemma as we are. Even more destructive is being dependent on this Love from our children.

Putting Step 1 into practice in the form of self-acceptance (or Unconditional Love in its deepest form) frees us from these old self-defeating beliefs and transforms Personal Responsibility into an act of ongoing Loving and patient care for ourself. We are learning to fill up our own hearts from the inside. We don't need to be so dependent on someone doing it for us. This does not mean we no longer need relationships. What I am referring to is a natural healthy balance of emotional maturity and therefore emotional security, which gives us a sense of independence and fulfilment. From this position of personal balance, it is then much easier to give as well as to receive.

The position of Total Personal Responsibility therefore is:

Clarity Box 4:1

✓ AS CONSCIOUS-AWARENESS, NO ONE CAN CONTROL MY THOUGHTS AND EMOTIONS. MY MIND IS ULTIMATELY WITHIN MY COMPLETE CONTROL.

✓ MY THOUGHTS, EMOTIONS AND ACTIONS, THEREFORE, ARE MY CHOICE, WHETHER THAT CHOICE IS A CONSCIOUS ONE OR NOT.

✓ WHEN I EXPERIENCE EMOTIONAL PAIN, IT IS NOT BECAUSE I AM A VICTIM OF WHAT OTHERS ARE DOING TO ME, IT IS BECAUSE I AM UNAWARE OF WHAT MY OWN MIND IS DOING TO ME.

✓ MY EMOTIONAL PAIN IS MY OPPORTUNITY TO EXPAND MY CONSCIOUSNESS FURTHER TOWARD MY ULTIMATE POTENTIAL OF UNCONDITIONAL LOVE.

Being an adult means that we have accepted the responsibility for our own life, including our own mind and our own needs. As a person of conscious-awareness, we become the wise parent to our own human-self, which is always like a child needing guidance. Loving, patient, ongoing care is what we truly needed as children. This child is still alive within us in every emotionally charged memory and conditioned belief.

Without the power of conscious-awareness, our human self is not able to grow beyond the capacity of an eleven-year-old child. Pay attention and observe yourself and others when conscious-awareness is lost and the primal self takes over. This is simply a factor of our human nature. We will always have this vulnerable human child within us to look after. The more we accept full responsibility for this fact, the more effectively this human child, that is our primal self, will be lifted up and held safely within our higher consciousness. Over a long period of time, our human mind is actually "obsorbed" into our higher-consciousness as a part of our evolution, provided that the genuine activation of our conscious-awareness is consistent enough. In fact, this process is occurring all the time as one of the primary purposes of our existence. We are always evolving one way or another. When we become conscious of this natural process, we can work with it and therefore greatly empower it.

None of us have had perfect parents and none of us *are* perfect parents. As adults, there is still parenting work left to do on ourself. This is a fact of life from which no one can escape. Step 2 is about accepting this responsibility of care for ourself and acting on it for our highest good and for the good of all those around us.

Accepting full responsibility for all that we think, feel, say, and do is a big step for many of us to take. The ego is constructed on the belief that other people are responsible for what we think and feel, and therefore how we act. As I continue to point out, the ego thinks like a dependent child, not an empowered adult.

Dominating others is still a form of dependency, no matter how powerful or clever we feel as the dominant one. As the dominant one, our dependency is on our ego power as a refuge from our fear-based misbeliefs about ourself and the world.

To understand this fundamental stance of Personal Responsibility and come to terms with it, it is important to realise that it refers predominantly to the mind. The dilemma that the great South African statesman, Nelson Mandela[12], found himself in is a good example of what I am talking about. As a young man he was an A.N.C. (African National Congress) activist struggling against the oppressive white South African government of the apartheid era. After fifty years of trying to bring change by peaceful means, the A.N.C. finally resorted to limited force in the form of blowing up physical infrastructure in order to disrupt government functioning. They did their best to not harm people in the process. Their focus was on physical installations. Mandela was eventually captured by government forces and

---

[12] http://en.wikipedia.org/wiki/Nelson_Mandela

charged with various crimes. The government knew Mandela was very influential and so they framed him by convicting him of crimes that were being committed by a more militant resistant movement, who were bombing public locations, killing many innocent people. As a result, Mandela found himself in prison for life. So here he was, locked up in jail for crimes he had not committed—locked up for fighting a just cause.

Clearly he was unfairly placed in a situation beyond his control. Surely he was now a helpless victim. Not so! While in prison, he was subject to torment and humiliation by the authorities who were keen to break his spirit. Mandela knew, however, that his mind belonged to him, and he used that knowing to great effect. He chose not to see himself as a victim. He chose not to indulge in anger and hate toward the government or the guards whose job it was to make his life difficult. Instead he faced his situation with acceptance and dignity. He embraced the experience and worked with it. As a result, while in prison, the guards could certainly control his movements, but they could not get a hold of his mind. He preserved his humanity and honoured the humanity of his guards, effectively neutralising any power they had to control his mind or break him in any way on that level. His actions also inspired the other prisoners, giving them hope and strength.

Not only did Mandela preserve his poise and dignity, he grew in emotional maturity and wisdom over the years of captivity. He was drawing on his own connection to the Life-Force, which meant his conscious-awareness was evolving more powerfully into his Higher-Self. His presence remained a symbol for justice in South Africa that helped to finally break down the white South African government. Even while in prison, he was a representative of truth—Unconditional Love and Total Personal Responsibility—and the truth continued to do the necessary work. Despite being in prison for twenty-seven years, Mandela was ready and capable of leading South Africa when the opportunity arose. Such is the power of conscious-awareness when aligned to Unconditional Love and Total Personal Responsibility.

Of course we can't all fill the shoes of Nelson Mandela. We can, however, work these same principles, this same power, into our own life and evolve in our own way and at our own pace. The important thing to understand is that these principles are real, whether we understand them or not, and they can work for us even as we are learning to understand them. The journey to conscious-awareness is a journey of increasing self-awareness and through this increasing self-awareness comes an increasing ability to care for our minds. The result is a deepening inner-peace and fulfilment that is not dependent on outside conditions.

As an adult human being, I am fully responsible for all that I think, feel, say, and do.

EMOTIONAL AWARENESS

Step 2 reveals the importance of confronting our self-defeating beliefs and our tendency to blame/condemn others and/or ourself whenever we feel emotional pain. Personal Responsibility is about opening up our hearts to our own human emotional vulnerabilities and consciously caring for them. This is in stark contrast to trying to bury them or feeling ashamed of them or getting angry at them.

From the results of my own studies of the dynamics of emotions, I have found that there are two basic levels to experiencing them:

1. **Free Emotional Response**
2. **Trapped Emotional Reaction**

1. Free Emotional Response

What can be called *free emotion* occurs in the present moment and is simply a natural higher-level sensory perception, not unlike sight, touch and hearing. As I have previously mentioned, Emotions/Feelings are the internal guidance system that is keyed into the Life-Force of Unconditional Love. When attuned to Unconditional Love, we experience the positive feelings that flow from it. When we are out of tune with this Life-Force, we experience the negative emotions that flow from the frightened human mind. For the sake of simplicity, where free emotions are concerned, I am placing emotions and feelings in the same box. Our emotions are therefore continually giving us genuine information about the condition of our own mind. I will deal with this more when exploring trapped emotional reactions. Free emotions are also giving us vital information about our environment and those we encounter. They tell us about our personal needs such as safety or Love etc.

This information helps our conscious-awareness know how to appropriately act in any given moment. For example, you may walk too close to the edge of a cliff and feel a wave of fear rush through you. This is your body/mind giving you an appropriate warning signal. Or on a more subtle level you may feel the presence of anger in the person with whom you are trying to communicate, and your body/mind feeds you signals that cause you to be wary. Of course our emotional responses can also be pleasant, such as when we are being shown loving kindness by someone.

2. Trapped Emotional Reaction

This is old emotional energy that has become trapped within our body/mind's memory network. It is like a negative emotional memory. In regards to the differentiation between feeling and emotion, this is emotion that is devoid of its higher feeling counterpart. Most of this *trapped emotion* is left over from our childhood when we did not always have the ability or opportunity to resolve situations that were psychologically damaging to us. As a result, we became confused and took on beliefs about ourself and the world that were not true (negative social conditioning). It is these misbeliefs that keep the emotions trapped within us. This trapped emotional energy is then instantly stirred up whenever the misbeliefs are triggered. Such confusion can then cause further emotional difficulty throughout the rest of our life, trapping even more negative emotional energy into our memory system.

Children are spontaneously emotional. Emotions dominate the way these young minds think. When children are happy, they are overjoyed, and when they are sad, it is the end of the world. Children are naturally emotional beings, which does not change until they are well into puberty and beyond when their rational mind gets a grip, for better or for worse, on their emotions.

Clarity Box 4:2

CHILDHOOD WOUNDS

CREATING MISBELIEFS / TRAPPED EMOTIONAL ENERGY

MISBELIEFS CARRIED OVER INTO ADULTHOOD

DISTORTED PERCEPTIONS OF REALITY LEADING TO FURTHER CONFLICT AND PAIN

FURTHER ACCUMULATION OF TRAPPED EMOTIONAL ENERGY

Unfortunately, evolving into adulthood means that we are liable to forget what it was like to be children. We seldom have patience for children who cannot act like adults, no matter how hard they try. When children are condemned and rejected for being emotional, for not being able to control their wants or emotional reactions, it puts them in an impossible bind. They desperately need our love, but they can't stop being children without having to endure the wrath of confused carers.

For children, this psychological damage comes in the form of believing they are fundamentally unworthy or wrong for simply being who they are, for simply having emotions, which cannot be true.

Such a confused belief is in direct conflict with our own higher knowing, which we all naturally have, even as a child. However, because children are so dependent on their carers, their higher knowing is often overpowered by the negative input from their cares and also by the need of the children to please their carers. There are many other situations in a child's environment that may lead to the child believing he or she is unworthy of Love, such as the child's parents splitting up, or suffering the death of a parent. Children naturally take such events in their lives very personally. They often blame themselves for situations that have nothing to do with them. If a parent is unaware of what is happening within the child's mind, much confusion can result, which can then be carried into adulthood.

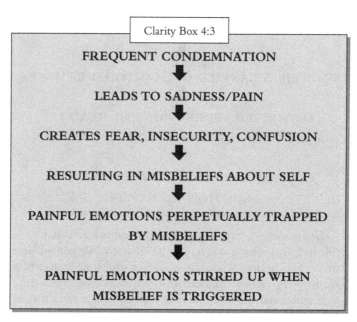

Clarity Box 4:3

FREQUENT CONDEMNATION
⬇
LEADS TO SADNESS/PAIN
⬇
CREATES FEAR, INSECURITY, CONFUSION
⬇
RESULTING IN MISBELIEFS ABOUT SELF
⬇
PAINFUL EMOTIONS PERPETUALLY TRAPPED BY MISBELIEFS
⬇
PAINFUL EMOTIONS STIRRED UP WHEN MISBELIEF IS TRIGGERED

Persona

To survive, children resort to creating roles and behaviours to please others in ways that don't match their true self. This inauthentic role-playing becomes our persona, the public face of our ego, and we live out these roles so much that we lose touch with who we truly are. For example, a boy may like reading and art, but his father may love football. His father puts him down for the things he loves. The boy abandons what he likes and tries to please his father by playing football, so much so that he takes on an identity as a football player, when all along it is not what is truly in his heart. No matter how good he gets at the game, he is still not fulfilled.

The more this persona is created, the more children lose touch with their higher consciousness. As a result, children frequently experience anger, sadness, despair, shame or disassociate from their emotions/feelings altogether. This of course continues into adulthood. We become bound up by "shoulds and shouldn'ts", rather than live our life by what genuinely feels right for us. Unhappiness and a lack of fulfilment is the result of this disconnection from our Higher-Self.

Over the years of our childhood, we may encounter these invalidating situations repeatedly. Often situations can be subtle and difficult to identify. Parents may simply misunderstand the child because of differences in character. This disconnection traps the child in an ongoing psychological dilemma. If these disconnections occur, children invariably develop beliefs about themselves and the world that are negative. These negative beliefs then continue to accumulate trapped emotional energy throughout childhood.

When these now unconscious misbeliefs are carried into adulthood, they are still going to be controlling the way we approach life. They will cause us to react to situations in distorted ways that unnecessarily create pain and conflict. As a result, emotional energy continues to be stored up in our mind in ways that add to the trapped emotional energy accumulated in childhood.

Clarity Box 4:4

NEED TO PLEASE CARER
⬇
LOOK FOR WAYS TO MAKE CARER HAPPY
⬇
PRETEND TO BE WHAT CARER WANTS
⬇
BELIEF IN NOT BEING GOOD ENOUGH AS SELF / MISBELIEF
⬇
DENY AUTHENTIC SELF AND HIGHER KNOWING
⬇
IDENTITY AS FALSE-SELF / PERSONA
⬇
LACK OF FULFILLMENT / PAINFUL EMOTIONS
⬇
ONGOING ACUMUATION OF TRAPPED EMOTIONAL ENERGY

Emotional Chain Reactions

As adults, we still hold mistaken beliefs such as we are unworthy for simply being who we are. In our subconscious minds, the self-condemnation remains. This inner-conflict is frequently triggered by our normal free emotional responses due to the similarity of feeling. The free emotion suddenly triggers similar trapped emotional energy (emotional memories) that has built up over time. When this happens, there is an instant chain reaction where the emotional charge contained within these associated memories is released into our present awareness, with often dramatic effect. This all happens in a split second and usually we don't recall the memories as such, we only feel the sudden emotional impact.

As a result, there is an over-reaction—a reaction that simply does not match what is occurring in the moment. Without us even realising it, old emotionally painful energy floods our minds. This in turn triggers our primal fight-or-flight reactions, and in so doing, distorts our ability to think rationally. For example; we see danger where there is none, such as violently reacting to an innocent comment. Another example is not seeing danger when it is there, such as complying with the inappropriate demands of an obsessively controlling partner to the point of significantly compromising ourself.

Clarity Box 4:5

BUILD UP OF TRAPPED EMOTIONAL ENERGY FROM PAST

SITUATION THAT TRIGGERS FREE EMOTIONAL RESPONSE

FREE EMOTIONAL RESPONSE TRIGGERS TRAPPED EMOTIONAL ENERGY

HEIGHTENED EMOTIONAL IMPACT DISTORTS ABILITY TO THINK RATIONALLY

UNHEALTHY EMOTIONAL REACTION DRIVEN BY MISBELIEFS AND TRAPPED EMOTIONAL ENERGY

Like free emotions, trapped emotional reactions can also be pleasant, at least in the short term. Such pleasant over-reactions can lead to addictions, for example, or falling in love inappropriately, or falling prey to the flattery of a confidence trickster. Trapped emotional reactions tend to be disconcerting because they have a habit of overriding our ability to think rationally and wisely. We lose touch with reality, in other words.

This dynamic within us is the root of all conflict in our life, because it distorts the very foundations of what we think is true. We react to the various difficulties in our life in a manner that harms us and those around us. Our distorted perceptions are continually creating difficulties for us that need not be there.

Trapped emotional energy is like flammable material just waiting for a spark to ignite it. The spark is our misbeliefs about the true nature of ourself. When triggered, our self-condemnation ignites the trapped emotional energy, which in turn ignites our instinctual fight-or-flight reaction, which then ignites more flammable material in the form of other associated painful emotional memories. In no time at all you have a raging bush fire burning out of control in your mind in the form of obsessive hate or obsessive love—neediness in other words. What fans these flames is fear—fear of not getting what we want, or fear of getting what we don't want—the mental trap of attachment and aversion.

To be consistently happy and fulfilled, I must be committed to taking full responsibility for the care of my emotional mind.

Conscious-awareness, empowered by self-acceptance and personal responsibility, is like a fire retardant. This essential self-care creates a growing awareness that there is a better way to deal with this destructive confusion. Ongoing conscious self-care creates an increasing awareness that this confusion is unlikely to be the truth of the situation, because of the volatile emotions that are being triggered. There is an awareness that unless we are living in the middle of a war zone, it is very unlikely that someone is really trying to harm us. The most that tends to be happening is that people are communicating to us unskilfully. They are simply being human like us. If we genuinely are in real danger, an activated conscious-awareness is more able to detect this and act appropriately to protect our wellbeing.

LIVING WITH YOUR EMOTIONS

When we are thrown into emotional turmoil, regardless of what is happening on the surface, underneath our level of awareness, old negative ingrained misbeliefs and emotionally charged memories are being triggered. This, in turn, causes us to be defensive or attacking or to shut down or to be dependent and needy. We are reacting from old emotional memories as though it is all happening again now. This is often called "shadow boxing." We are just fighting with the ghosts of our past.

This confusion often causes us to withdraw our love from those we care about the most, such as our partner and children. In other words, those who we depend on the most emotionally, whom we have opened our heart to the most, are also the closest to our deepest vulnerabilities. As a result, they are the ones who will most likely trigger our emotional wounds, and in turn, suffer our reactions. We all display this destructive dynamic in some way in our lives, and the degree to which this dynamic is active is the degree to which we cannot function in the way we would like.

As part of our healing process, this trapped and pressurised emotional energy needs to be released in appropriate ways. Some examples are: counselling, emotional release therapy, journaling, meditation, art, physical exercise, and other forms of expression that do not cause harm to anyone.

The mental confusion that keeps trapping this emotional energy needs identifying and *re-parenting* through wise counselling and in-depth therapy and/or our own persistent emotional processing. We must learn how *not* to be fooled by the misbeliefs that tell us to condemn ourself or another and replace this confusion with ongoing loving acceptance and compassion. Our misbeliefs keep us trapped in destructive life-patterns.

Every adult has a responsibility of care toward their own negative conditioning. All functioning adults have the ability to care for their own mind. What we need is faith in ourself, and a common sense willingness to reach out for help when needed.

Negative emotions are not wrong. They are simply delivering a message to our conscious-awareness, telling us that our mind is in a state of confusion. The important thing, therefore, is to understand what trapped emotional energy is trying to tell us.

Trapped emotional energy is like the cries of a hurt five-year-old child. What the five-year-old is saying in this hurt state of mind is often confused fantasy. We can't rely on the immediate content of what is said other than the fact that the child is hurt and confused. It is then up to the carer of that child to calmly investigate further as to what is going on for the child, rather than falling into being a part of the child's confusion. Conscious-awareness, empowered by Love and Wisdom, is the loving carer, who soothes the fears of our lower survival mind and its ego by appropriately looking after the genuine needs of our body/mind.

When we consistently give ourself the essential gift of Unconditional Love, it can then naturally and easily flow on to others.

Combining Unconditional Love with Personal Responsibility is the key to change; it is the key to overcoming all difficulties in our life. Steps 3 and 4 are about putting these principles into practice.

See Appendix 1, 2 and 3 on pages 355, 359 and 363 for a list of negative emotions and their definitions, as well as a list of positive affirmations that can be used to consciously counteract the confusion associated with these disturbed emotions.

5 KEYS TO CARING FOR YOURSELF

Below I have listed five essential factors or keys to caring for yourself. The clients and students that I have worked with over the years, who have truly succeeded in overcoming their difficulties and who have gained a significant level of mastery over their lives, have been the ones who based their lifestyle around all these important factors of self-care.

1. Daily Journal
Keeping a daily journal is a cornerstone to caring for yourself. Without it, real penetrating clarity into your confusions and recurring troubles is unlikely to be found. Just thinking about things alone is too foggy and flighty. Once you have written something down, you have plucked it out of your whirling mind

and captured it onto the paper. You can then delve into it even further without being so distracted by other thoughts.

Finding the discipline to keep a daily journal can be difficult at first. Our ego tends to be lazy and naive. It assumes the great rewards in life will just magically happen without any work. Also, our initial resistance is a good indication as to how much we have learned to habitually tune out from ourself. We look for others to take responsibility for our essential wellbeing and as a result, we are prone to neglect ourself.

Sitting down at your journal each day is like sitting down over coffee as the mentor and loving guardian of your friend, your human-self. If you resent and want to avoid your special friend (who you live with twenty-four hours a day), you are not going to be motivated to take proper care of your human-self. Do your best therefore, on a daily basis, not to give way to the confusion of your human-self, your ego. Take care of that confusion instead by giving it expression in your journal before doing your best to process this confusion. The exercises I have placed throughout this book are there to be used as a guide for this purpose.

Regularly writing out your issues, thoughts, emotions, and feelings with the 5 Step Process as your guide, will enable you to uncover your confusion and clear the emotional backlog. It is an essential tool for learning to take care of the issues that you have as the conscious-aware adult, rather than being lost in these issues like a powerless child.

Your life is your business and you are its manager. It is your responsibility to ensure that you don't end up emotionally, physically, and spiritually bankrupt. Love, harmony, and abundance are already yours. The doorway to all this is within the heart of you. Your conscious-awareness and consistent action in the spirit of Unconditional Love for yourself is the key. Your daily conscious connection with your human-self is the foundation, the rock, that your entire life is built on.

This is your own personal workbook. No one is going to mark it. It does not have to be neat and tidy. You don't have to write things that are profound—we often do when we don't mean to. Journaling is often about just scribbling out the confusion that is cluttering up your mind.

If you are concerned about confidentiality, which people often are with good reason, then simply throw the sensitive parts of it away after you have written it. Before you do, write a summary of the insights, goals and strategies that you want to hold in your mind and keep that with you. The peace-of-mind and clarity that you will gain from the process will stay with you.

Some of my clients set up a secure file on their computer that can be only accessed with a password. One of my students uses a special password protected email box for this purpose, which only she can access. She then emails her journal entries to herself.

Journaling is also about keeping a focus on your personal growth—keeping yourself pointed consistently in the right direction. It is about self-acceptance and personal responsibility. If you persist, in a short time writing in your journal will become a treasured and routine part of the day.

It is also a good reality check, because neglecting your journal is a sure indication that you are neglecting yourself. On the other hand, you don't have to be too rigid about it either. If you skip a day or two here and there it is not the end of the world. Nevertheless, being persistent and consistent is the key to success.

Keeping a daily journal is a way of having a genuine and meaningful relationship with yourself and once you are settled into the routine, it only takes a couple of pages a day to keep your life on track.

Writing in a journal is about:
- Getting to know yourself.
- An opportunity to plan your day.
- An opportunity to express, get in touch with, and define your emotions, feelings, needs and concerns.
- Keeping track of emotional issues that tend to build up and interfere with your peace of mind and wellbeing and to explore ways of taking care of these issues.
- Uncovering and challenging self-defeating beliefs/perceptions/conditioning and the resultant negative self-talk.
- Taking responsibility for, and working with, the challenges in your life. This can come in the form of:

- Reminding yourself of the principles of lovingly caring for yourself.

- Letting go of your need to blame or judge situations, yourself or others as wrong, and instead focus on what your needs are and how to initiate action to take care of them.

- Contemplating on the solutions rather than dwelling on what you perceive or imagine are the problems.

♦ Setting goals and assessing your progress each day without self-condemnation.

♦ Deepening your connection with your Higher-Self by opening your mind to higher understanding without setting any limits. Some ways of achieving this are:

  - Contemplating the nature of Unconditional Love.

  - Contemplating the nature of Total Personal Responsibility.

  - Contemplating what it is to *be* the Higher-Self

  - Opening your mind and heart to guidance that is available to you from higher planes of consciousness.

When you can consistently accept yourself as you are, and keep a daily focus on your life, you can, one day at a time, make great changes in your life.

Meditation

Meditation can also be a part of this process. Meditation is about practicing being totally present and tuned into yourself as a detached, consciously aware observer. Even as your conditioned survival mind keeps on reacting, meditation helps you to be the peaceful observer of those reactions, and in the process, heal those reactions. It is a powerful tool for learning to see reality as it is, beyond old distorted conditioning. Meditation enables you to know yourself, accept yourself, and work positively with what you find. If you combine meditation with journaling and reading (which can all be seen as a part of meditation), you have for yourself a powerful process that will effectively reprogram your mind and change your life.

There are four main forms of meditation: relaxation, concentration, awareness and healing. **Relaxation meditation** is for letting go of tension and replenishing energy. **Concentration meditation** is for strengthening your will/discipline and for transcending the lower mind, which is essential for building a solid foundation for your conscious-awareness. **Awareness or insight meditation** is for developing clarity so as to increase your ability to work directly with your human-self and to also more deeply connect to your Higher-Self. **Healing meditation** focuses on healing the body and mind. An ongoing meditation practice tends to become a combination of these four forms.

Also, meditation is not just about sitting for extended periods of time. The practice of meditation should lead to an ongoing state of what Buddhism calls "mindfulness", where you are able to effectively tune into yourself at any time, even in the midst of activity, as a process of maintaining a state of conscious-awareness. In fact, mindfulness and conscious-awareness are really the same thing. See pages 84, 97 and 263 to 267 for more on meditation.

There are many simple books and CDs about meditation available today. There are also many good meditation teachers who offer courses and ongoing groups.

Be wary of any teachers or meditation doctrines that claim that their meditation technique is the best and only way. There is no one type of meditation that suits everyone. It is better to learn from various techniques and philosophies and develop your own meditation "tool kit" base on, but not limited to, the four forms of meditation that I have already mentioned

2. Education and Inspiration

Education: Studying self-help and self-empowerment books is essential to our personal growth and wellbeing. Look at this statement carefully. Note how I used the word "study" and not just "read." When we study something, we read it more than once and even make our own notes. It is of little use to read a self-help book like a novel and then expect it to make a difference to our lives. We must study such books, do the exercises, and endeavour to put them into practice. If we do this, the same book will reveal more to us each time we review it. This is how we learn anything. The same goes for self-help audio and audio-visual materials. This is a sure way to reprogram our minds in order to kick out those old misbeliefs that keep blocking us from Love, serenity, joy, and abundance.

It is also important to make a distinction between "self-help" and "self-empowerment" books. We need to learn how to take care of our inner-selves—our emotions and states of mind—by studying self-help books. We also need to learn how to effectively act and create in the world and to stay motivated, and we do this by studying self-empowerment books.

It is important to be aware that the more empowered you try to become, the more you are likely to expose your misbeliefs and vulnerabilities. Self-care is essential, therefore, to support self-empowerment.

Inspiration: Few of us stop to think that being inspired is our own responsibility. This is an essential aspect to being self-motivated. Accepting this responsibility may mean making the effort to find that person, group, or program that has the right message for us, and the message we need to hear naturally changes as we change. It is all part of keeping our consciousness focused in the right direction.

Persistent, consistent, focused thought inevitably manifests that thought into physical reality, provided that thought has the counterpart of consistent action. Your unconscious mind or human-self is doing this for you all the time but it often creates what you, as the conscious self, don't want. Learn to create consciously, in line with the laws of consciousness and you will have what you *do* want. Being inspired keeps your thoughts and creative energy on a higher plane.

3. Counselling/Therapy/Life Coaching
See page 12.

4. Personal Sharing and Development Groups
See page 14.

5. Look After Your Body
Another obvious telltale sign that we are not caring for ourself is the way we take care of our bodies. I am not going to talk

at length about healthy diet and fitness. We all know what this means, and there are countless books and other material on the market that can guide us in this area. As always, common sense is the key.

We also need to get real about excessive alcohol or indulging in mind altering drugs (not including appropriately prescribed medication). This is all about tuning out, which is self-abuse. Despite the initial euphoria or energy boost drugs and alcohol give to some people, it inevitably fragments the mind and pulls it down into the blind and primal depths of fight-or-flight. In this state of mind, we tend to not care what harm is being done to the body or mind. A downward spiral is inevitable.

If you find yourself still justifying this sort of lifestyle to yourself then you are clearly still not willing to take real care of yourself. In reality, you have a power within you that is far superior to any drug or drink. As your consciousness expands through consistent self-care, dependency on artificial props naturally falls away. The infinite power of the Universal Life-Force is all we need.

Consciously caring for yourself may include going for regular walks, taking up a form of Yoga or something similar, playing sport, and making the time to prepare wholesome meals. Neglecting your physical fitness, under-eating or over-eating, rigid and obsessive diets or frequently eating poor quality foods means that you need to accept and Love yourself more.

Rest and Recreation
Rest: We need to make a distinction between rest and recreation. Rest is about the cessation of activity. A round of golf is not rest, it is recreation. Rest is essential for healing and rejuvenation of body and mind. Rest in the form of meditation is one of the best ways to learn how to relax. Relaxation meditation is very easy to do. Just sitting on a grassy slope looking out over a lake while letting go of the issues and business of your life is a relaxation meditation. If you can't sit still for any length of time, then you need to get in touch with why, because if you don't, you are liable to have a very short life or a very large medical bill or both.

Meditation is also about having a restful mind. We can have a restful mind while being active, and indeed this is the goal one would wish to achieve. A restful mind is a mind that has clarity, balance and detachment. Usually we have to start this practice by sitting down and doing it in a more concentrated form before we are then able to take it into our daily activities. The 5 Step Process that you are beginning to learn by reading this book is a powerful meditation that we can take with us wherever we go.

Recreation: Like rest, having fun is also essential for healing and rejuvenation. All too often we get on the treadmill of thinking that we can't relax and be happy until we achieve this or that, or until a certain person treats us "properly". Meanwhile we are wasting our opportunity to enjoy life now. Happiness is a choice. It does not always depend on outside circumstances. We can literally choose to have fun whenever we wish, and this is essential for healing and personal growth. The challenges that we face in life, even if willingly faced, impacts our body and mind in many ways. As our consciousness expands, our whole body and mind is going through a refinement process. Our body and mind needs to rest and find enjoyment in order to have time to fully recover. We need these gaps in our daily responsibilities to relax and have fun for the same reasons we need sleep.

If we don't make the time to rest and have fun, we soon lose our motivation and vitality, and we may even burn out. Like a restful mind, a joyful mind is a clear mind. A clear mind is a creative mind—one that looks for solutions, rather than worries about problems—hence "re-creation". Furthermore, once you have connected up to your personal sharing group, there is a good chance you will find someone to share fun times with and with whom you can also relate to in a healthy life-enhancing way.

EXERCISE 6
SEPARATING FACT FROM FICTION

Our human minds have an amazing ability to create their own imagined reality and then transpose that imagined reality onto actual reality to the point of not knowing the difference. We do this by adding imagined information to the actual information that we are taking in about a real event. Here is a hypothetical example: you may make an innocent comment to me about my looks, simply noting something that you find interesting, even praiseworthy. I assume you are putting me down and think that I have to defend myself. As a result, I angrily tell you to mind your own business. To make matters worse, I look at you with suspicion from that moment on.

This misunderstanding occurred because I imagined that you were trying to put me down, when in reality I had no information about the motives behind what you said. Without me being aware of it, my mind imagined a motive and added this to the picture. Furthermore, I held you responsible for what my imagination added. I didn't realise that you had inadvertently triggered a set of painful memories from my childhood. Even though I had mostly buried these memories, my fight-or-flight defences were still on a hair trigger around this issue. My primal mind was still trying to protect me in its limited way.

This is something that is happening all the time. We are projecting our own imagination onto the reality in front of us. One of the main reasons our mind dose this is for self-protection. In reality though, we are unconsciously trying to protect ourself from our own painful emotional memories. We have become so used to doing this as a part of our conditioned ways of thinking. We are convinced that what we imagine is real. We are not aware that this added information comes from our own mind and is the product of our own poor relationship with our own self. We are still believing that we are not worthy in some way. We are trying to protect ourself from this unconscious thought. It is the confused child within us who is still dominating our thinking.

What makes matters worse is that we tend to be very resistant to looking at this confusion directly, because of how deeply it has become a part of our defence system. We are loath to let go of what we have added to the moment. After all; what if we are right? *Unfortunately we are wrong most of the time!* This is a major part of the reason why we create our own suffering. This is also one of the major reasons for relationship breakdown. We end up not having a relationship with our chosen partner at all. All we end up seeing and fighting with is our own painful memory-driven imagination that we are projecting onto our chosen partner (refer to "Letting Go" in Chapter 7).

There are other reasons, a part from **conditioning from painful memories**, that explain why we unconsciously project our imaginations onto the moment and then make negative judgements as a result. Here are two other examples:

Social conditioning: We are all brought up within certain family traditions that do not necessarily apply to other families— even to the people next door, or to the people across the street, or even to our cousins. When we are children, our family unit is our main world and we unconsciously grow up to think that the rest of the world "should" be the same. If we encounter significant differences then we unthinkingly conclude that "those different people" are a bit strange, or worse.

The same unconscious thinking applies also in larger groups. We regard our country's culture as normal, and the culture of some other countries as weird and therefore inferior.

Character Differences: My strongest character trait may be thinking and therefore I love to analyse things. Your strongest character trait may be feeling and so you love taking care of other people. Another person's strongest character trait may be strength of will and that person loves to challenge his or her self in sport and leadership. As a result, we communicate and relate differently, even within the same family unit. Our natural born character differences can lead to confusion and conflict.

In this context, therefore, if your behaviour is different to what I am used to, according to the conditioned programs in my mind, I judge you as being wrong in some way. All I really know is that your behaviour is different to what I am used to. The rest is what I have added to the moment. I am afraid of your differences and push you away to protect myself. I am afraid you won't meet my needs. In reality, my discomfort has nothing to do with your behaviour. My discomfort is created by my own misguided assumptions about you. I create my own suffering.

We can also make the reverse mistake and make positive assumptions about things that we don't really know about. Advertisers are tricking us into doing this all the time. When it comes to making important decisions, we must guard against our mind's tendency to project its hopes and dreams onto what we are dealing with.

In regards to conditioning from painful memories, we are *afraid of our own past*. In contrast, when it comes to social conditioning and character differences, we are *afraid of the unknown*. Either way, it is all about unnecessary self-protection. It is the problem of allowing our primal, survival, blindly conditioned minds that are out of touch with reality to run our lives. To live constructively in reality, we must wake up our conscious-awareness. The following exercise is designed to help us do just that.

Read the whole exercise through before you start, in order to help you gain a better feel for it. Be aware always that there is no perfect way to do any of these exercises. The more you have a go at doing them, the more awareness they will help you gain, and the more skilful you will become in your own process of healing, awareness, and growth. Your conscious-awareness is in an ongoing process of expansion.

Sorting out the facts

1. Write about in detail in your journal the problem that you want to deal with.
2. Describe what you think and feel about the situation and the people concerned.
3. Now take two separate pieces of paper and place a different heading on each one. On the first piece of paper, place the heading, "Facts". On the second piece of paper place the heading, "Fiction". Now prepare to be absolutely honest with yourself.
4. On the Fact page, read through the notes that you have written about the problem that you want to deal with and list in point form the things that you actually **know** about the situation and the people in it.

5.   Be aware that no matter how intuitive we think we are, we cannot read another person's mind—certainly not with any real accuracy. Rarely do we know the full motives behind our own words and actions. Motives are complex and many layered. We cannot truly know what the complex motives are behind what another may say or do. All we can ever do is guess or speculate. This list is about what we actually know. It is not about what we speculate.

6.   The only real way to find out about the motives of another's behaviour is to communicate to them. In the process, we must be prepared to genuinely listen to them with an open mind and talk things through with them. That way the person in question is given a chance to process their own thoughts and feelings and understand their own behaviour, which they, themselves, may not understand at first.

7.   When we do try to talk to the person in question, he/she may not be very receptive. He/she may be evasive or even a bit aggressive. We don't know the reasons behind that either. The person might be afraid to open up because of his/her own inner struggles. Most people, if approached with kindness and patience however, will open up in time. With the right approach, most issues can be worked out.

8.   There are a very small percentage of people who are genuinely dishonest and full of malice, who we are better off avoiding. Such people are soon revealed in this process of communication.

9.   The truth is: the vast majority of people do not want to be in conflict with us, any more than we want to be in conflict with them. The unnecessary conflict occurs because we are all just jumping at our own shadows. Learning to skilfully own and manage our own fears and insecurities is what makes the difference.

10. We cannot gain the clarity to approach communication constructively until we can see above our own fears and insecurities.

11. Complete your Fact list and review it a few times just in case non-factual information has crept in.

Sorting out the fiction

12. Now, in your Fiction list, write down in point form all the imagined information that you wrote in your journal about the problem. Review the list a few times to make sure you have all the information.

13. Consider what I mentioned before about how the mind is trying to protect itself from past painful memories and also the unkown by projecting imagined information into the moment.

14. Write about each point from this perspective and do your best to identify past conditioning, whether it is painful memories, social conditioning or the way you personally relate from the perspective of your own character type.

15. Write down the insights that come to you.

Establishing a clear vision

16. Finish the exercise by exploring better ways to approach this problem where you are not making other people wrong because of your own fears and insecurities.

17. Make sure that you don't make *yourself* wrong for being human. All these exercises are for the purpose of compassionately caring for your own mind and setting yourself free from suffering.

CHAPTER FOUR SUMMARY

1. To be healthy, well-adjusted and positively motivated, I must accept my personal responsibility to Love myself unconditionally.
2. For many of us, we associate being responsible and disciplined with the controlling and repressive demands of authoritarians.
3. When we were children, we were often condemned for not getting things right.
4. All discipline must serve Love and ultimately lead to greater personal freedom.
5. If approached with self-acceptance and self-care, trial and error can be a fulfilling journey of self-discovery.
6. As children, when we lack a real emotionally intimate connection with our primary carers (including wise disciple), over and above having our material needs provided for, we often grow up still feeling emotionally needy and dependent.
7. Without this vital intimacy in childhood, our connection with our Higher-Self is impaired.
8. Because of our confusion, we expect Unconditional Love from other human beings when they are no better at giving love than we are.
9. The solution to this dilemma is to access our own innate source of Love, our Higher-Self.
10. Every adult has the potential for conscious-awareness, which enables us, as adults, to access our own internal source of Love.
11. Our children depend on us for this consciously aware Unconditional Love.
12. What this necessary self-Love leads to is a healthy balance of emotional security, which gives us a sense of independence and confidence.
13. With this Love I can take care of my own human-self, the child within me, and have better relationships with others.
14. The child I once was is still alive within me in every emotionally charged memory.
15. As adults, there is still parenting work to do on ourself.

16. Being conscious-awareness gives me the ability to take responsibility for all that I think, feel, say, and do.

17. Step 2 reveals the importance of examining my beliefs/attitudes and my tendency to condemn myself or others when I feel emotional pain.

18. There are two basic levels to experiencing emotions:
    a) FREE EMOTIONAL RESPONSE, which is the genuine information our natural emotions give us about our internal and external environment in each moment that is congruent with the present moment.
    b) TRAPPED EMOTIONAL REACTION, which is old distorted emotional energy that has become trapped within our body/mind's memory network due to carrying misbeliefs in our mind. When triggered, these emotional reactions are out of place with the present moment.

19. Most of this trapped emotional energy is left over from our childhood when we did not always have the opportunity or ability to resolve situations that were psychologically damaging to us.

20. Being so vulnerable, children often blame themselves for situations that have nothing to do with them.

21. Misbeliefs, that trap emotional energy in childhood, carry over into adulthood, further compound the misbeliefs, and accumulate more trapped emotional energy.

22. This confusion causes us to withdraw our love from those we care about the most, such as our partner and our children.

23. Self-defeating subconscious misbeliefs keeps trapped in destructive life-patterns.

24. To survive, children resort to creating roles and behaviours to please others in ways that don't match their true self. This inauthentic role-playing becomes our persona, the public face of our ego, and we live out these roles so much that we lose touch with who we truly are.

25. As a child, we may have also had a character that was sensitive or difficult to manage, which can compound the situation. We are not necessarily a blank slate at birth.

26. Nevertheless, the weight of responsibility is on parents to skill themselves up for the task of parenthood. It is the

parent's challenge to constructively work with and reduce, or hopefully help their child overcome negative traits.

27. Combining Unconditional Love with Total Personal Responsibility is the key to overcoming all difficulties in my life.

28. As part of my healing process, trapped emotional energy needs to be released in appropriate ways.

29. The mental confusion that keeps trapping this emotional energy needs to be indentified and *re-parented* through wise counselling and in-depth therapy and/or my own persistent emotional processing.

✓ **Take loving responsibility for your mind. Your life depends on it.**

✓ **Wise discipline will set you free.**

✓ **Be the wise and compassionate parent to your inner-child.**

✓ **Gladly learn through trial and error. That's the natural way.**

✓ *NEVER GIVE UP. SUCCESS IS INEVITABLE!*

STEP 2
TOTAL PERSONAL RESPONSIBILITY
PART TWO

IDENTIFYING THE EGO'S BLIND SPOTS

There are common ways in which our ego gets confused about the realities of life and then, as a result of these confusions, creates for itself an unsatisfactory life of hardship and suffering. In this chapter I will highlight what I see as the most destructive of these confusions and then elaborate on them. I have already touched on some of these, but it is useful to spell them out, because it is so hard to find clarity around these confusions. Our ego's entire game is based on them. We live our life from the basis that these confusions are reality and then wonder why our human existence does not make sense.

As with the deeper understanding of Unconditional Love, I am not expecting you to immediately comprehend what I am laying out for you here for the very reason that this is where our ego is most blind. This is why we keep suffering. This is why we find it so hard to change. Our ego does not want to see these fundamental realities. We will scoff at them; intellectualise them away; attack them; ignore them, but our suffering continues. Our ego wants the suffering to stop, but it does not want to stop doing what it is doing that is causing the suffering, because its game is, on some level, satisfying its illusions and short-term gratifications. Like a child, our ego can't let go of the sweets that rot our teeth in order to work toward a bigger, more life-sustaining goal. But the suffering continues and our ego finds itself trapped in the nexus of its own illusions. There comes a point where we just *have* to look, where we have to wake up to our ego's games and become conscious. As always, accepting personal responsibility to Love ourself unconditionally, provides a compassionate sanctuary in which our ego can be dismantled. It is like a safe cocoon where we can transform ourself from blind ego into the majestic butterfly of conscious-awareness. The old form must die to make way for the metamorphosis that will eventually free us from suffering. The phoenix is an ancient symbol that also tells the story of this metamorphosis. This flaming, majestic bird of magic rises from the ashes of its own vanquished ego.

The ego's main blind spots are:

✗ **The misbelief that fear is an impenetrable wall.**
✗ **The misbelief that Love comes from somewhere outside us.**
✗ **The misbelief that someone or something can cause us mental/emotional suffering.**
✗ **The misbelief that Life has no meaning.**
✗ **The misbelief that we are all separate.**

You may have expected more, but we are looking at life now on a fundamental level. I could just boil it all down to the last point, but that would be too steep a climb to the peak of reality. What I am presenting to you is already a very steep climb for most. As I have said before, I am cutting some essential doorways into your mind so that you can look out at a bigger picture of reality. You will understand more and more about this new picture as time goes on. When the time is right for you, you can step through these doorways and experience that new reality and the freedom that comes with it.

THE MISBELIEF THAT FEAR IS AN IMPENETRABLE WALL

ODE TO FEAR

In days of downturned eyes and wounded heart,
I lay prostrate at your feet.
You were my master then.

I was your faithful servant,
Dared not look at your terrible presence.
You shrouded me in comfortable darkness.

My imagination you ruled with your skillful ways.
I kept your commandments and kept my distance
From those who walked with open eyes.

With you as my god, I thought I was greater than all,
And afraid I was less than the rest, until
My heart lay dying on your battle field.

Wounded and bleeding I lay,
I could fight no longer,
Gone was my strength and my weapons were lost.

Beaten, I surrendered to the enemy,
And prepared myself for death,
But somehow Life came instead.

Only a false self lay broken on this battlefield of delusion.
A new Self rose from these ashes of defeat.
In my transformation I saw the world anew.

Today I too walk with open eyes,
And see you as you are,
As you unwittingly lead me to my Self.

Your flaming breath is but hot air.
Your terrible presence a facade.
Your commandments lies and falsehoods.

My imagination truth now rules.
My commandment is now Love.
My heart is filled with the presence of the One.

So much of what this book is about is learning to face our fears and see that they have no basis in reality.

Fear is a factor in our life in part because our physical body/mind operates on mere mortal survival, the same as the animal kingdom. Fear is the driving force on this level of reality. This fear is then accentuated because human beings have the added power and potential of consciousness. As a result of consciousness, we don't have the comfort of simply being our instincts and being at one with nature like the animal (the oneness that we can and must eventually experience has to be sought at a higher plane of consciousness). We are independent thinkers and therefore have to figure things out for ourself. As a result, mental and emotional confusion is the special suffering that human beings have to contend with, way beyond what an animal has to experience. This added potential, if misused, can degrade a human being to a lower level than the animal kingdom, or if used skilfully it can lead us to the heights of spiritual enlightenment where we become a guiding Light for all humanity and a loving and wise guardian of this world.

Fear is only an impenetrable wall to the extent that we identify ourself solely as a survival mind with a body, an ego in other words. From this level of limited awareness, life is survival of the fittest. It is nothing but a glorified chook yard in which we all fight for what we perceive as the limited scraps of love and fulfillment. Every chook plays its own game in order to survive. Some of us dominate to survive. Some of us hide. Some of us try to be very, very nice to everyone in the hope that they will be nice to us. Some of us rebel and try to create another chook yard where it all ends up looking just the same as the previous one. Some of us try to out-think all the other chooks. Underneath it all is fear.

In the chook yard of the ego world, comfort is the highest refuge from fear. Comfort does not get rid of the fear. Fear is still waiting outside the door to ambush us when the comfort slips away. The ego can only find its comforts in the material world by consuming more and more of what brings it comfort, including kindness from other people. This seeking of comfort is about avoiding what we find uncomfortable—back to the trap of aversion and attachment (see pages 47 to 48). We are always, therefore, in a position of powerlessness over the conditions of life, no matter how materially successful we might seem. Just read about the rich and famous in the magazines. Despite supposedly having everything, true happiness and peace of mind is still illusive. We envy them nonetheless, thinking that if we had all those resources we could somehow do it differently. But that is the ego deluding itself again. In the chook yard of the ego world, we are not the masters of life, we are just trying to bargain with it. Fear is still the master.

Of course, if you are rich and famous and also have a significant level of conscious-awareness, then that is a different matter. You would know what is truly important in life and you would make good use of your privileged position by serving humanity as best you can, which many public figures are now doing—a sign of humanity growing up. Service is the opportunity and the challenge of all those in a privileged position in this physical world. Self indulgence is the dire temptation.

The Life-Force of Unconditional Love does still filter into the ego's chook yard world. We couldn't survive if it didn't. You might recall my "fish in the ocean" metaphor in Chapter 3 on page 62. Good childhood conditioning allows the ego to unconsciously rest in the true sanctuary of Unconditional Love. To the degree where this is evident, is the degree where a healthy personal balance or self-esteem is evident. Nevertheless, the chook yard level of existence is still there. It is just a more pleasant chook yard to hang out in, so long as you don't want to be too different.

True conscious-awareness, as I have already pointed out, is at one with Love, or at least becoming so, and is consciously aware that it is. On a mental/emotional level in particular, conscious-awareness is not dependent on the material world. It is not threatened by it. Conscious-awareness, on some significant level, knows itself as something eternal, the Higher-Self that is an essential part of the Universal Life-Force. Such a knowing cannot be arrived at intellectually. It can only be known through the experience of opening our heart to Life, which is the same as facing our fears.

It is in facing our fears and stepping off that cliff of ego illusion that we discover the limitless power of our Higher-Self, hence the ego's inevitable dilemma. To escape its suffering, the ego has to essentially die in order to awaken into true consciousness, and to our ego, facing our fears can feel like we are indeed dying at times. Our ego inevitably has to face what it believes it cannot possibly face. Suicide is sometimes the tragic result of the ego-dying process. Killing the body, however, is mistaking the nature of the problem. Suffering occurs in the mind, and that is where it must be resolved. The confusion will continue with or without a body until clarity is found. What are dying are our illusions about the nature of reality and our attachments to those illusions. We think these delusions are an essential part of our identity, when in fact they are not. Our real Self awaits hidden beneath these illusions, waiting for the chance to be set free.

What the ego does not comprehend at first is that it *is* consciousness, which cannot die. Consciousness just keeps on adapting and expanding through every experience of physical life and beyond. The irresistible pull toward our Higher-Self dictates that the ego inevitably must face what it perceives as unfaceable and surrender to what it expects to be annihilation. Instead, conscious-awareness emerges from the ashes of ego illusions like the phoenix. Ego always underestimates itself because it can't see beyond the lowly confines of the chook yard existence that is created by its misbeliefs. In reality, our ego's illusions are dying all the time as we evolve and mature, but these are just little deaths, brief moments of recognition of our mistaken beliefs that are not too threatening. Occasionally though, a big wakeup call comes that shakes what we think are our very foundations. The fiery dragon named personal crisis corners us and pins us to the ground. In the heat of this crisis, our ego's façade is burnt away and we are left exposed to the fire of unavoidable change, loss and, if we are willing to face the experience, transformation.

Suffering is what initially motivates us to step off the edge of our ego delusions and into the unknown world of consciousness. It would be nice if we all could evolve calmly, gradually and willingly. This is not the ego way though. The ego's way is avoidance, because it clings onto what it knows, which is its own illusions. What the ego does not realise is that the Life of the human being is not its body, or even its conditioned mind, it is conscious-awareness. The body/mind is just a vehicle for the experience. The whole point of Life is to wake up, and everyone eventually will (this statement opens up a mystery that I will address in the next chapter). Our ego fights against the higher laws of Life and it must inevitably lose. Every attempt to avoid reality will simply push it that much closer to the edge of its own undoing.

Death on the ego level of limited survival is seen from the perspective of conscious-awareness as a birth into Life. The temporary pains of that dying process are accepted by those on "the path", even welcomed in a way, due to the immense reward that it brings. Those in the ego world think that seekers after true self-realisation are mad. The ego can't comprehend why one would search out and welcome the very thing that ego desperately avoids.

If self-realisation is the true purpose of life, then suffering is like the hand that shakes us to wake us up. It is a gentle shake at first, but becomes increasingly insistent the more ego resists the call.

To be operating from conscious-awareness is not about rejecting the ego world of survival. That would be indulging in aversion, which would simply drag us back down again. We are still in this ego world, but we can also see beyond it. We are responding more from the motivation to Love and not reacting so much from fear. We offer acceptance to the ego world of illusion, but our very presence is, nevertheless, going to change it. When we live our life based on the higher Laws of Consciousness, it is going to be either confronting to the unconscious egos around us or inspiring to those who are ready to awaken. Unconditional Love is the driving force that is evolving humanity slowly toward justice and harmony, despite the fear and confusion that still has the majority in its grip.

Facing our fears and working through them is therefore essential for realising our potential, for raising our consciousness to where our suffering can be solved and/or transcended. Conscious-awareness is the conqueror of fear and the world of illusion that fear creates. The act of facing our fear is an affirmation of that which we truly are.

The spirit of the adventurer, or the sporting thrill seeker, are good examples of the Soul's desire to conquer fear. The satisfaction of climbing a mountain, or the thrill of leaping off a cliff with a parachute strapped to our back, is the euphoric feeling of experiencing ourself as an indestructible Soul. It is the power of our conscious-awareness piercing the veil of our ego's perceived limitations.

We don't have to climb a mountain or leap of a cliff tied to a parachute to experience that power within us. Opportunities to face our fears, to face our ego's delusions are kindly presented to us by Life every day. Our wisdom grows on the ashes of our vanquished fears and delusions.

THE MISBELIEF THAT LOVE COMES FROM SOMEWHERE OUTSIDE US

ONE LOVE

We stand hand in hand looking back,
Seeing how our roads merged together.
We look ahead and wonder,
Whether it will be one road or two.

I look at you and you at me,
What do we really know of each other?
Apart from a strange familiarity in the heart,
From where a mystery love springs forth.

Will you change? I know I will.
Will that matter? I hope it doesn't.

Does this love come with a freedom clause?
Will I be free to be who I am? Will you?

Do I know you? Do I know me?
My hidden pain calls to me, tugging at me.
What will you think when it comes calling?
Do you also have a room that you don't dare visit?

They say love is about sharing.
Does this include our pain and our fear?
All is beautiful now but what then?
Will my shame shut you out?

I offer my love to you freely.
Why not offer my fear and pain as well?
Can't this too be a beautiful gift?
Perhaps a gift of my humanity.

If I give myself to you completely,
And try not to blame myself on you,
Will you do the same for me?
Will I be able to keep my heart open?
I wonder if God loves this way?
Perhaps that's how he does it.
Is that how he loves us in spite of ourselves?
Is this how we can love ourselves as well?

I come unveiled to share my thoughts with you,
Tentatively feeling my way into your secret room.
Your door opens to me ever so slightly.
Then in the lighted darkness we make a pact.

We give ourselves to the Light,
And open ourselves to each other,
We accept the gift of each other's pain,
And share in the one divine Love.

The mistaken belief that we will experience Love only when someone else gives it to us is a very hard illusion to conquer. This is the very reason why fear on a mental/emotional level exists. This is the very reason why human beings suffer. This is the reason why our ego searches for Love like a hungry ghost, who is attached to the world but cannot be ultimately satisfied by it. The reason why Love is so illusive is because we are looking for it in the wrong place. To use a simple metaphor, it is like looking for your glasses, thinking they are lost, when all along they are on your face and you have been looking *through* them in the process of looking *for* them. We are looking for Love, searching, searching, when all along we *are* that Love.

This is why the persistent act of *being* Love inevitably reveals the true nature of ourself, just as facing our fear does. For our ego though, letting go to the Love that we are already, means letting go of trying to convince or force the world around us to love us. "What if I don't get what I want?" the ego cries, not seeing that all its controlling and manipulating is actually choking the love that it is trying to cling onto. Our ego's world is based on fear-driven control of the world around it in the pursuit of comfort, like a child trying to build and zealously protect a house of cards in the midst of a raucous party.

The world of conscious-awareness, on the other hand, is based on a deep intuitive knowing that Unconditional Love is the true reality and that consciousness *is* Love and therefore Life never ending. It is the knowing that we *are* eternal consciousness, that we *are* Life itself. It is the knowing that our physical life in this material world is only a brief assignment designed to further deepen our realisation of who we truly are. It is the knowing that reality is our guide and our protector. It is the knowing that our ego must die in order for us to be free.

The profound peace of conscious-awareness arises from a sense of deep security found in the still, silent gap between attachment and aversion. The hungry ghost has realised that it is a beautiful radiant spirit, no longer lost, but at home in the stillness, the heart of the Higher-Self. All it takes is a shift in perspective on what Life is all about for the true reality of Life to start revealing itself. The awakened spirit of conscious-awareness is then free to participate in the world without the unnecessary struggle of trying to get Love from the world when the world does not have it to give.

When we live with conscious-awareness, creating fulfilling relationships becomes so much easier. When we are the loving guardian of our own human-self, we are less inclined to look to our partner to prop us up emotionally. We are able to accept and take responsibility for our own humanness, which also means letting go of our need to control others in order to feel secure. We can let go of the control games. We can stay more present in our own still, centred space, even when those around us may temporarily be in their ego. We are not so threatened by their humanness, because we know how to take care of our own humanness. We can instead offer patience and respond with Love. This in turn helps those who are struggling to stay centred find their own way back to their heart of awareness, which is what the opening poem is all about.

In this atmosphere of freedom, we love to go home, because home reflects the sanctuary we each have in our heart for our own humanness. In this place of mutual acceptance, it is easier to open up and reveal our vulnerability to one another. We are not dumping our issues on one another. Nor are we trying to fix one another. Instead, we are each sharing our process, our human journey with one another.

Love is then but a focused, meditative breath away (refer to the Higher-Self meditation on page 84). It is our inner-sanctum created by our own conscious-awareness, which then overflows as loving kindness to those around us. When the physical body loses its grip on life, the spirit simply finds itself even more at home in Love, free of its physical limitations. Fear, for this awakened consciousness, has become an indicator of mere confusion, a doorway to further awakening. For conscious-awareness, there is no risk to living in this physical world, because there is nothing real that can be lost. For conscious-awareness, every level of our existence, whether pleasant or unpleasant, simply becomes an experience that expands our consciousness. When we have awakened into conscious-awareness, we are able to live courageously, because we have learned to die consciously. We are able to consciously negotiate the death-throws of our ego each time we break through our ego's delusions. We can even accept and consciously flow with the death of our physical body. For the ego, these are the two greatest fears. When we are living in our conscious-awareness, we know that Love is the very essence of our own Self.

"I am that", is a statement often encountered on the spiritual path, which means I am Light/Life/Love itself. I cannot be harmed. I cannot be reduced. I can only expand.

When I truly, consciously, responsibly Love myself, my humanity, I am loving everyone, humanity itself. There is no separation. There is only the appearance of separation, created by a world full of egos, as we act out our confusion.

On our journey to self-realisation, we are, of course, going to experience ourself being Love and being ego at the same time. We have a foot in both worlds. It takes a while to accept this and know how to work with the awakening process. This is what this book is about.

THE MISBELIEF THAT SOMEONE OR SOMETHING CAN CAUSE US MENTAL/ EMOTIONAL SUFFERING

CAPTURED

I captured a heart and held it close.
It was the answer to all my prayers, this heart.
The prospect of dreams fulfilled,
And a life to be lived.
A perfect match that would forever last.
So I held it tight just to make sure.

I captured a heart and held it close.
It was the answer to all my prayers, this heart.
The life I dream and the life I live,
Hasn't yet been a perfect match.
I must convince this heart it's mine,
And hold it tighter just to make sure.

I captured a heart and held it close.
It was the answer to all my prayers, this heart.

The life that I dreamt and the life I live,
Is still growing father apart.
Why can't you see you're my perfect match?
I can feel you slipping but I can't let you go.

I captured a heart and held it close.
It was the answer to all my prayers, this heart,
Or at least I though it was so,
But now the dream is lost and I will surely die,
Don't you realise what you have done to me?
I pin the heart down so it can't get away.

I captured a heart and held it close.
It was the answer to all my prayers, this heart,
Or at least I thought it was, but now it has died.
I loved this heart so how could it die?
My perfect dreams have fallen apart.
What will I do now for a heart?

To hold others responsible for what we think and feel is a belief that is taken as truth in the ego world. "You make me so angry!" "Now that they have done this to me, I am ashamed to show my face in the world." "I feel so good when he's with me. I couldn't bear to be without him." "I don't want you speaking to other men. You belong to me." The soap opera of the ego world is endless. As a result, the ego world is a tangled mess of pain and conflict.

Ego clings onto people, places, and things in an attempt to find refuge from suffering and gets angry and looks for someone to blame for its mental/emotional pain when that attachment is threatened. The blamed person then reacts to the blame and lashes back at the blamer. This further convinces the blaming ego that its delusions are true and the tragic dance of conflict and pain continues on and on. This is why it is such a blind spot where seeing reality is concerned. Ego is like an infant playing with something sharp. It keeps stabbing itself and experiencing pain without realising that it is the cause of its own suffering. Our ego keeps stabbing itself with its own mind, with its own misbeliefs.

The sharp object is our own unconscious self-condemnation placing self-condemning meanings on what others say or do.

On the deepest level, consciousness cannot be hurt because it is at one with Light/Life/Love. One's ultimate worthiness, on this level, is without question. Trying to hurt or offend someone who is truly awakened is like slashing a sword at nothing. The sword encounters nothing because there is no ego left to strike. What you will get from a fully realised person is compassion, which is a quality of Unconditional Love. The awakened one will see right through you to the illusions that are driving your deluded behaviour. The awakened one, who you are attacking, will see their own self in you, at a time when they too were deluded. As a result, the awakened one will only have compassion for your suffering. What you will experience is them disarming you with kind words that will speak directly to the needs of the vulnerable child within you, and to your heart, in an attempt to help you address those needs more constructively. If you disregard this kindness and continue to attack, the awakened one will simply walk away, leaving you with the necessary experience of your self-inflicted suffering.

You won't often encounter someone with that level of awareness. What you are more likely to experience, if you pay attention, is someone awake enough not to hold onto their reaction for long. Such a person will have the awareness that will enable them to soon realise that their reaction to your attack is their own ego hurting itself. They will let go of any offence that they have taken on and do their best to resolve the matter with you when the situation is more calm.

For one who is becoming conscious, a moment of conflict is seen as an opportunity to heal his or her own confusion. On the other hand, when we are caught in our ego, the moment of conflict is just another confirmation that we are a victim and that our violent reaction, on whatever level, is supposedly justified. Therefore, if you see yourself as a victim, you are not seeing reality as it is. Keep looking. In the centre of your suffering is a doorway to freedom.

Conscious-awareness is the power of choice, but in a way, there is no choice. To explain what I mean, I will paraphrase the great philosopher and spiritual teacher, Krishnamurti[13] (May 11, 1895–February 17, 1986): The ego thinks it has choices, but it is deluding itself. If you want peace, happiness and fulfilment, there is in fact only one choice ever to make, and that is Love. Love is wisdom. Love is peace. Love is freedom. Love is reality. Love is the only true state of sanity.

When we are living from conscious-awareness, we choose Love, because we know that Love is the only thing that works in order to free us from suffering. If a choice other than Love is made, suffering is the result, so we realise that this means we must be confused and we will search within our own mind for the source of the confusion and then make another choice based on a greater level of awareness.

Suffering is no longer seen as the enemy who rampages through the shaky sanctuary of our comfort zones. Suffering is instead seen as the teacher who is showing us how to be free, like a fierce, but wise, Zen Master. Within conscious-awareness is the potential and the power to take full command of our own thoughts and therefore our emotions. Accepting total personal responsibility for everything we think, feel, say, and do in the spirit of Unconditional Love, steps us into that potential where Life becomes our teacher in every moment. This courageous and powerful stance, known as the way of the "sacred warrior"[14][15], enables us to look at each situation that confronts us in life with a very different perspective. The ego keeps finding excuses to blame others for the way it feels, but the sacred warrior has made a stand and now serves only Love. As the sacred warrior, we refuse to accept the ego's spin on things, because we know this only reduces us to being a powerless child. Instead, we face the fear and follow the disturbed emotion into our own self, allowing it to flow through our awareness, no matter how it feels. We know that any prolonged painful emotion is the product of

---

[13] Krishnamurti J. (2007). *The Collected Works of J. Krishnamurti*. Motilal Barnasidass.

[14] Nelson Mandela. *The Sacred Warrior: The liberator of South Africa looks at the seminal work of the liberator of India*. Times Magazine Article (Dec. 31 1999) http://www.time.com/time/magazine/article/0,9171,993025,00. html

[15] Trungpa C. (1995). *Sacred Path of the Warrior*. Shambhala. U.S.A.

deluded thoughts, conscious or unconscious. We know that these destructive emotions, and the deluded thoughts behind them, say nothing valid about the true nature of ourself or the world around us. So we hold steady, feel and observe the emotional disturbance within us from the transcendental position of this higher awareness. Inevitably the ego's delusions are revealed and the very Light of conscious-awareness sweeps them away like fog being evaporated by the sun.

At the same time, our painful emotional energy is released and healed by that same Light of Love that is held within our open heart. This state of awareness is also known as Christ Consciousness, or Clear-Light Buddha Mind and similar expressions from other traditions.

We are then better able to respond appropriately to whatever situation we are in, because we are no longer so blinded by our own delusions. We have become the solution in that moment, rather than adding to the problem.

If we are not willing to sincerely take this stance of total personal responsibility as best we can each day for our own mind, we are at risk of remaining deluded about the true nature of ourself. True reality will more likely be lost to us.

There is only one choice if we want to be free from suffering.

THE MISBELIEF THAT LIFE HAS NO MEANING

SILENCE SPEAKING

I talked softly so they would not shout at me.
I gave in because they were more powerful than me.
I pleased them with a smile so they would not reject me.
I ran away because they were bigger than me.
Then one day the silence said that I was only frightened of myself,
And I thought, yeah, I guess that's how it works.
And I saw how the world fears, and I saw the fear grow.

I became dominating so they would not overpower me.
I became their ruler so they could not control me.
I spoke loudly so they would always hear me.

I grew large so they could not stand over me.
I learned to fight so they could not hurt me.
Then one day the silence said that I was only fighting myself,
And I thought, yeah, I guess that's how it works.
And I saw how the world fights, and I saw the fighting grow.

I reached out in kindness and some were kind back to me.
I served them humbly and some were grateful to me.
I open my heart to them and some welcomed me.
I tended their wounds and guarded their secrets and some repaid me.
I gave love freely regardless and in return some even loved me.
Then one day the silence said that I was only loving myself,
And I thought, yeah, I guess that's how it works.
And I saw how the world loves, and I saw the Love grow.

Having read this far into the book, it would be obvious to you by now that I see Life as ultimately meaningful, that it has a definite purpose and that purpose is ultimately good in the highest sense of the word.

In the world of ego, life is basically meaningless. The primary goal is to pursue comfort and to gratify our physical, emotional and mental needs on a limited survival level. Life itself remains a mystery, which we actively avoid looking at too deeply in the fear that the foundations of our comfort zones might be threatened. Things like spirituality, the paranormal, clairvoyance, telepathy, life after death, even the ramifications of quantum science, we may find uncomfortable and even frightening. We seek refuge from these mysteries in fundamentalist religion or empty materialism.

In fundamentalist religion, no matter what variety, someone else tells us what to think or what not to think. We find comfort in being better than the non-believers and from this position we may busy ourself trying to save others from clinging to the wrong god; that's if we don't decide to kill them instead for their "evil ways".

The way religious doctrine has evolved over the last two millennia has led to a widespread rejection of all that is spiritual. The orthodox Christian belief that we will end up in hell for eternity for committing various sins, including not believing in a particular brand of "saviour" (irrespective of whether you are from another culture that has never heard of that particular saviour), has repulsed our common sense, and that is just one example. Where Christianity is concerned, much of this type of doctrine was added to the scriptures by the medieval church in an attempt to control the masses. To add to our rejection of religion, the church authorities themselves have been negligent in practicing the principles they supposedly preach.

The East has its own doctrines that defy common sense, such as being reincarnated as an animal of some sort if you don't live a wholesome life. The belief that reincarnation extends on for eons and eons, rendering the goal of enlightenment seemingly beyond reach, I believe also leads to apathy and hopelessness in the hearts of those who need real meaning in their lives. Such doctrines are not supported by experiential evidence and are rejected by those who are in touch with Perennial Wisdom—the knowing of their own Higher-Self. Various disempowering forms of ancestor worship have also bound generations up in superstition. All this type of doctrine that flies in the face of common sense is in fact religion created by our confused ego and not from any sense of aware-consciousness. This is why it does not make sense. This is why it does not lead us out of suffering.

Ego has not been able to comprehend Perennial Wisdom. Instead we have reduced the great teachings, that were supposed to empower us and free us, down to a childlike fearful worship of an angry authoritarian god—a typical ego driven tyrant.

In the next chapter I will lay out a framework that reveals the common teachings from the true masters throughout human history that transcend all the conflicting doctrines of the ego. You will see how this framework appeals to common sense and gives real insight into life's important questions. See Chapter 6, "Karma, Reincarnation and Enlightenment" on page 166.

For those of us who don't care to look more deeply at the subject of spirituality, and therefore break through the dogmatic façade of religion, there has been nothing left but to escape into materialism.

With materialism however, enough is never enough. In the West we have invented this thing called a "consumer society", where we indulge in what is called "consumerism", and for years now we have been eagerly exporting this to the rest of the world.

With consumerism we need economies that constantly grow, and therefore, increasingly consume the earth's resources so that we can keep consuming more and more material things. This is of course supposed to fulfil us. Instead we have created a rat-race and a spiralling crime rate—a society of the haves and the angry have-nots.

Because consumerism is driven by ego, it is inevitably out of balance with the laws of Life. Our environment has suffered systematic destruction since the beginning of the industrial revolution. This destructive game is driven by "needy children" who can't let go of the sweets that rot their teeth, for the sake of a larger, more important goal, such as environmental sustainability. Look at how hard it is for us to accept the temporary pain of setting carbon emission reducing targets in order to minimise the dangerous effects of global warming. Just the effect of all the megaton's of this pollution on our health over the last fifty years should have been enough to prompt us to put a stop to it. In the West we have been satisfied that we have been able to insulate ourself from the negative effects of out-of-control materialism with all the comfort that it brings. What we haven't been able to avoid is the negative health effects of all the industrial and automotive pollution, and the effects of the rat-race lifestyle that we have created. Cancer and heart disease on epidemic levels are just two examples. Even with all this suffering we are not ready to wake up. Now we have created an entire shift in the earth's environmental balance. Will we pay attention to the prompting hand of suffering? How much shaking will we need to wake up and stop destroying our own environment?

There is nothing wrong with technology and trying to make our lives more comfortable and manageable. The imbalance is not about that. The imbalance is about our egos using material things to indulge our emotional neediness, which, in reality, can never be satisfied in this way. Our neediness thinks it needs more and more of what we don't really need. You cannot get an emotional need fulfilled by a material thing. Only Unconditional Love can fill that need. Technology, therefore, is misused to serve short-term profit for multinational companies who pander to our neediness. Selling something like Coca Cola to third world countries is a perfect example. As a food supplement, it has no value. As something that appeals to emotional neediness, it is very powerful. Here you have people in need of healthy food being served up a product that threatens their health, but sold as something good. Another example is technology that would truly serve the highest good of humanity, such as clean power, being neglected over the past century because it was not as profitable in the short-term.

This is how it is in the ego world. Ego is constructed out of confusion. We are, nevertheless, all looking for fulfilment and an important part of this fulfilment is having a real meaning to our lives, whether we relate to it in that way or not. Ego is trying to fulfil these needs, but like the small child, it doesn't know how. The childlike ego has been left to its own devices and now the house is a mess and the children have descended into conflict and squaller. Ego is like a child who, out of fear and ignorance, refuses to grow up.

It is not a matter of condemning the ego world. The ego is a normal phase along the evolutionary cycle of humanity's consciousness, but we can't remain for too long being dominated by this short-sighted way of being. We each must take responsibility for our own mind and evolve accordingly.

True meaning can only be found on the level of conscious-awareness and within the Universal Laws of Consciousness. Conscious-awareness is the parent guardian within us and the Laws of Consciousness are the good parenting guide. It is here that all things come into harmony and comprehension.

THE MISBELIEF THAT WE ARE ALL SEPARATE

NOT LIKE ME

I look them over and find we have nothing in common.
I step into their space and their eyes reject me.
I listen to their voices and their tone is cold and uninviting.
I put out my hand and they take it with apprehension.
They all sit isolated from one another,
Huddled in their own little world.
I catch a glimpse of myself in the window pane,
And suddenly realise that I look just the same.

> *By the night's end they are sharing their feelings,*
> *And I discover they are just like mine.*
> *Funny; I thought we had nothing in common.*

The belief that we are all separate is again the result of our ego identifying itself as a body with a mind serving only that body, trapping itself on the level of survival of the fittest.

For someone who is living on the level of conscious-awareness, the act of harming another to gain benefit for oneself, for example, is regarded as absurd. To conscious-awareness, it is obvious that harming another will inevitably directly or indirectly harm oneself. For example, the anger that festers in the population of a nation, that is being exploited by the industries of other powerful nations, exploding onto the world scene through acts of terrorism. It is easy to self-righteously judge the savage acts of the terrorist, but we turn a blind eye to acts of industrial terrorism that so-called responsible nations have been carrying out for the last century or more. Every act has a consequence.

What we do on a daily basis has ramifications for every living thing on this planet. When we have millions of out-of-control egos on the loose, the consequences become grave.

On the level of conscious-awareness, a sense of oneness with all beings, including this planet that nurtures our life, naturally arises. The more our mind unites with Unconditional Love and Total Personal Responsibility, the more we are in tune with the Universal Life-Force—the Life-giving ocean that flows through us all. We no longer identify ourself as a separate body. There is a genuine, intuitive feeling for all beings as though they are in some way a vital part of our own being. This is not the ravings of idealistic "bleeding hearts". This is the natural effect of an evolving consciousness becoming in tune with the natural Laws of Life. The effects of conscious-awareness are so powerful that it is not necessary to become a spiritual master to make a profound difference to your life. As the great Theosophist and metaphysician, Alice A. Bailey (June 16, 1880-December 15, 1949) put it:

> "Goodwill is man's first attempt to express the
> love of God. Its results on earth will be peace.
> It is so simple and practical that people fail

to appreciate its potency or its scientific and dynamic effect. One person sincerely practising goodwill in a family, can completely change its attitudes. Goodwill really practised among groups in any nation, by political and religious parties in any nation, and among the nations of the world, can revolutionise the world." Alice A. Bailey "*The Problems of Humanity.*" p. 7.[16]

By accepting total responsibility to Love yourself unconditionally, you are not only doing yourself a great service, but humanity also. When your own mind is at peace, the effects of your inner-harmony positively influences all those around you. You become an inspiration for others, who naturally seek your counsel. Your decision making becomes wiser and thus more in tune with goodwill and cooperation toward others, whilst also displaying a deep strength of character that attracts respect from others. What is good for you, from the perspective of true conscious-awareness, is good for everyone.

The Universal Laws of Life are very elegant and simple, which is why they inevitably confront our ego's confusions, but if we are brave enough to keep our heart open to these laws of Life, they will heal us, awaken us, and set us free.

If I see myself as a victim, I am denying the reality of the power and beauty of my conscious-awareness. My mind belongs to me. The key to peace and happiness is in my hands in every moment. Having absolute faith in this reality, no matter what my old misbeliefs have to say, means I give myself the maximum opportunity to heal and grow through every experience.

---

[16] Bailey A. A. (1964). *The Problems of Humanity*. Lucis Press Ltd. New York.

CHAPTER FIVE SUMMARY

1. There are common ways (ego blind spots) in which our ego gets confused about the realities of life and then creates for itself an unsatisfactory life and frequent suffering as a result of these confusions.

2. We live our lives from the basis that these confusions are reality and then wonder why our human existence does not make sense.

3. Our ego wants the suffering to stop but it does not want to stop doing what is causing the suffering, because its game is satisfying its unconscious illusions and short-term gratifications.

4. To rise above suffering, we have to wake up to our ego games and become conscious. As always, accepting personal responsibility to Love ourself unconditionally, provides a compassionate sanctuary in which our ego can be dismantled.

5. The ego's main blind spots are:

   ✗ **The misbelief that fear is an impenetrable wall.**

   ✗ **The misbelief that Love comes from somewhere outside us.**

   ✗ **The misbelief that someone or something can cause us mental/emotional suffering.**

   ✗ **The misbelief that Life has no meaning.**

   ✗ **The misbelief that we are all separate.**

✗ **The misbelief that fear is an impenetrable wall.**

1. Fear is a factor in our lives in part because our physical body/mind operates on mere mortal survival, the same as the animal kingdom.

2. This fear is then accentuated because human beings have the added power and potential of consciousness. As a result, mental and emotional confusion is the special suffering that human beings have to contend with, way beyond what an animal has to experience.

3. This added potential, if misused, can degrade a human being to a lower level than the animal kingdom, or it can

lead us to the heights of spiritual enlightenment, where we become a guiding Light for all humanity.

4. Fear is only an impenetrable wall to the extent that we identify ourself solely as a survival mind with a body, an ego in other words.

5. In the chook yard of the ego world, comfort is the highest refuge from fear. Comfort does not get rid of the fear. Fear is still waiting outside the door to ambush us when the comfort slips away.

6. The ego can only find its comforts in the material world by consuming more and more of what brings it comfort, including kindness from other people.

7. On a mental/emotional level in particular, conscious-awareness is not dependent on the material world. It is not threatened by it.

8. Conscious-awareness, on some significant level, knows itself as something eternal, the Higher-Self that is an essential part of the Universal Life-Force.

9. It is in facing our fears, it is in stepping off that cliff of ego illusion, that we discover the limitless power of our Higher-Self.

10. Our ego inevitably has to face what it believes it cannot possibly face.

11. To escape its suffering, the ego has to essentially die in order to awaken into true consciousness, and to our ego, facing our fears can feel like we are dying at times.

12. Suicide is sometimes the tragic result, but the problem is not located in the body. Suffering occurs in the mind, and that is where it must be resolved. The confusion will continue with or without a body until clarity is found. Killing the body is mistaking the nature of the problem.

13. Suffering is what initially motivates us to step off the edge of our ego delusions and into the initially unknown world of consciousness.

14. Death on the ego level of limited survival is seen from the perspective of conscious-awareness as a birth into Life.

15. If self-realisation is the true purpose of life, then suffering is like the hand that shakes us to wake us up. It is a gentle shake at first, but becomes more and more insistent the more ego resists the call.

16. Facing our fears and working through them is therefore essential for realising our potential, for raising our consciousness to where our suffering can be solved and/or transcended.

✗ **The misbelief that Love comes from somewhere outside us.**

1. The reason that Love is so illusive to our ego is because we are looking for it in the wrong place.

2. For our ego though, letting go to the Love that we are already, means letting go of trying to convince or force the world around us to love us.

3. "What if I don't get what I want?" the ego cries, not seeing that all its controlling and manipulating is actually choking the love that it is trying to cling onto.

4. This is why the persistent act of being Love inevitably reveals the true nature of ourself, just as facing our fear does.

5. The profound peace of conscious-awareness arises from a sense of deep security found in the still, silent gap between attachment and aversion.

6. The awakened spirit of conscious-awareness is free to participate in the world without the struggle of trying to get from the world what the world can't give.

7. When we live in conscious-awareness, creating fulfilling relationships becomes so much easier.

8. We are able to accept and take responsibility for our humanness, which also means we are able to set other people free to been be themselves.

9. In this atmosphere of freedom, we love to go home, because home reflects the sanctuary we each have in our heart for our own humanness.

10. For conscious-awareness, every level of our existence, whether pleasant or unpleasant, simply becomes an experience that expands our consciousness.

11. When we have awakened into conscious-awareness, we are able to live courageously, because we have learned to die consciously, on the level of our ego, and even when it comes to letting go of our physical body.

12. When we are living in our conscious-awareness, we know that Love is the very essence of our own Self.

✗ The misbelief that someone or something can cause us mental/emotional suffering.

1. Ego clings onto people, places, and things in an attempt to find refuge from suffering and gets angry and blames others for its mental/emotional pain when that attachment is threatened.

2. Our ego keeps stabbing itself with its own mind, with its own misbeliefs. The sharp object is our own unconscious self-condemnation placing self-condemning meanings on what others say or do.

3. On the deepest level, consciousness cannot be hurt because it is at one with Love. One's ultimate worthiness, on this level, is without question.

4. Trying to hurt or offend someone who is truly awakened is like trying to slash the air with a sword. There is no ego left to strike.

5. For one who is becoming conscious, a moment of conflict is seen as an opportunity to heal his or her own confusion. On the other hand, for an unawakened ego, the moment of conflict is just another confirmation that it is a victim and that its violent reaction, on whatever level, is justified.

6. If you see yourself as a victim, therefore, you are *not* seeing reality as it is.

7. When we are living from conscious-awareness, we choose Love because we know that Love is the only thing that works in order to free us from suffering.

8. Accepting total personal responsibility for everything we think, feel, say, and do in the spirit of Unconditional Love, steps us into that potential where Life becomes our teacher in every moment. This courageous and powerful stance is known as the "way of the sacred warrior".

9. Suffering is no longer seen as the enemy who rampages through the shaky sanctuary of our comfort zones. Suffering is instead seen as the teacher who is showing us how to be free, like a fierce, but wise, Zen Master.

10. As the sacred warrior, we refuse to accept the ego's spin on things, because we know this only reduces us to being a powerless child.

11. There is only one choice if we want to be free of suffering, and that is learning the art of being Love.

✗ The misbelief that Life has no meaning.

1. In the world of ego, life is basically meaningless. The primary goal is to pursue comfort and to gratify our physical, emotional and mental needs on a limited survival level.

2. The ego seeks refuge from uncertainty in fundamentalist religion or empty materialism.

3. The way religious doctrine has evolved over the last two millennia has led to a widespread rejection of all that is spiritual.

4. Ego has not been able to comprehend Perennial Wisdom. Instead we have reduced the great teachings that were supposed to empower us and free us, down to a childlike fearful worship of an angry authoritarian god—a typical ego driven tyrant.

5. For those of us who don't care to look more deeply at the subject of spirituality and therefore break through the dogmatic façade of religion, there has been nothing left but to escape into materialism.

6. The imbalance is about our egos using material things to indulge our emotional neediness, which, in reality, can never be satisfied in this way, so we need more and more of what we don't really need.

7. You cannot truly fulfil an emotional need with a material thing. Only Unconditional Love can fill that need.

8. It is not a matter of condemning the ego world. The ego is a normal phase of the consciousness of humanity on its way to growing up, but we can't remain for too long being dominated by this short-sighted way of being.

We each must take responsibility for our own mind and evolve accordingly.

9. True meaning can only be found on the level of conscious-awareness and within the Universal Laws of Consciousness. Conscious-awareness is the parent guardian within us and the Laws of Consciousness are the good parenting guide.

✗ The misbelief that we are all separate.

1. For someone who is living on the level of conscious-awareness, the act of harming another to gain benefit for oneself, for example, is regarded as absurd.

2. Every act has a consequence. What I do on a daily basis has ramifications for every living thing on this planet.

3. On the level of conscious-awareness, a sense of oneness with all beings, including this planet that nurtures our life, naturally arises.

4. By accepting total responsibility to Love yourself unconditionally, you are not only doing yourself a great service, but humanity also. When your own mind is at peace, the effects of your inner-harmony positively influences all those around you.

5. The Universal Laws of Life are very elegant and simple, which is why they inevitably confront our ego's confusions, but if we are brave enough to keep our heart open to these Laws of Life, they will heal us, awaken us, and set us free.

✓ **Take loving responsibility for your mind.**
✓ **Forgive yourself for being human.**
✓ **You are not a victim, you are empowered Conscious-Awareness.**
✓ **See your fear, face your fear, don't be your fear.**
✓ **Gladly learn through trial and error. That's the natural way.**
✓ *NEVER GIVE UP. SUCCESS IS INEVITABLE!*

STEP 2
TOTAL PERSONAL RESPONSIBILITY
PART THREE

KARMA, REINCARNATION AND ENLIGHTENMENT

Surely I am a mystery worthy of investigation,
A challenge worth facing,
A wonder worth knowing,
Nothing grander to be sure.

In the last two thousand years, humanity has made many great technological advances, but when it comes to the question of true wisdom, the *science* of morality, we have progressed very little. Here I emphasise the word "science" to steer the concept of morality away from religious moralising, which all too often has little to do with what truly works to bring peace, harmony, joy and ultimately Love into human affairs. Despite our religious teachings and material technology, fear, ignorance, prejudice and greed still prevail, along with all the suffering and destruction that it causes.

We can spend years studying in school and then university and still be no closer to the answers to these fundamental problems facing the world. We are taught so much "materialistic knowledge", but in all this time we are taught so little wisdom.

Nevertheless, the seeds of wisdom have been sown at frequent intervals throughout human history, and those seeds are indeed showing signs of germination in the human mind on a large scale. Real universal values that reflect the core principles of Unconditional Love and Total Personal Responsibility are becoming more evident in human affairs. Despite the suffering, conflict, and inequality that still plague this world, humanity is becoming more of a global community. Freedom, equality, dignity and a fair and reasonable standard of living for all is a common ideal now. Humanity is slowly evolving beyond the "survival of the fittest" mentality. Humanity is becoming more conscious. This is inevitable and unstoppable. This is the irresistible internal pull that is the evolutionary process of conscious, a process that is lifting humanity far beyond mere Darwinian evolution. This is the process of enlightenment.

We are each a living cell in the body/mind/spirit of humanity. Humanity evolves because we, as individuals evolve. Even though humanity still has a long way to go, the evolution of our consciousness is speeding up. This is because more people are becoming consciously receptive to the guiding Light of the Higher-Self. A new common awareness is emerging. This is not another organised religion. It is the awakening of perennial wisdom within the hearts of an ever increasing percentage of humanity.

As I carefully explained in the introduction, I am not presenting here another dogma. This is a framework of knowledge that will enable you to perceive a bigger reality. It is a stepping stone along the journey to ultimate awakening. This knowledge will help you understand why life works the way it does and how you are a meaningful part of that life. It will help you understand that truth and justice does prevail, but you have to step back far enough to see how that works itself out. This framework must appeal to your common sense, the knowing that is your Higher-Self. Exploring this knowledge is simply a matter of loosening up what you think you know, stepping into this framework, and observing yourself and the world through it. You can step out of it again whenever you want. You are the one in charge of your own mind and therefore, your own life. If you are ready for this next step, a bigger Life is waiting to be revealed to you.

I will start this process by outlining the various elements that make up this framework. Once this is done, I will then piece it all together and show you how it works.

THE UNVEILING OF PERENNIAL WISDOM

Knowledge of Reincarnation in Western and Eastern Culture

Reincarnation refers to every human being having a Soul, a spiritual presence within us that does not die when the body dies. The Soul is the consciousness that makes the human being what it is. Instead of passing out of existence, the Soul re-enters physical life in a new body for the purpose of continuing on the experience of Life. With each life experienced, the Soul slowly gains increasing awareness of its creative power of consciousness while restricted to a physical body/mind. After many such lives, the Soul reaches a stage of its development where it realises itself to be the self-responsible authority of its own experience in this physical world. This important stage of awareness prepares the Soul for the next and final leg of its grand journey. This final stage enables the Soul to further realise itself as a living expression of the Universal Laws of Consciousness. In other words, the Soul achieves enlightenment.

There are perhaps four main benefits to enlightenment. The first benefit is we have mastered our mind and all there is in the physical world to such a degree that we are beyond suffering. The second benefit is we can help others free themselves from suffering. The third benefit is we are no longer required to re-enter the physical world in a physical body with all its limitations in order to further our evolution. We have broken free of the cycle of being attached to death and rebirth, which is known in the East as samsara. The fourth is that we are finally one with Universal Love.

The knowledge of reincarnation had almost become lost in the West and obscured by dogma in the East. At the time of Christ it was taught by some sections of Judaism and also by some early movements born out of the teachings of Christ and also the classic Greek philosophy of Plato[17] (428/427 BC–348/347 BC) and Pythagoras[18] (c. 570–c. 495 BC). The framework of reincarnation, karma and enlightenment puts the power and responsibility for one's own salvation squarely in the hands of the individual. Over the centuries, after the crucifixion of Jesus Christ, this self-responsible philosophical stance came to be in direct conflict with orthodox Christian doctrine, which gives an external Christ all the power over our Souls and the Orthodox Church the full power to interpret the doctrine. Constantinus Augustus, known as Constantine 1[19][20], was the first Roman emperor to formally accept and support Christianity. He reigned from 306 to 337 AD. Constantine had a need to create a centralised religious authority that would help him establish and maintain control over the fractured Roman Empire. The notion that each individual could be self-responsible did not gain favour with those who saw themselves destined to rule. As the Roman Empire slowly crumbled over the following centuries, the Christian Church felt the need to assert even more centralised control over the masses as a way to compensate for the insecurity of those turbulent times. The Eastern Roman Emperor Justinian 1[21], who reigned between 527 and 565 AD, became the champion of Christian Orthodoxy. He mercilessly suppressed all opposing religious/spiritual activity and philosophy. The teachings of Origen Adamantius[22] (185-254 AD) was perhaps the last public bastion of alternative thought within Christianity. His theology included a Plutonic influenced framework of reincarnation. In 543, Justinian effectively put a stop to any further official support for Origen's more spiritual interpretation of Christian doctrine.

---

[17]   http://en.wikipedia.org/wiki/Plato

[18]   http://en.wikipedia.org/wiki/Pythagoras

[19]   http://en.wikipedia.org/wiki/Constantine_the_Great#Religious_policy

[20]   Metzger B. M. (1997) *The Cannon of the New Testament: Its Origen, Development and Significance.* Oxford University Press. New York.

[21]   http://en.wikipedia.org/wiki/Justinian_I

[22]   http://en.wikipedia.org/wiki/Origen

The philosophy of reincarnation was nevertheless kept alive by underground movements such as the Masonic traditions[23].

In the East, no one centralised religious authority formed and the philosophy of reincarnation remained an important aspect of the culture. The highest forms of spiritual teachings rarely reached the masses, however, who were submerged in the superstitions and corruptions of the of the various priesthoods that lived off the offerings of the common people[242526]. The masses were still kept ignorant by teachings that were too obscure, complex, and disempowering. Buddhism[27] (established around 600BC) became the main alternative to the corrupt priesthood of the time. Buddha re-established a straightforward path to self-realisation where each individual is regarded as self-responsible. Despite dogma and over-intellectualisation creeping in, Buddhism remains one of the clearest and most popular of the orthodox teachings of self-realisation.

In both East and West, perennial Wisdom has been taught to us by many highly evolved individuals throughout human history. These Wisdom teachings were designed to introduce us to the transformational power of Unconditional Love and Personal Responsibility. Due to the nature of the human ego however, their message repeatedly became a tool for the less evolved masses and their leaders to justify very ungodly deeds. Only a few could truly hear and understand the real message. Religion became a form of control and a promoter of unthinking obedience, rather than a promoter of true moral advancement and consciousness development. As a result, pride and selfishness has been able to spread its roots everywhere.

In the West, science and philosophical thought eventually rebelled against religious dogma and the age of "enlightenment" (beginning in the 1700's) began[28]. Unfortunately, rebellion is a

---

[23] Hall M. P. (2006). *The Lost Keys of Freemasonry.* Tarcher; illustrated edition. U.S.A.

[24] http://en.wikipedia.org/wiki/Eastern_religion

[25] http://en.wikipedia.org/wiki/Comparative_religion

[26] Omvedt G. (2003) *Buddhims in India: Challenging Brahmanism and Caste.* Sage Publications. California.

[27] http://en.wikipedia.org/wiki/Buddhism

[28] http://en.wikipedia.org/wiki/Age_of_Enlightenment

reaction that is born from a distain that at least partially blinds the rebel. Due to this reaction, all notions of spirituality were also rejected by this purely materialistic scientific revolution, and as a result, the intuitive power of higher consciousness became invalidated and suppressed. Science therefore exposed itself to the ravages of pride and selfishness as well.

Today we have a technological age that is morally backwards. In mainstream scientific institutions we are free to think so long as it's along purely materialistic lines. In mainstream religious institutions, blind obedience to childish dogma is still demanded. We have been literally taught by science and religion alike, not to look within our own heart, or to put it another way, we are told by both what we are supposed to think, regardless of what we are intuitively feeling. Where free, open minded and intelligent investigation of spirituality and consciousness is concerned, both science and religion try to bind us in unthinking dogma.

It is ludicrous that there are fundamental questions about life that mainstream science still resists touching. A few examples of these untouchable questions include:

- Is there life/consciousness after death?
- How is it that some people have powerful extra sensory perceptions of various kinds?
- Is there real evidence for reincarnation?

Science is supposed to impartially investigate natural phenomena, no matter what it is. Try researching these questions in a mainstream university and you may find yourself out of a job. If we turn to religion for answers to such questions, we certainly get answers, but these answers are like stories we would tell to children, not to sophisticated intelligent adults. An abundance of solid evidence is available to those who wish to honestly investigate such phenomena, and many have risked their reputation by doing just that. Even though the results of their investigations have been largely suppressed by mainstream institutions, it can still be found[293031].

The New Wave of Perennial Wisdom

Perennial Wisdom however, cannot be lost. The shortcomings of religion and science motivated many individuals to search more deeply for real answers to human suffering. As a result, beginning around the mid 1800's, a new wave of spiritual knowledge began entering the consciousness of humanity. All over the world individuals received this knowledge in many different ways and in many different forms, but essentially the message was the same, with the emphasis always being on Unconditional Love and Total Personal Responsibility. The new age of Spirituality had been born. Since that time, some of the greatest spiritual texts that have ever graced the minds of humanity have emerged. I give some examples further on in this passage.

Today we have all the information we need to transform humanity into a just and harmonious society that can live also in harmony with our environment. All we need now is the will to put it into action, and this will is rapidly building. As I have said, there is a long way to go, but a definite awakening is occurring, comparatively speaking, within a critical mass of humanity. This growing network of awakened individuals is making its presence felt in the affairs of humanity on every level. This will only increase as time goes on, because once consciousness is awake, nothing can hold it back.

I am not going to reference other writers and scholars as expected with an academic approach. This knowledge is now a part of my own heart and much of it comes through directly from my Higher-Self. Nevertheless, I will to give you some examples of the knowledge that has come through over the past one hundred and fifty years to give you a starting point for further research. Bear in mind that these examples are by no means the whole picture. Let your heart also guide you in your search. As you sincerely look for knowledge of the truth beyond your ego

---

[29] wikipedia.org/wiki/Reincarnation_research

[30] http://en.wikipedia.org/wiki/Reincarnation

[31] http://www.near-death.com/reincarnation.html

comfort zones, that truth will extend its hand out to you—it is a conscious, living force.

In the 1860's in France, a highly educated and morally evolved individual, who came to be known as Alan Kardec[32] (1804-1869), began investigating the spiritual phenomena that was evident at the time. He soon found himself to be a catalyst for a certain type of spiritual knowledge that presented itself to him through highly skilled spiritual mediums whenever he was in their presence. He realised that even in the presence of different mediums, the knowledge seemed to be from the same source. He began compiling this information and noted how quickly his study of these teachings was raising his own consciousness. He soon had at his disposal a comprehensive reformation of the Christian doctrine, freed from ego corruption and complete with the knowledge of reincarnation, Karma and enlightenment. Despite this knowledge being radical for the time, the power of its Wisdom spoke for itself. A whole international movement evolved around this knowledge that is known as Spiritism. These works and other books that have flowed from this tradition also give great insight into the nature of life after death.

In Russia, a unique individual named Helena Petrovna Blavatsky[33] (1831-1891) brought through a great body of higher esoteric spiritual knowledge in a series of books and together with an American named Colonel Henry Steel Olcott[34] (1832-1907) formed what is known as the Theosophical Society. Alice A. Bailey[35] (1880-1949), who was a member of the Theosophical Society for a time, then brought through a further body of knowledge between 1925 and 1949.

Around that same time, great exponents of the Eastern Swami tradition began travelling to the West, such as Swami Vivekananda[36] (1863-1902), and Paramahansa Yogananda[37] (1893-1952). They introduced the West to the highest forms of

---

[32] http://en.wikipedia.org/wiki/Allan_Kardec
[33] http://en.wikipedia.org/wiki/Helena_Petrovna_Blavatsky
[34] http://en.wikipedia.org/wiki/Colonel_Henry_Steel_Olcott
[35] http://en.wikipedia.org/wiki/Alice_A._Bailey
[36] http://en.wikipedia.org/wiki/Vivekananda
[37] http://en.wikipedia.org/wiki/Yogananda

the Hindu tradition which, unlike orthodox Christianity, for example, embraced all spiritual traditions.

Buddhism began to enter the West, particularly after the Second World War, from countries such as Japan, China and Tibet. The Theravada traditions of Buddhism flowed in from countries like Burma, Thailand and Sri Lanka.

In the 1960's in the West, a popular rebellion against rigid conservative values and the Vietnam War burst onto the scene in the form of the protest movement/flower-power/free-love era.[38] Despite the chaos of that movement, it led to a mass searching of alternative answers to the important questions of life and the new age of spirituality found new levels of recognition. Westerners began travelling to the East in search of enlightenment. Many came back to the West having found what they were looking, becoming important teachers in their own right. Richard Alpert, who came to be known as Ram Dass[39], and Jack Kornfield[40] are good examples.

In the 1970's a profound text came through a research psychologist at Columbia University, which came to be known as "A Course in Miracles".[41] This text speaks from a Christian perspective, but concentrates purely on wisdom and is designed to help the individual transcend their ego. Some call it Christian Zen.

There is also the Sufi tradition, a purely spiritual teaching from the Islamic culture and the Kabala from the Jewish culture. Taoism also has its modern forms.

In the late 1990's a man named Neale Donald Walsch[42] wrote a series of books called "A Conversation with God". Walsch, a suffering and lost seeker of answers found himself conversing with a higher consciousness who answered his, at first, angry cry for help and a conversation with this high source of consciousness began. The knowledge that came through quickly helped Neale get back on his feet and when his works were published, people

---

[38] http://en.wikipedia.org/wiki/Counterculture_of_the_1960s

[39] http://en.wikipedia.org/wiki/Ram_Dass

[40] http://en.wikipedia.org/wiki/Jack_Kornfield

[41] Foundation for Inner Peace (1996). *A Course in Miracles* (2d ed., newly rev.). Viking Penguin. New York.

[42] http://en.wikipedia.org/wiki/Neale_Donald_Walsch

found it to be a common and relatable dialogue that many were longing to have with the God of their understanding. Neale has become a good representative for the average seeker. The humble, conversational style of these books belies their depth.

Another great body of knowledge that is worth noting is the study of "near death experiences"[43] or NDE's as they have come to be known. This is where an individual dies but is either brought back to life through medical intervention or comes back spontaneously, sometimes miraculously, defying medical explanation. While undergoing the death process, these individuals report having had a profound experience of a higher consciousness that is often also spiritual in nature. Many people are deeply changed on many levels by such an experience. Their consciousness appears to receive a radical boost, often leading to great insight into life beyond physical death. There have been so many reported incidences of NDE's from all over the world that many important studies have now been done on the subject. Such studies find that these experiences have many common elements and seem to follow a set of natural laws that also correlate to perennial wisdom.

This is a brief and by no means complete snapshot of what is now at our disposal. I have mostly concentrated here on important works that have been "channelled" in the more classically direct spiritual way. Some of these works are very deep and not easy to understand at first. There are also countless spiritual teachers and writers, such as myself, who work more directly with people and who endeavour to provide stepping stones into healing, awaking and self-realisation.

ONE SOUL, MANY LIVES

The Soul's Great Journey

We start out each life as a new born babe, and so too does the Soul when it starts its journey in the physical realm bonded to a human form. At the start of its journey into the physical realm, the Soul has the potential of spirit, of the Higher-Self, without, at first, the power of conscious experience to awaken and strengthen

---

[43] http://en.wikipedia.org/wiki/Near_death_experience

its awareness. Like the new born babe, the inexperienced Soul is at the mercy of the elements. It simply provides the Life-Force to the human form along with the dynamic consciousness that pulls it beyond animal instincts and into its own journey of evolution. At first, the Soul's consciousness is not experienced enough, not powerful enough to take full control of the human mind and instead the more primal, survival, human mind takes over and the Soul just goes along for the ride. The result is the human ego.

For the Soul, being born into the physical realm is like a bird being put in a cage and then drugged. The experience is one of limitation, restriction and confusion. The cage is the human mind thinking that it is a body and nothing else and that it must survive in a world of fear and lack. The challenge for the Soul is to break free of this cage like the butterfly struggling to free itself from its cocoon. This challenge evolves the Soul from a new born babe to a radiant Light of conscious-awareness that no chain can hold.

The Soul is not doomed to being repeatedly reborn into the physical realm for eons and eons, as is claimed in some Eastern doctrines. That is not much better than an eternal hell. Although it varies greatly, you could consider a more realistic figure of about one to two hundred thousand years and within that time perhaps ten to twenty thousand lives. In other words, the Soul is here to experience, grow and evolve toward a definite goal. Against the backdrop of this greater journey, each physical life becomes but a brief assignment for the Soul. At first though, the ego knows nothing of this. We assume that this life is it, depending on the culture in which we are born. Under the weight of the primal mind, our physical needs are paramount and in each physical life the Soul mostly loses any awareness it may have gained of its greater potential.

The purpose of the first stage of the Soul's journey is experience. It comes into physical existence in order to experience all facets of human life, all manner of personalities and many different roles such as mother, father, son, daughter, master, servant, artist, king, warrior, scholar, and so on. The Soul is also here to experience all psychological states that are the product of humanity and its choices. This first stage covers the major part of the Soul's human journey, where most Souls still are today.

The human being is no longer part of the animal kingdom and pure animal instincts are not enough to guide us. We must rely on our sense of moral knowing, our conscience, our first rudimentary link to our Higher-Self, but this knowing is weak at first and we lack the wisdom of experience. As a result, we fall into fear and confusion and descend into the chook yard of the ego mind. Unaware of the power of Love and Wisdom available to us from our Higher-Self, we descend into competing for what we think are limited resources. Injustice, pain and suffering are the result.

The Guiding Hand of Karma

Here we come under the guiding hand of Karma. In most doctrines of old, and especially to the ego, Karma is seen as the punishing hand of an angry father-god or a cold, impersonal life-force. In reality it is the guiding hand of Love ensuring that we all reach our destiny.

Because Karma is Unconditional Universal Love, Unconditional Universal Love is therefore the benchmark for human behaviour. It is like the vibratory note of a beautiful, pure, perfect musical chord. Any action that does not resonate in harmony with this pure note of Universal Love, sets off a discordant vibration that must, at some point in time, be brought back into harmony. In other words, any action that is not in accord with this ultimate form of Love, must be corrected at some future point in time as a part of learning how to *be* Love.

Karma can also be beneficial. Good actions lead to good outcomes and good relations that can extend beyond a given life. Often the benefits of good action may not be possible to experience until a later life. Of course, beneficial Karma that comes from good actions must be via a sincere selfless giving of oneself. You can't buy good Karma—the misguided desire to do so has been a corruptive influence in many religions, including Christianity and Buddhism.

Karma is simply about cause and effect on a grand scale. It all appears to be mysterious, because the effects usually come in future lives when we are not consciously aware of the initial cause. This may seem unfair, but the lesson is really for the Soul, not so much the ego, which is limited to only one physical life. The Soul has one life as well, but of course that can last for thousands of years. This may point to a different interpretation of the Christian doctrine of one life.

We all have free will, which is essential because a vital part of what we are here to learn is to be conscious creators. At first, out of ignorance and fear, we create pain and suffering along with everything else we create. We are nonetheless always within the bounds of Karma and so the ego can only go so far off track before the guiding hand of Karma comes into play. Karma is the Wisdom side of Love. It is that which teaches us Total Personal Responsibility. It is teaching us that only Love is real, that only Love works and that all else is an illusion. We are free within those boundaries however, to experience creating from illusion. Just look out your window or on the television at what we have collectively created so far.

We are here to become powerfully conscious, and you cannot be conscious of something without being able to compare it to something else. If all we have ever known is Love, how could we consciously know Love, how could we experience it? It is like the young adult's desire to independently venture out into the world, no matter how wonderful a sanctuary one's family home has been. We must go forth and create our own life. This desire is a part of being human, and it is also a quality of the Soul. Coming home is all the more exquisite for the experience of not being there, helping us appreciate home so much more. For the Soul, home is Unconditional Love—the Universal Life-Force, but it journeys out so far into the human mind that at first home is a dim memory that it almost forgets.

We at first do not trust the truth of Karma though, because of the seeming injustice that we see all around us. How can Karma/God/Universal Life-Force be Love if it allows innocent children to suffer and die, poverty to go unchecked, tyrants to live to an old age while their subjects suffer in prisons and deaths camps? How can Karma be Love when we lose our loved ones and when natural disasters occur?

If all we are is a body and its primal mind, then there would be no real answer to these questions. This physical world however, along with our physical bodies and physical identities, is the vehicle for the experience of Life, not the Life itself. It is like touring around the countryside in your car as part of a holiday. The car is your body. You as the driver are the Soul. It is you as Soul who has the living, conscious experience, not the car, your body/mind. All that is physical is impermanent. Soul is the intelligent consciousness and Soul cannot die. For Soul, all experience is vital to its evolution, so on this level, nothing is lost. There is only gain. Even the brief experience of being a child dying in disease ridden poverty is of vital importance to the Soul. This, of course, confronts the sentimentality of the ego that identifies itself as a mere physical body caught in the limited world of attachment and aversion.

The hand of Karma goes largely unseen to the untrained eye. The power of its guiding hand takes effect in between lives and determines certain factors for the next birth into human existence. This is why many tyrants appear to escape justice. When they are in the physical world, tyrants are in the realm of their own free will and can do with it whatever they like. When their physical life ends, however, the tyrants, thinking that they are all powerful, are confronted with ultimate power and the full consequences of their actions. I will speak more about this later.

The opportunity for the tyrant in that physical life is to learn about the nature of power, destructive or constructive. The experience for those whose lives are directly affected by the actions of the tyrant could be lessons of endurance, of acceptance, of courage, of compassion for others who are suffering and so on. It can also be an opportunity for Karma to work itself out in the lives of some who were also tyrannical in a previous life.

It is a mistake, however, to think that Karma is the reason for all our challenges. Most of our suffering in a particular life, in fact, is caused by what we think and how we act in that life. Karma does, however, add other largely unavoidable factors to our life that we simply, for the sake of our awakening and evolution, must work with.

Indications of Soul Maturity
Another factor is what could be considered the *maturity* of the Soul, in other words, the degree of experience, and therefore Wisdom, that the Soul has gained over time. This determines how skilful one is when it comes to facing life's challenges. For

example, a Soul may be, for whatever reason, born to parents who mistreat their children. Let's consider the story of two brothers, John and Bill. John is an experienced Soul, whereas Bill is an inexperienced Soul. For John, there is within his intuition a strong sense of his own principles of what is right and wrong. He suffers at the hands of his misguided parents, but he can see beyond their influence. He has an unbreakable optimism that allows him to endure his difficult circumstances. In adulthood, whatever emotional woundedness he carries from his childhood experiences, he openly faces and works through and learns even more about life in the process. John has been able to fall back on the conscious-awareness he had attained in previous lives. He is not necessarily aware of what these prior experiences are; he just knows deep in his storehouse of intuition what the Universal Laws of Life are about.

Bill, on the other hand, does not yet have this storehouse of intuitive knowing. There is, as yet, little inner-foundation for his character to stand on. As a result, he depends far more than John on the guidance of his parents and bases his identity on what they say he is and what they do to him. Bill therefore, becomes lost in confusion and heads down self-destructive pathways in life. He sees himself as a victim and thinks everybody owes him his happiness, but at the same time rejects the helping hand of others, even that of his brother, who does his best to help him. At some point in his future lives Bill will have the same level of fortitude that his brother John has, but for now, life is just about deepening his experience of human nature and working through his Karma.

Soul experience also determines the degree and variety of talent displayed by individuals. For example, why an individual easily masters the art of music as though it is the person's "second nature" (a revealing term in itself), while other music enthusiasts have to learn the hard way.

Despite outward appearances, it is unwise to be quick to judge the Soul experience of another individual. The karmic circumstances of another individual are invariably far too complex to fathom. For example, an experienced Soul may be finely ready in this life to take on some extremely heavy karma that would crush most individuals. This individual is naturally significantly destabilised by the challenge, and may even take more than one lifetime to master this dynamic, but master it this Soul will, and make great strides toward enlightenment in the process. To an outsider, however, this experienced individual may seem otherwise for a time while old negative personality patterns are being worked through present day consciousness.

The Character of the Soul

Another factor is the Soul's own character, over and above the character of the physical body/mind. Every Soul has its unique note, its part to play, which is maintained throughout its entire journey. Even though the physical personality changes from life to life, underneath, the Soul is influencing that personality with its own enduring character. For example, I am a philosopher in the field of psychology. This is very much influenced by my Soul, who seeks understanding as its special purpose, and has now a certain level of experience. Another Soul's specialty may be power and leadership. Another's may be beauty in the forms it creates, such as with art, music, dance and so on. Every Soul is unique in the part that it plays and no part is more important than the other. This influence may not always be so evident in every life, but it shows itself overall. No matter what physical personality we may take in the future, or have taken in the past, the character of our Soul will have an ongoing influence. As we reach the latter stages of our evolution, the Soul will be the dominant factor in our physical life. Soul character determines our ultimate motivations and interests. It determines the way we inevitably serve humanity as an advanced Soul, nearing the completion of our path to enlightenment.

Know Your Character

Our own unique character (both Soul and physical body/mind) plays a major part in the way we approach the world. Our childhood conditioning is laid on top of our natural born character and this conditioning is strongly influenced by the way our unique character interacts with those around us. For example: Your father may have a strong will, which he uses to be successful in business. He is an action man and has no time for "sentimentality" or "pointless navel gazing" as he may regard feelers and thinkers. As his child, if you are a feeling type or an intellectual, your father may not relate to you. You may not gain his acceptance and approval—something that children crave from their fathers. If you are also a strong-willed type, you may identify with your father and seem like the favoured one, or you may have a mind of your own and find yourself locked in a battle of wills. The dynamic would change again if this dominant parent was the mother instead of the father.

Or for instance, a mother may have suffered for years from undiagnosed depression and associated anxiety. Because of this her children have been under the heavy cloud of her sadness and in constant fear of further upsetting their mother. They would experience frequent emotional abandonment, due to their mother not being able to connect to them when needed. A strong willed child may become angry and rebellious, chafing under this oppressive atmosphere. A feeling child may try to take care of the mother, thinking that mother's feelings are the feeling child's responsibility. A thinking child may also try to rescue mother with problem solving or withdraw into a fantasy world. Once again the dynamic would change if it was the father who was suffering from chronic depression.

Character influences can be life-enhancing, such as when there is a natural harmony between parent and child, or dysfunctional when there is character disharmony. The challenge for us is to recognise all that occurs in our life is placed there to help us be more conscious. Therefore, a father who does not approve of you is, on the Soul level, helping you to claim the personal power of achieving approval of yourself, independent of your father. A mother who is depressed and shut off emotionally from you is giving you, as an adult, the opportunity to consciously learn how to Love and nurture yourself. When we look at it this way, our wellbeing as adults still ultimately depends on our commitment to self-acceptance, self-awareness and compassionate personal responsibility.

What influences our behaviour patterns is complex, but by looking at your childhood conditioning and your character, you have most of what drives you in your grasp. Using the 5 Step process will enable you to uncover the dynamics of your conditioning. There are many systems for assessing a person's character, but a good place to begin is to use the simple designations of Feeling, Thinking, and Willing.

Feeling/Emotion:

Those of us who have feeling/emotion as our strongest quality see the world in terms of "us". We naturally think in such a way as to include others in our personal circle. Because of our feeling sensitivity, we are very aware of how others feel, to the point of actually being able to feel other people's feelings. If we are prone to being fearful, then we may tend to cut ourself off and isolate ourself, because we are simply too emotionally vulnerable to open ourself up to people. On the other hand, we may have a tendency to lose ourself in other people. We tend to have trouble with boundaries. We become emotionally dependent and allow ourself to be compromised for the sake of hanging on. As a result, we fall victim to those who gain satisfaction from dominating others.

We have a greater tendency to take criticism to heart, because we are more likely to blame ourself when things go wrong. We are more inclined to think conflict is our fault than somebody else's. We are the tragic victims and the hopeless care-takers.

However, when we are in touch with ourself and self-empowered, we have the best people skills. We are sensitive and caring, while at the same time allowing others to stand on their own two feet. We make great teachers, group facilitators, counsellors, social workers etc. We are the best listeners, having great empathy for other people's problems. We make sure everyone in the group is cared for. In business we are the best networkers or personnel officers. We have fine intuitive minds that can also possess psychic abilities. We are often great exponents of the creative arts and appreciate beauty in all things.

Thinking/Knowledge/Intellect:

Those of us who have thinking as our strongest quality see the world in terms of "them". We are the great observers and analysers.

If we are prone to being fearful, we can be aloof, quirky, and even paranoid, due to interpreting what we observe in a negative or distorted way. Because we are too busy observing and analysing, we tend to forget to connect with people, and in particular, our own self. People, for us, can be seen as mere objects and we can be manipulative and cruel as a result. We can be very critical, genuinely seeing what is wrong with the world, but because of our own negative self-worth issues, we forget to pay attention to what is right and beautiful.

When we are in touch and self-empowered, we make great problem solvers and inventors. We make great entrepreneurs, or the creative thinker behind the scenes with great intuitive insight. We can be the laser-focused scientist finding breakthrough cure for a disease, or the professor or investigator weaving together and making sense of mountains of seemingly conflicting information. We can read between the lines and understand the secret workings of life, and ask questions that other people don't even think to ask. Our work becomes dedicated to compassionately serving humanity instead of our insecure ego.

Action/Will/Power:

Those of us who have will as our strongest quality, see the world in terms of "me". We follow our own vision and go our own way. We are the great leaders and adventurers.

If we are prone to being fearful, we may tend to be aloof, arrogant, wilful, stubborn, and/or aggressive. We can be dictatorial, insensitive, and tunnel-visioned. If something goes wrong, it is usually seen as somebody else's fault. We may also use avoidance as a defensive tool, which we use to cut people out of our life, or even cut ourself off from our own thoughts and feelings by locking away parts of our mind that are disturbing to us.

When we are in touch and self-empowered, we are great statesmen. We are courageous trail-blazers. We battle the odds and win, inspiring others in the process. We are the positive thinkers and the motivational speakers. We are visionaries perceiving the next great step forward. We love to lead and we can do long, hard, physical work. Get behind us and we will pull you through. Our disciplined and focused mind can also give us extra sensory perception (ESP).

While the action person leads the way, the thinking person plans the way, and the feeling person makes sure that everyone finds their way. You may be able to recognise yourself as leaning more toward one of these three qualities. However, we are all combinations of the three, and sometimes it is hard to define. Often, due to flaws in our upbringing, we are not even aware of some sides of our character. Having your character analysed by an expert can be of great benefit. Armed with this new information, we can observe how we interact with the world and learn much in the process. If we can be honest with ourself about our limitations and not let pride get in our way, we gain an opportunity to take greater command of our lives.

Perhaps the best known and the most versatile of the systems of character analysis are: Myers-Briggs personality types[44], The Enneagram[45], Astrology[46], and Numerology[47].

Table 5 on page 187, uses the "Seven Ray System"[48][49] of character designation, which is quick to grasp in its simple form. It uses the primary designations of Will, Feeling, and Intellect and then continues with their combinations. Table 5 outlines some positive and negative traits of each type. The positive qualities of a particular type are Love-based and the negative are, of course, fear-based.

The diagram then points out the way of integration for each type; in other words, what qualities that need to be consciously learned by an individual to balance out one's character during the span of a lifetime. For example, Feeling types, generally speaking, would need to develop Will (strength, discipline) and Intellect (clarity, insight, detachment) in order to effectively benefit from this naturally strong feeling ability. This would balance the Feeling type's tendency to lose themselves in their emotions and

---

[44] Myers, Isabel Briggs; McCaulley Mary H.; Quenk, Naomi L.; Hammer, Allen L. (1998). *MBTI Manual (A guide to the development and use of the Myers Briggs type indicator)*. Consulting Psychologists Press; 3rd ed edition.

[45] Beesing, Maira (O'Leary, Patrick; and Nogosek, Robert J.). *The Enneagram: A Journey of Self-Discovery*. Dimension Books.

[46] Oken A. (2006). *Alan Oken's Complete Astrology: The Classic Guide to Modern Astrology*. Nicolas Hays, Inc; 1 edition

[47] Millman D. (1993). *The Life You Were Born to Live: A Guide to Finding Your Life Purpose*. HJ Kramer.

[48] Bailey A. A. (1995). *The Seven Rays of Life*. Lucis Press Ltd. New York.

[49] Michael D. Robbins M. D, Ph.D (1990) *Tapestry of the Gods: Volume 1*. University of the Seven Rays Publishing House. California.

lose touch with their personal boundaries. Without developing will and intellect, their naturally strong feeling ability would instead become a liability. A good level of conscious-awareness is needed to bring these different traits together in a way that positively enhances the individual's feeling ability, which will always be the prominent part of the person's character.

Use this diagram to help yourself gain insight into your character and to your path of integration.

Table 5. Character Types and Their Path to Integration

PATH TO INTEGRATION

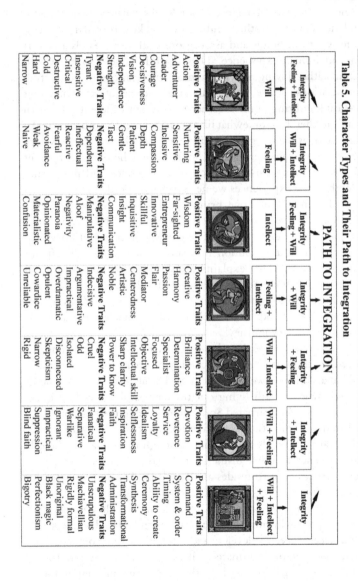

Will	Feeling	Intellect	Feeling + Intellect	Will + Intellect	Will + Feeling	Integrity
Integrity = Feeling + Intellect	Integrity = Will + Intellect	Integrity = Feeling + Will	Integrity + Will	Integrity + Feeling	Integrity + Intellect	Will + Intellect + Feeling
Positive Traits	**Positive Traits**	**Positive Traits**	**Positive Traits**	**Positive Traits**	**Positive Traits**	**Positive Traits**
Action	Nurturing	Wisdom	Creative	Brilliance	Devotion	Command
Adventurer	Sensitive	Far-sighted	Harmony	Determination	Reverence	System & order
Leader	Inclusive	Entrepreneur	Passion	Specialist	Service	Timing
Courage	Compassion	Innovative	Flair	Focused	Loyalty	Ability to create
Decisiveness	Depth	Skillful	Mediator	Objective	Idealism	Ceremony
Vision	Patient	Inquisitive	Centeredness	Intellectual skill	Selflessness	Synthesis
Independence	Gentle	Insight	Artistic	Sharp clarity	Inspiration	Transformational
Strength	Tact	Communication	Noble	Power to know	Faith	Administration
Negative Traits	**Negative Traits**	**Negative Traits**	**Negative Traits**	**Negative Traits**	**Negative Traits**	**Negative Traits**
Tyrant	Dependent	Manipulative	Indecisive	Cruel	Fanatical	Unscrupulous
Insensitive	Ineffectual	Aloof	Argumentative	Odd	Separative	Machiavellian
Critical	Reactive	Negativity	Impractical	Isolated	Warlike	Rigidly formal
Destructive	Fearful	Paranoia	Overdramatic	Disconnected	Ignorant	Unoriginal
Cold	Avoidance	Opinionated	Opulent	Skepticism	Impractical	Black magic
Hard	Weak	Materialistic	Cowardice	Narrow	Suppression	Perfectionism
Narrow	Naive	Confusion	Unreliable	Rigid	Blind faith	Bigotry

Soul Mates

Another important factor in our Soul's journey is our special relationships with other Souls. As we make our way from life to life, we form bonds and associations with other Souls as a part of our human experience. These karmic bonds can be created from either loving and harmonious associations or conflicting associations. These bonds can create forces of attraction that repeatedly bring Souls together to play out different roles with one another. It is somewhat like the friends and enemies we make at school as we are growing up in a particular life. Here we are growing up together in the school of Life where we learn about Love and consciousness. These karmic bonds add power and depth to the experiences we need to have in order to evolve.

The bonds of Love bring opportunities for a far deeper intimacy where a more powerful experience of Love, and also of loss, can be experienced. These beautiful bonds of Love help to speed up our evolution in a similar way to facing difficult circumstances. This explains in part why we have a natural affinity with some people and not with others.

Such "Soul groups" are not rigidly set though. We are always forming new bonds and associations as we make our way along our evolutionary journey.

Even when we die, these special bonds of Love continue between disincarnated Souls (Souls who are no longer in physical form) and also between disincarnated Souls and incarnated Souls (Souls who are still living out their physical life on the Earth plane). As a disincarnated Soul, we may be in the position to aid a loved one while they are still living out their earthly life. Other disincarnated Souls are advanced enough to have a specific role as a teacher to other disincarnated and incarnated Souls. Our experiences of spirit guides and angels are largely accounted for in this way.

In regards to bonds of a conflicting nature, they are often for the purpose of burning off karmic debts and if faced with courage and acceptance, to develop and strengthen our consciousness-awareness, which ultimately all life experience is for. Facing the conflicting experiences in this way is the quickest and most effective way to put the conflict behind us. Karma cannot be avoided. It will follow us until it is worked through, for it is of our own making and is a part of our own unique energy stream that is the very reality of what we are. Our eventual enlightenment depends on it. Remember that Karma is not punishment; it is the guiding hand of Love.

FRIENDS

There was a time when we were strangers.
We stood from each other aloof and a little proud.
I imagined that we had little in common,
And that the bonds of friendship were not ours to share.

Now we stand together,
Guardians of each other's deepest thoughts,
Thoughts we rarely even share with ourselves.
At times I could swear you are my second nature.

I remember the first time you opened yourself to me.
It came out of the blue.
Next thing I knew we were Soul mates,
Traversing life's journey together.

At times we don't always agree.
Sometimes we even argue,
Lost for a while in our fear and pride,
But then the sacred bond of friendship always pulls us through.
We see each other from afar,
And tell each other things we cannot see.
At times I don't like you for your honesty,
But then love you all the more.

My life has greater meaning with you walking by my side.
But I know if we should drift apart some day,
In my heart your memory would always stay,
For knowing you my friend has helped me more truly know myself.

Putting the Pieces Together

When you put these pieces together—Karma, Soul's degree of experience, Soul's character, our special relationships with other

Souls, as well as human body/mind character and conditioning mentioned previously, you have what makes us all unique as human beings. It explains the differences in ability and opportunity that we see amongst human beings all over the world. This is why these factors are beyond the ego's ability to explain. In an attempt to make sense of things, the ego concludes that we are somehow lucky or hard-done-by or that it is just God's mysterious way and it is beyond our possible understanding.

In reality, we are all at some point along the evolutionary path of the Soul. There are always Souls leading the way before us, and there will always be others following along behind. Our worthiness in the eyes of the Universal Life-Force of Unconditional Love is the same no matter where we are on that path. In fact, the special and essential responsibility of those who are further along the path is to be a representative of Unconditional Love to those following behind. Of course this fact is not really comprehended until we have awakened into some level of conscious-awareness.

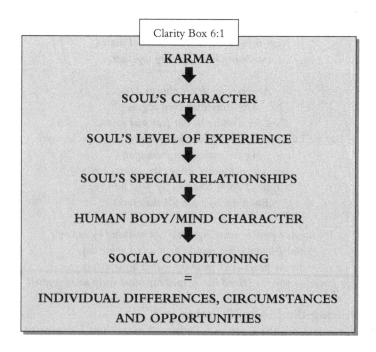

Clarity Box 6:1

KARMA
⬇
SOUL'S CHARACTER
⬇
SOUL'S LEVEL OF EXPERIENCE
⬇
SOUL'S SPECIAL RELATIONSHIPS
⬇
HUMAN BODY/MIND CHARACTER
⬇
SOCIAL CONDITIONING
=
INDIVIDUAL DIFFERENCES, CIRCUMSTANCES AND OPPORTUNITIES

EVOLUTION AND ENLIGHTENMENT

THE SECRET OF THE VOID

I look about me and see only the darkness of a moonless night.
I reach out for support but feel nothing,
As if floating untethered in a starless space.
I turn inwards but encounter memories I try to avoid.
I panic and run, but I run in circles.
I lash out to strike my foe but wound only friends.
I collapse exhausted and surrender to the void,
And in the void the silence speaks,
And in the stillness the Light reveals its secret.

Now that we have some important pieces of the puzzle, let's put them all together and see how the Soul makes its way from first entering the human body/mind to full enlightenment. In the process you may gain a better understanding of why your life is unfolding as it is and gain insight as to how you can make the most of this experience.

The Inexperienced Soul

Because of the infant nature of the Soul when it begins its great journey toward enlightenment bonded to the human form, it mostly forgets what it is. For a long time the Soul is lost in the physical realm. It identifies itself solely as a physical body/mind, even in the way it approaches and relates to its spiritual yearnings. Due to its very limited conscious-awareness, a very inexperienced Soul is not really conscious as such in between lives. Death is indeed like a form of sleep. Its new births into the human form are designed for it by the guiding hand of some greater consciousness. As I have already stated; the purpose of this first stage of evolution is the experience of human nature in all its facets. In many ways the experience is at first quite random. The Soul just ventures forth with its own uniqueness and makes of its experiences what it can. As experience grows, so too does the consciousness of the Soul. This consciousness then gradually creates an awareness of itself in between lives that is still at first predominately identified with the physical realm. As the Soul continues to evolve, it eventually becomes more aware of itself as spirit and a new identity at this level begins to form.

At first we are barely equipped to survive and our lives are simple and often short. Like a child, we are not yet aware that we are learning and evolving. Life is just happening and yet there is an accumulation of knowledge and experience from every life lived. As we slowly evolve and thus gain more sensitivity and intelligence, our desire and drive for more material comfort and fulfilment increases. This is the natural process of evolution. This is the nature of a child even under the guidance of an aware parent.

As the Soul makes its way in this unaware state, Karma becomes a factor in its life through its positive and negative interactions in the world. At the end of each life, the actions of the Soul are weighed up by the guiding hand of Karma and a new course is set. A new life is started a fresh with little or no awareness of the previous life.

The forgetting of previous lives is very important. In every life, everyone gets a fresh start, no matter what they may have done in the previous life; otherwise it would initially be very hard to grow and evolve. We are born, Karma permitting, as a beautiful innocent babe who naturally attracts love and nurturing. Imagine if you knew your child was a serial killer in his previous life and that he killed your daughter or even yourself. Such memories would complicate things greatly. A Soul would have to be at a very high point of evolution before it would know how to constructively handle that sort of awareness. The forgetting therefore is essential for the new roles to be played out between Souls and for Karma to be worked through. To continue the previous example, your child now has an opportunity to do things differently and to make amends for previous mistakes.

Due to our lack of awareness at this stage of our Soul's evolution, Karma is worked though mostly beyond our understanding. All we know is that, despite our best efforts, we encounter certain challenging conditions and circumstances. These challenges nevertheless evolve us and add to the accumulation of knowing in our Soul's intuition. If we dominate another, we in turn learn what it is to be dominated. On the other hand, if we have a tendency to allow ourself to be dominated, sooner or later circumstances will arise that will motivate us to stand on our own two feet. Karma never lets us go too far in one direction without creating a counter force to balance things out.

When you observe the circumstances in your life, therefore, it is essential to try to contemplate on them from this perspective. You are not being punished by some cruel god. You are instead being given opportunities to see things differently. You are being given opportunities to become aware of how your own mind is getting confused and how it is creating its own suffering.

Don't be too concerned about trying to figure out what part of your experience is due to Karma and what is due to your own thoughts and actions in this life. The same goes when observing others. Such things are rarely easy to identify, because of the obvious complexity of Karma. The factors behind Karma are more than we can know in our limited awareness during a physical life. Karma has to deal with the interrelations of every human being over every lifetime. The complexity of that is mind-blowing. As the old saying goes, it is not so much what happens to us, it is how we deal with it that makes all the difference.

There are times when we are made aware of a cause of a karmic circumstance, an issue from a previous life that is having an effect on us now, to give us insight that will help us work through that experience. A sincere willingness to accept Total Personal Responsibility for our life helps to invoke such information into our awareness. Such information sometimes comes into a person's awareness as I am guiding them through a meditation process as part of their therapy.

Overcoming our difficulties is about learning to choose in accordance with our higher knowing. The Universal Laws of consciousness are there to guide us and awaken us to this higher knowing in each life so that we can continue to grow. Through the experiences that we gather from one life to the next, our grasp of this perennial Wisdom slowly increases. This Wisdom, accessed through our intuition, enables us to see beyond the limited vision of the ego's survival mind.

The Evolving Soul
As we continue to gather experience and grow accordingly, our conscious-awareness in between lives awakens. A conscious

existence beyond this world begins to blossom. This creates new learning opportunities for the Soul

As a part of a "near-death-experience" (NDE), people often report experiencing some sort of review process of their entire life whilst time somehow stands still.[50] Most of us have heard the expression, "my life flashed before my eyes". This profound process unfolds in a way that enables them to experience their life, not just from their own perspective, but also from the perspective of all the other lives they have touched, both positively and negatively. One's consciousness in some way merges with the ocean of consciousness that binds us all together. During the process, those experiencing this phenomenon usually find themselves held in a state of ecstatic peace, where there is a heightened level of awareness, but no hint of condemnation from self or any other source. Occasionally though, the experience can be a rude awakening for an individual who has led a misguided life, or simply because a jolt of some kind will be motivating for the individual. NDE's appear to be tailor made for each individual as a part of their overall awakening process. This review experience reflects one aspect of what the evolving Soul is now naturally able to experience in between its physical lives.

The Soul, in between lives, also gains the ability to be aware of its previous lives. This new awareness enables us, as disincarnated Souls, to assess what is the best path to take in the life to come. We are now becoming the author of our own destiny. Our successive lives are now more predetermined, due to the intentions we have set for ourself. We are now more conscious on a Soul level of what we need to achieve in a particular life in order to further our evolution. We don't always accomplish everything we set out to do, because we still get a bit lost in our forgetfulness. That is not so important. We always learn something and there will always be another chance of experiencing what we need to experience.

Another opportunity that is now available to the Soul in between incarnations (physical lives) is to live out its ideals in what is known as the "astral plane". This is a higher dimension of pure thought/feeling that is a reality in itself. Dreaming is a dim reflection of this dimension. This astral experience is available as

---

[50] http://en.wikipedia.org/wiki/Life_review

part of humanity's evolution. The astral plane is, therefore, just a more subtle extension or dimension of the physical world, with its own natural laws that are governed always by Unconditional Love and Total Personal Responsibility. Many people are naturally aware of this plane of existence due to their intuitive or psychic abilities.

As the Soul is awakening to the possibilities of its growing awareness, on the astral plane, it now has the opportunity of gathering together with other like-minded Souls to create a new reality drawn from common ideals. Unlike our physical lives here on Earth where everyone is thrown in together, which challenges the Soul in many important ways, the natural laws governing the astral plane divide it into many levels. These levels represent common states of consciousness. The more aware one is, the higher the level of the astral plane one can access.

As a result of an increasing capacity for consciousness on the part of many Souls, there is an increasing capacity to experience this new realm of Soul life in between physical lives. It is a bit like opening up new territory in an unexplored part of this physical world with other like-minded people with the purpose of trying to create a sort of utopia. This is a reflection of the heaven depicted in many religious doctrines. These growing ideals are not fully attained however, until they are also accomplished in this physical world, with its higher degree of difficulty. It is like putting theory into practice.

Idealism, therefore, is another sign of a growing Soul consciousness. Even though we are unlikely to remember our life as a Soul in the astral plane, we are nonetheless possessed with a strange desire to live out certain ideals, however skilfully or unskilfully that may be. Pursuing such ideals usually lifts us above the ego chook yard and into altruistic endeavours. It is the beginning of the expression of a more universal form of love.

The astral plane, however, is a two edged sword. In the physical world there is a lag time between what we think and what we create with that thought. It takes time and persistent focus of thought and associated action to physically create something. This is not so in the astral world. It is more like a world of lucid dreaming, a world of our imagination. When we think it, we create it. This is wonderful if our thoughts are lifted up into the ideals of Love and goodwill. All too often though, we leave this physical world deeply set in a state of fear, confusion and negative passions. Fear-based religion and the fear of eternal hell have a lot to answer for where such Soul confusion is concerned. Leaving the body does not end our state of mind. This confusion remain imbedded in the Soul, distorting our conscious-awareness until it is healed. The negativity of our thoughts can drag us into a world of common thought that can reflect our conception of hell, except with this hell, we create it for ourself. We remain stuck in our negative thought creation until our thought processes change, resulting in a new experience. This inevitably wakes us up to the power and the consequences of our thoughts. This constitutes a powerful lesson for the Soul. If we are not conscious enough to wake up to this self-created hell, we are eventually pulled free by a higher consciousness and given a new birth.

This self-creativeness explains why many NDE experiences follow along cultural lines. One individual may see Christ, another Buddha, and another a beautiful garden. Another person may experience nothingness because that reflects their belief that there is nothing after death. Such experiences constitute the first stages of a Soul waking up out of its limited physical consciousness. The less experienced the Soul is, the more the astral experience will reflect its own ego conditioning. For the more evolved Soul, the astral experience will increasingly reflect their deep capacity for loving kindness and wisdom, and themselves as spiritual beings in their own right, independent of the Earth plane.

A Graphic Example of Karma at Work
Self-awareness on the level of the astral plane gives Karma new opportunities to awaken the Soul. Let's take the tyrant as a graphic example of how the ultimate power of Karma can work itself out in the astral plane.

For a start, to be a successful tyrant, you have to be very intelligent in order to gain and maintain so much control over a population while keeping your enemies suppressed. You also need to have a very strong will and a big ego to the point of thinking that you are somewhat godlike yourself. You would also tend to be underdeveloped morally. You would have little to no feeling for others. The Soul of the tyrant would no doubt be specialising in power and has leaned too far into the negative aspect of this ability. Even so, a high level of evolvement would be needed to be a tyrant of any real note, such as a despotic dictator who rules for many years.

So the tyrant dies, thinking that more than likely there is no life after death and therefore no real consequences to his actions (let's call this Soul a "he" for simplicity sake, even though Souls don't actually have a gender). The first rude shock the tyrant would get is that he still exists. Confusion, horror and perhaps many other emotions are likely to follow. The tyrant may even try to re-enter the physical world to continue his tyrannical ways, but of course he has no physical body and nobody other than the occasional psychic can see him. He is then confronted with the reality of the Life-Force of Supreme Consciousness. In his arrogance and unbridled pride, he may try to deny this force and rebel against it, but his once all powerful will is rendered futile in the face of the most powerful force there is. He is instead confronted with the life experience of every person he has harmed in a way where he literally experiences being that person in their suffering and yet he knows he is experiencing it. At first he thinks that there is no escape. In this realm there is no sleep and no escape from reality. The mental/emotional anguish is enormous. He fights, he bargains, be pleads, but all is futile. The Life-Force has no interest in his passions and his conniving thoughts. It is only interested in what is in his heart. This is the only thing that is real where a person's morality is concerned. He has, through his own actions, created for himself his own tailor-made hell.

Even with all this suffering, this Karmic process is still not about punishment. It is designed to wake up this powerful, yet misguided Soul. Because of his strong intelligence and awareness, Karma does not need to give him a new birth and subject other Souls to even more suffering at his hands. Instead, it can hold him in this state for as long as is needed. Indeed it could take a few centuries of Earth time to break down this degree of self-will and pride in a way that could not be done during his physical lives. Inevitably there comes a point in this process where the tyrant's ego breaks down, surrenders and genuinely cries out for mercy or just simply accepts the consequences of his actions and gives himself to what may come. In that instant, mercy is by his side in the form of some sort of loving guidance that will begin to educate him in the laws of Love and compassion.

Due to his already high level of evolvement, his awakening is now quite rapid and his sudden recognition of the true reality of Light/Life/Love is profound. He now finds himself, not in his self-created hell, but in self-created bliss. Everything now makes sense. He now regards all his suffering as a small price to pay for the bliss of this profound self-realisation. He is now one with Love and now sees the road ahead and the part that he is to play in service to all other Souls. He also sees the Karma that is left for him to repay on the physical plane. Due to his natural courage and power, he chooses a fast track to complete his enlightenment. He chooses a series of lives of extreme suffering and selfless service to others. He now knows what he is and he now knows that the physical plane is his opportunity to complete his journey as a Soul.

When observing an individual in a state of extreme suffering that may seem very unfair, you can know that they are advanced Souls by how serenely they accept and deal with the experience. They are often comforting those around them who are horrified at what they see. Despite their physical suffering, they are at peace. These advanced Souls are operating from a higher level of intuitive knowing than those around them.

Fortunately there are not too many tyrants of that order around. The path for most of us is far less dramatic and more orderly in our stages of self-realisation.

A More Typical Journey Between Lives

A more typical experience of the transition of one life to the next is as follows. Let's make this subject a female and call her Jane. Jane dies from the normal complications of old age. She is not quite sure of what to expect. She has not been one for religion, but in the last few years she has opened her mind to things spiritual. Even so, there was no real depth to her contemplations. At the moment of death she is aware of her body lying lifeless on the hospital bed as though she is looking down from the ceiling. She is confused for a moment but then a calm washes over her. She sees her youngest daughter in the room calling for a nurse who comes to the bedside. She is aware that her daughter is upset, but somehow knows that she will be fine. She then thinks of her husband who died some years before her. Before she knows it, her husband is right there beside her. He is younger than he looked just before he died. He looks like he did at the prime of his life at around the age of forty. She also notices that there is a sort of luminescence to his appearance. A great presence of Love envelopes her as her husband tells her that everything is fine and to go with him. She is vaguely aware that he spoke directly to her mind, that he didn't use words as such.

The next instant Jane finds herself floating off with her husband toward a wondrous light that seems to envelop them more and more as they draw nearer. Some sort of tunnel effect is experienced on the way toward the light as well as a sense of great speed. Jane then finds herself before other beings who appear to be just pure Light. The Love they radiate is immense and in no time Jane finds herself reviewing her previous life whilst in telepathic report with these Spirit Guides. Her husband is again no longer with her but the Love she is now feeling is so enveloping that this does not disturb her. She experiences a blissful calm as her life review unfolds.

Jane becomes aware of how she avoided facing a certain challenge with her mother at the age of twenty three that would have enabled her to break out of an old pattern of subservience. She allowed her mother's dominance to discourage her from pursuing a career as a doctor. Her mother's father was a doctor. He abused her mother as a child and her mother grew to despise him and also his profession. Her mother eventually faced her pain in her mid fifties and in the process realised that she used dominance as a way of protecting her vulnerabilities, being a power Soul that she was. This completed for her a Karmic lesson. Even though Jane's mother made amends to her later in life, Jane had missed her chance to follow a path that would have well suited her own Soul's speciality. She becomes aware of a stream of former lives where this pattern of avoidance developed. In one of these particular lives Jane was a male. She saw that her mother in that life had been his (Jane's) domineering wife. This most recent life was an opportunity to make amends to herself in order to correct the mistake of allowing others to take control of her.

As Jane continues to review her life just past, she becomes aware of how other opportunities presented themselves to her, via the hand of Karma, which helped her do at least some work on the avoidance issue. She observes how a period of conflict with a bullying supervisor at her workplace forced her to face her fear of speaking out. Another situation gave Jane a chance to face a similar fear when she confronted her eldest daughter, who had neglected to pay back money Jane had lent her. Jane saw how she did well facing both those challenges, having been fortified by her regrets of not pursuing the career of her choice.

The life review now raises Jane's awareness to a period in her life when she gave way to self-pity and unnecessary grief after her husband died. Jane could see how she lacked confidence in herself and feared life on her own. She was able to experience how her youngest son felt when she was not fully there for him during his fight with cancer. Even though she was held in a state of deep, loving peace, Jane could still experience all her son's fear, pain and loneliness as though it was her own. Jane saw how her self-pity had clouded her awareness at the time when her son most needed her support.

Jane also observes how she was able to genuinely touch people with her compassion in her more conscious moments and was aware that this quality was becoming well developed in her. She experiences each beautiful moment from the hearts of the recipients of her compassion. She experiences the feelings of gratitude, comfort and an increased sense of security from an elderly neighbour Jane regularly visited and cared for. There came the experience of her son when he was nine, when his beloved pet dog, Spot, was killed by a car. Jane experiences how he felt when she tenderly held him for over an hour as he poured out his grief. She experienced how her long, gentle talk with him about life and death that night brought him comfort and understanding. Then she felt his joy and excitement when she surprised him with a new puppy a few weeks later. She realised that it was this experience in particular that helped her son forgive her when she wasn't there for him during his time of trial later in life. Many other experiences pass through Jane's awareness, some instances she was not aware of until now.

Jane finds her awareness expanding in every direction as the full degree of her Soul consciousness gradually returns, and yet it all feels so natural. Her review process draws to a close, but she is aware from her interaction with her guides, that they will continue to work together on her life path before she returns to another physical life.

Jane also finds her awareness drawn to those she left behind, in particular her eldest daughter, who is struggling with conflicting emotions after Jane's death. In no time, Jane finds herself at her daughter's side, accompanied by another spirit guide. Jane is given guidance on how to send her daughter feelings of comfort and happy thoughts by gently merging with her mind. Fortunately Jane's daughter is receptive. Jane is able to stimulate certain warm memories she shared with her daughter. This helps her daughter constructively face her guilt for not being at Jane's bedside at her death and also motivates her to work through the resentment that she held toward Jane over the conflicts that they had at times. This simple act of loving kindness by Jane saves her daughter from suffering years of metal turmoil over these issues. Jane is able to deepen her experience of how disincarnated Souls can aid their incarnated loved ones without interfering with their free will.

Many other insights came to her awareness as a part of this learning opportunity. She remembered a time during the transition stage at the end of a former life, where she had become trapped in her own mental/emotional confusion after she left her body. She had grown up within a rigid and misguided religious community that she had eventually rejected. She had not successfully processed her guilt for leaving and she still held deep fears of some sort of hell for the sins she perceived she had committed, even though she knew she had to be free to live her own life.

When Jane, or Hillery (who she was known as then) died, she was afraid to go to the Light and her fear and confusion prevented her from perceiving the Spirit Guide, who was there to help her. Hillery wandered around in the lower levels of the astral plane that are very close to the Earth plane with many other lost Souls. None of the Souls were connecting to one another. They were all lost in their own particular confusion and were even frightened of one another. Using his telepathic abilities to gently stimulate her positive memories, Jane's Spirit Guide managed to coax her to an old mentor who was still living on the Earth plane. Her old mentor, a former pastor in the same religious community, had a much higher understanding of spirituality and was also clairvoyant. He sensed Hillery's (Jane's) cry for help and was able to speak directly to Hillery's mind and sooth her fears. He informed her that there was no hell in the sense that she was taught by the misguided elders at her old church and that loving guides were waiting to take her to a place of acceptance and compassion that would be like a wonderful sanctuary. Even though Hillery was still fearful and confused, she became hopeful enough for her heart to open to the Love that was waiting there for her. In that instant the bubble of her confused mind that was trapping her was burst and she was able to perceive her Spirit Guide and found herself bathed in that now familiar blissful peace.

Despite Jane not successfully taking all the opportunities that she could have while incarnated in her last life, she has nonetheless further expanded her conscious. She now rejoins a dimension of the astral plane that was new to her after her previous physical death. Now it is familiar territory. She feels like a student who has been away from school for twelve months on some sort of student exchange program to another country. It is familiar but there are new experiences to get used to as well.

Jane is now also aware that her need to be with her husband of her life just past is not so urgent. She is aware that they share a close bond, but there are many other Souls that Jane feels deeply connected to as well. Her awareness is linked with them all now, as well as the awareness that she is in a world of affinity where like-minded Souls gather together. She is home.

In her astral world Jane is aware of beings who are at various higher levels of advancement. She also knows that her awareness as a Soul is still limited. There are still many dimensions that are beyond her ability to participate in or even comprehend. For example, during this period in her astral world, she is visited by a particularly beautiful Soul of great advancement. Upon meeting, Jane instantly knows this being as her father, Bartholomew, in a previous life. This connection prompts them to project to one another the form they carried during that time on Earth together. He was an advanced Soul even then. Jane was Bartholomew's son then and gained great benefit from that relationship. The bond between them became very deep and he has been an important guide for Jane ever since. At this time they work together on Jane's life path as he helps her gain awareness of new possibilities in her Soul's evolution.

Bartholomew exists in a higher dimension that Jane finds difficult to understand. There, beyond at times even the higher dimensions of the astral plane, Bartholomew participates in a type of collective intelligence known as a causal entity. Bartholomew informs Jane that he is there now even while he is with her. It is too much for Jane as yet to comprehend and they go back to concentrating on her life-path work.

In reality Jane does not have a form as such, any more than she has a gender. Forms are often projected to one another as a recognition of significant connections during times on Earth. At Jane's level of consciousness, one's physical lives are still very much a source of Soul identity.

At some point in time Jane is called by great beings of Light to complete her life-path work in preparation for her next incarnation. There is some definite emotion felt by Jane, because she is aware enough to know that physical life is often a tough assignment. With the aid of these great beings she is made aware of some aspects of her next incarnation, and she even has some influence as to the course that will be set. She is aware of the connections with certain other Souls who will be an important part of her coming life. She is therefore aware of the general plot, but many aspects are kept hidden. She also gains a new level of determination to awaken out of the slumber of her unconscious ego in this coming incarnation.

Jane's connection with the Soul, who was her husband in her life just past, will continue. They will be partners again. They both share a deep desire to awaken during this coming incarnation and have made a strong commitment to support one another in their common journey toward enlightenment. Jane is made aware that her name in this coming life will be Barbara.

Upon re-entering the physical plane as a new born babe, Jane's new Soul knowing becomes intuitive feelings that are stored deep within her heart, ready to be retrieved in her teenage years or young adulthood. Can she respond to that mysterious call in this coming life? Can she break through into a real level of conscious-awareness this time with the aid of the loving hand of Karma and her ever growing inward determination to be a conscious Soul in the physical world?

The Advanced Soul

As Souls become more advanced, like Jane's beloved Bartholomew, they come to identify themselves as pure spirit. They occupy larger and larger vistas of the astral dimensions and beyond. Physical death for them is simply a returning home from an assignment. A new incarnation for them is much more purposeful. Having now mastered their consciousness to a large degree, they are now actively involved in some sort of service to humanity, according to their Soul's specialisation. The challenges of serving humanity as pure spirit and also in a physical body on Earth now becomes a major part of their Soul growth experience.

There comes a point of Soul advancement where there is no more need to return to a physical body. One has even evolved beyond being Soul and is now basically the Higher-Self that beckoned the Soul ever forward over the long millennia of experience. Enlightenment is achieved but the evolution of such spiritual entities continues on into even higher vistas of cosmic consciousness. The cosmos is now their domain. Depending on one's field of speciality, some enlightened Souls choose to stay closely connected to humanity. Some even return to Earth with a special mission to perform, such as Christ or Buddha or some other great avatar that has graced the Earth during times long past.

During this current time on Earth, such great beings are choosing to remain behind the scenes. They are instead the relay stations for the Universal Spiritual knowledge that is pouring into the consciousness of humanity at this time. The avatar today is the mass of open hearted Souls endeavouring to pull humanity beyond its technological and material arrogance and into a higher moral awareness. Goodwill and cooperation on a world scale is now the objective and its achievement is inevitable, no matter how long it takes.

For all of us though, once our conscious-awareness has awoken during our physical life, the path to eventual enlightenment is rapid compared with the first stages of blind experience. This is because we are now consistently going with the flow, even if we do still veer off track on a regular basis.

One of the greatest mistakes we make at this stage of conscious-awareness, however, is to grasp at enlightenment. We want to escape from the world rather than master it, which only serves to keep us bound to it. We try to fool ourself into thinking that we can skip the hard road of healing and integrating our human-self fully into the sanctuary of our heart of conscious. The quickest way to enlightenment is to forget about enlightenment and instead concentrate solely on being the representative of Unconditional Love to our own human-self and to all other beings. Being Love *is* being enlightened.

There is no need to fear the death of the physical body any more than there is a need to fear our life *in* a physical body. All that you need in order to successfully live your life in peace and harmony is within you. All that you need to heal your emotional wounds and mental confusion and to grow accordingly is also within you. Accept what is right in front of you in your life and open your heart to it and embrace it. Make your choices and create your life with courage and integrity. Live your life to the full with the willingness to feel all there is to feel and to see all there is to see.

Life is abundant on every level. Only your own confused mind can deprive you of this richness. The profound peace of conscious-awareness is the treasure of all treasures. It is the foundation of all that you are in this physical world. It is the fountain head of all your potential. Only your own conscious-awareness can open the door to the Love that will set you free once and for all.

MISTAKEN

I stared at my form in the mirror and thought it ugly,
But I was mistaken.
I reached for my heart and felt only fear,
Thinking there was nothing else,
But I was mistaken.
I journeyed into my mind and found myself unworthy,
But I was mistaken.
I steadfastly pressed forward and pierced a heavy veil,
Behind which shone a dazzling light of purity unfathomable,
And at the same time felt that this was truly me,
Was I mistaken?
I think not.

CHAPTER SIX SUMMARY

1. Reincarnation refers to every human being having a Soul, a spiritual presence within us, that does not die when the body dies. Instead of passing out of existence, the Soul re-enters physical life in a new body for the purpose of continuing on the experience of Life.

2. With each life experienced, the Soul gains awareness of its power of consciousness until it reaches a stage of its development (after many lives) where it realises itself to be the self-responsible authority of its own experience as a living representative of the Universal Laws of Consciousness, enlightenment in other words.

3. There are perhaps four main benefits to enlightenment: 1. No longer being subject to suffering. 2. Ability to help others overcome suffering. 3. To no longer be required to re-enter the physical world in a physical body with all its limitations, in order to further one's evolution. 4. Being one with Universal Love.

4. Science is supposed to impartially investigate natural phenomena, no matter what it is, including consciousness, life after death, ESP and spirituality.

5. Beginning around the mid 1800's, a new wave of spiritual knowledge began entering the consciousness of humanity. All over the world individuals received this knowledge in many different ways and in many different forms, with the emphasis always being on Unconditional Love and Total Personal Responsibility.

6. Since that time, some of the greatest spiritual texts that have ever graced the minds of humanity have emerged.

7. We start out each life as a new born babe, and so too does the Soul when it starts its journey in the physical realm, bonded to a human form.

8. The Soul is the potential of spirit, of the Higher-Self, without at first the power of conscious experience to awaken and strengthen its awareness.

9. Like the new born babe, the Soul, at the beginning of its journey into the physical world, is at the mercy of the elements. It simply provides the Life-Force to the human form along

with the dynamic consciousness that pulls it beyond animal instincts and into its own journey of evolution.

10. At first, the Soul's consciousness is not experienced enough, not powerful enough to take full control of the human mind and instead, the more primal survival mind takes over and the Soul just goes along for the ride. The result is the human ego.

11. The challenge for the Soul is to break free of the delusions of ego like the butterfly struggling to free itself from its cocoon. This challenge over its many lives evolves the Soul from a new born babe to a radiant Light of conscious-awareness that no chain can hold.

12. Soul is here to experience, grow and evolve toward a definite goal, which is enlightenment. Against the backdrop of this greater journey, each physical life becomes but a brief assignment for the Soul.

13. This entire journey may take around one to two hundred thousand years, but can vary greatly from Soul to Soul.

14. The Soul is also here to experience all social roles and psychological states that are the product of humanity and its choices.

15. The human being is no longer part of the animal kingdom and pure animal instincts are not enough to guide us.

16. Our sense of moral knowing, our conscience, is our first rudimentary link to our Higher-Self, but this link is at first weak and easily overridden by our lower nature.

17. As a result we fall into fear and confusion and descend into the chook yard of the ego mind. Unaware of the power of Love and Wisdom available to us from our Higher-Self, we descend into competing for what we think are limited resources. Injustice, pain, and suffering are the result.

18. Here we come under the guiding hand of Karma. In most doctrines of old, and especially to the ego, Karma is seen as the punishing hand of an angry father-god or a cold, impersonal life-force. In reality it is the guiding hand of Love ensuring that we all reach our destiny.

19. Because Karma is Unconditional Universal Love, Unconditional Universal Love is the benchmark for human behaviour.

20. Any action that does not resonate in harmony with Love sets off a discordant vibration that must, at some point in time, be brought back into harmony.

21. We all have free will, which is essential because a vital part of what we are here to learn is to be conscious creators.

22. At first, out of ignorance and fear, we create pain and suffering along with everything else we create. We are nonetheless always within the bounds of Karma and so the ego can only go so far off track before the guiding hand of Karma comes into play.

23. Karma is the Wisdom side of Love. It is that which teaches us total personal responsibility. It is teaching us that only Love is real, that only Love works and that all else is illusion.

24. We are here to become powerfully conscious, and you cannot be conscious of something without being able to compare it to something else. If all we have ever known is Love, how could we consciously know Love, how could we experience it?

25. Many of us have difficulty trusting a higher, universal conscious or God, because of the suffering and injustice that we see all around us, but this suffering is created by the ego mind, not by Karma/God.

26. We are all given free will to create what we choose in any given life. It is between physical lives when Soul comes under the absolute power of Karma. Karma sets the course, the challenges and opportunities for the next life.

27. A tyrant may appear to escape justice during the term of that physical life, but once death arrives, this deluded Soul comes face to face with the ultimate power of Karma. There is no escape.

28. A very inexperienced Soul has little to no awareness within the spiritual realm in between physical lives. The higher forces determine the course of the next life and the Soul, with its free will, lives out that life as best it can, ignorant of the higher guiding forces.

29. As the Soul evolves, conscious-awareness in between physical lives grows. The Soul increasingly becomes aware of the purpose of its existence, which is to expand its consciousness to a state of being Love/Wisdom on all dimensions.

30. Conscious-awareness in between physical lives as a discarnate Soul, enables the Soul to experience itself as an astral being within the astral plane, a dimension that is purely on the level of thought/feeling, something like lucid dreaming.

31. On the astral plane, unlike the physical Earth plane, like minded Souls gather together to explore evolving ideals. These realms are where the notions of heaven come from.

32. This growing idealism or awareness of the principles or science of Love/Wisdom is then reflected in the desires and motivations of physical lives of the evolving Soul. This can take the form of a desire to grow consciously, of altruism and of selfless service, for example.

33. The lower levels of the astral plane can also be a gathering place for Souls still caught up in fear and negative passions. This is where the notion of hell comes from, but this is a self-created hell that can end the moment one's thoughts turn toward Love.

34. The self-created realms that reflect heaven or hell teach the Soul about the nature and consequences of its own thoughts and actions. The more evolved the Soul, the more Karma can teach that Soul within the astral plane about the true nature of itself, whether in the hell realm or the heaven realm.

35. This period of learning within the astral realms lasts as long as it is beneficial for the Soul. The Soul then returns to Earth for more experience in a physical body living out a physical life.

36. Inevitably a Soul awakens to the true nature of itself, at least on a rudimentary level, during a period of a physical life. This leads to some form of spiritual awakening.

37. As the Soul continues to evolve, conscious-awareness gradually heals, integrates, and replaces the lost and suffering ego. The Soul, even whilst in a physical body, recognises that every experience is an opportunity to realise itself as Love itself.

38. This is a very important stage on the way to enlightenment. This Soul now rarely creates negative Karma. Instead it is ending (burning) all the negative Karma that it has previously created. In other words, one by one it is shattering its ego

delusions and rapidly expanding its consciousness in the process.

39. As an inexperienced Soul the journey is slow and often arduous. As an advanced Soul, the challenges are welcomed, progress is rapid and enlightenment is only a handful of lives away.

40. A highly evolved Soul increasingly exists within the higher realms of the astral plane and beyond, until its need to return to a physical body is outgrown. This is what is known as enlightenment. This Soul may still choose to return to Earth in physical form to carry out some form of service for the benefit of humanity.

41. The experience/age/maturity of a Soul determines an individual's strength of character and depth of intuition as well as the Soul's natural intelligence and talent.

42. An inexperienced Soul will be easily confused and led astray by the negative influences in his/her environment. A person with an advanced Soul will have an intuitive knowing of the higher Laws of Consciousness and will cut his/her own path in life, regardless of negative influences.

43. We are all somewhere along that path of advancement. At this stage, most of humanity is still within the inexperienced Soul stage, even though there is increasing advancement into mature and advanced Soul ability. This is why there is still much chaos in the world today while change is rapidly occurring.

44. The more advanced you are as a Soul, the more responsibility you have to be a representative of Love to those who are not as evolved.

45. The Soul has its own character or specialisation that influences every life, subtly at times, stronger at other times, especially as the Soul gains the upper hand in an individual's consciousness. This influence continues even as the physical body/mind character changes from life to life, depending on the experience needed.

46. The 3 main pathways that one's character can take, whether on a Soul or physical personality level, are: 1. Feeling/Emotion 2. Thinking/Knowledge/Intellect 3. Action/Will/Power.

47. We are each a combination of varying strengths of these qualities in a given life.
48. It helps to gain some awareness of your character type.
49. Perhaps the best known and the most versatile of the systems of character analysis are: Myers–Briggs personality types, The Enneagram, Astrology, Numerology and the Seven Ray System of character designation from the works of Alice A. Bailey.
50. Another important factor in our Soul's journey is our relationship with other Souls.
51. As we make our way from life to life, we form bonds and associations with others Souls as a part of our experience as human beings. These karmic bonds can be created from either loving and harmonious associations or conflicting associations.
52. These bonds create forces of attraction that repeatedly bring Souls together to play out different roles with one another.
53. They add power and depth to the experiences we need to have in order to evolve.
54. There is always room for forming new bonds and associations as we make our way along our evolutionary journey.
55. Even when we die, these special bonds of Love continue between disincarnated Souls (Souls who are no longer in physical form) and also between disincarnated Souls and incarnated Souls (Souls who are still living out their physical life on the Earth plane).
56. As a disincarnated Soul, we may be in the position to be able to aid a loved one while they are still living out their earthly life.
57. Other disincarnated Souls are advanced enough to have a specific role as a teacher to other disincarnated and incarnated Souls. Our experiences of spirit guides and angels are largely accounted for in this way.

- ✓ You are an eternal Soul on a journey of consciousness expansion.
- ✓ Life is Love and is designed to ensure you inevitably succeed.
- ✓ Accept total responsibility to Love yourself unconditionally and the guiding forces of Life will have the opportunity to aide your progress.
- ✓ Treat all beings with loving kindness whilst always honouring yourself.
- ✓ *NEVER GIVE UP. SUCCESS IS INEVITABLE!*

CHAPTER SEVEN

STEP 3
LET GO & TUNE IN

A BRIEF INTRODUCTION TO STEP 3

Letting go reveals how to step out of the ego games of blame, conflict and manipulation, and step into the freedom of healing and personal growth. To change our life, we need to focus on and take total responsibility for our own reactions to the world, and the people in it. We do this by tuning in to our own physical sensations, emotions and thoughts, in the spirit of loving acceptance and compassion for ourself as best we can on a daily basis. Our life simplifies dramatically when we accept that the cause of our suffering is our own confused thinking and the solution to this suffering can be found in the sanctuary of our own heart and Soul. By staying in touch with ourself in this way, we come to experience the healing power of Love, as our vulnerable human mind is embraced within our open heart of conscious-awareness. By becoming our own source of Love, we gain the power to heal all past wounds and confidently manage our future. We gain a great focus of power to change our world by first healing and changing any part of our own mind that is not motivated by Unconditional Love for ourself and all others. Through this process, we gain clarity of mind and the ability to act wisely. We are truly awakened to the reality that all life experience is an opportunity to grow in awareness, Love, and empowerment. We can change our experience of the world by healing ourself.

BARBARA AND BRYAN'S STORY

Continuing the story with Bryan . . .

During my day at work I had a lot of what I call rats running around inside my head. I couldn't help expecting my boss to come into my office and start giving me a hard time. He came into my office several times, but it was like business as usual. He seemed to get over the disagreement we had yesterday easily enough, why couldn't I? This thought made me even more determined to take good care of my mind. During my break, I sat on my own and read a couple of personal development handouts on the subject of anger and conflict, like I promised myself. By the time I finished reading; a few insights had to come through for me. I realised I was stuck in my old self-rejection mindset again. I was waiting to be condemned for my mistake and my defences were on high alert. A lot of memories of different scenarios from my past surfaced in my mind. They were all to do with conflict issues and this feeling of rejection, and a lot of anger on my part. The reading material was just what I needed.

My break was soon over and my day got busy after that so I couldn't give it much more thought. However, I think tuning in at lunchtime like that helped me relax a bit for the rest of the day. I felt more centred.

On my way home, though, I could feel a growing knot in my stomach as I wondered what mood Barbara was going to be in—shades of the not so good-old-days. When I walked in the door, I was greeted with Doogle, the dog, running around my feet as usual, but there was no sign of anyone else. I figured the kids were probably doing their homework. I then heard Barbara's voice calling out to me from what I guessed to be the study at the other end of the house. There was a gentleness in her voice that helped me feel more at ease. I walked into the study where she was sitting and put down my brief case. I immediately saw the book in her hand as she reached up from the reading chair to hug me. The book was her own self-help manual she likes to read. It's not stuff I relate to that much but it seems to work for her. She'd obviously been doing her own tuning in during the day. The knot in my stomach dissolved as we talked.

I got so used to the chaos of the old days when we would get lost in the blame games. Even the kids seem to be different now. They are now more care-free and yet disciplined, like they care about themselves more. Like today, I can still find myself facing the old drama play that once dominated my mind and dragged me down.

"If you need some quiet time," Barbara said, "I'll get some dinner on and call you when it's ready."

Her kindness touched something in me that almost brought me to tears. I kissed her and she headed for the kitchen. I reflected on the fact that these special moments are becoming more frequent and I shook my head when I thought about how our marriage almost ended.

After saying hello to the kids, I closed the door of the study and took out a couple of books from my drawer in the writing desk. One was the main book I was reading to help me get in touch with myself. The other was a journal that I use to scribble out my often wayward thoughts and emotions and then process them.

I had an urge to put the books away and hang out with Barbara in the kitchen. I just wanted to drink up her kindness, which was fair enough I guess, but I want to give more to the relationship and not just take from it like I've done in the past. More importantly, I wanted to give to myself.

I remember the words I heard spoken at a relationship seminar I attended some time back. "Put yourself first, then your partner, then your children, and then the rest of the world." This seemed very selfish to me at first. It went against my social conditioning. Surely we must put our children first, and then our partner, then work and maybe I come next. But as the seminar progressed, I understood what they were talking about. I realised they were talking about love and wisdom. If I don't give this to myself first, in other words, learn how to love and care for myself first as a responsible adult, then I would have precious little to give to my partner. Then what would our partnership give to our children—another role-model of immaturity, conflict and emotional repression? I tried that one. I decided to scrap it for the new model, which has worked wonders.

I began to write out my thoughts and emotions about the conflict I had with my boss. I have learned that it is best not to worry about how the words come out, but rather be spontaneous and free flowing—after all, that's how emotions are. What flowed out was a lot of anger and resentment. Soon, though, the other memories that came to me at lunchtime began to surface again. Another incident at an earlier job came to mind, and some incidents with my elder brother and also of being bullied at school. My father then came into the picture and I could see more clearly the pattern that was emerging. They were incidents of not being treated with consideration, as though my feelings and thoughts were irrelevant. I could feel the anger and resentment burning within me, and shame as well. I put the pen down and sat with those emotions for a while, going right into them like I'd been taught.

While I was sitting there feeling this dark energy within me, my mind kept wanting to race off into the drama and the blame games. I was feeling victimised all over again by these memories, but then I started to feel like I shouldn't feel that way and I got annoyed at myself, and felt stupid for being so weak. But then I caught myself as I began to beat myself up. I remembered the acceptance step and my right to be human. I remembered I was there to compassionately care for myself.

My annoyance soon began to soften and be replaced by a deep sadness, along with some tears. I could sense how abandoned I felt as that child. I remembered with a greater sense of understanding how the normal everyday mistakes that a kid makes were often used as weapons against me, or as a reason to ridicule me. I could feel the wounds alive within me—my inner-child waiting now for me to accept him as he is and truly listen to him and feel him. Soon I found myself imagining that I was hugging him and it seemed for a moment that he was real. More tears flowed from both of us. I then took him by the hand and brought him home; my home; my heart. The images that formed in my mind as I read John Bradshaw's book, "Homecoming"[51], earlier in the year, embraced me once again and I could literally picture myself taking me, as a little boy, out of that house of my past and into my heart, the sanctuary that I have for myself now.

That little boy is now my responsibility. I feel this as a conviction that is now strong within me and I feel the power that

---

[51] http://en.wikipedia.org/wiki/John_Bradshaw_(author)

216

comes from it. I like to think I know what it means to be an adult these days, and more than anything else, I believe that it is this understanding that enables me to feel good about myself.

I now felt a renewed softness toward myself—a sense of caring that makes everything okay. My balance was now renewed. A few more layers peeled off the old onion of my human baggage.

It is easy for me to see now what had happened yesterday. I could see how my boss, Ted is his name, accidentally triggered a minefield of old anger, resentment and shame when he clumsily ticked me off about the job order I had mislaid. Suddenly I was one very pissed off ten-year-old, and who knows how old my boss's mind suddenly became. We must have looked a real sight as we slugged away at each other. After Ted had left my office, my old emotional memories continued resurfacing. The angrier I got, the more I hated myself without even realising it. All I could see was how hard-done-by I was, but as a reaction, I felt more and more self-destructive. All reason had flown out the window.

Talking to Ted constructively about it tomorrow was now a possibility. This morning it would have been totally out of the question. Barbara tapped on the door to call me for dinner. I made a mental note to do some more reading on the subject after the kids and I had done the washing up, and also to thank Barbara for being in my life.

THE PATHWAY TO HEALING

In this chapter, I will be introduce the important working principles for healing your painful emotions and self-defeating thought-patterns. To further enhance your awareness, I have included a preliminary set of exercises. I will then take you deeper into the process of healing your mind and finish with a comprehensive exercise that is designed to help you break through old negative conditioning to new heights of healing and peace.

Step 3 is about putting steps 1 & 2 into action by actively opening up to your human-self. In other words, taking real care of your mind and body by being your own loving and responsible guardian, who is totally committed to the highest principles of Unconditional Love and Total Personal Responsibility.

As the one who is learning to tend this garden of your mind, you must learn how to dig deep, because the roots of mental confusion and the emotional pain that it causes go very deep and spread very wide. To be a skilful gardener you must learn how to work with your emotions and undo your mental confusion on an ongoing basis. Step 3 is the most important step when it comes to healing your emotions and misbeliefs and changing your life on a deeper level.

Unfortunately this is the step we most often skip over or simply neglect. It is the hardest step for the ego to comprehend. At first we are rarely willing to accept, or able to grasp how deep this commitment to ourself needs to be. The ego wants to quickly get the pain over with so it can get back to its comfort zones, or it wants to grasp at the rewards of success without fulfilling the required personal development work. At some point down the track though, the ego finds itself disappointed and disillusioned in the face of the next challenge for which it is unprepared.

Step 3 takes us above and beyond the ego's limited capacity. The ego has a basic fear of facing and working directly with our vulnerable emotions, due to its limitations. As a result, we try to analyse them away, burry them or blame them on someone else. In contrast, Step 3 is about letting go of this fear-based ego control, opening up and allowing the emotional energy to flow into and through our heart of conscious-awareness and Higher-Self for healing. We still need to think, but it is thinking in coordination with the intuitive feeling of our Higher-Self. Step 3, Let Go and Tune In, is about our conscious-awareness building a bridge of acceptance and healing to our human-self. This enables our vulnerable human-self to be lifted up into the loving and wise arms of our Higher-Self.

Here our aware ego is learning to step aside and simply occupy itself by keeping the door to the Higher-Self, our compassionate heart, held open via our commitment to accept our humanness. Our heart of consciousness, filled with loving intentions, becomes a sanctuary for the old emotional wounds of the past (trapped emotional energy/wounded inner-child) to flow into. It is here that our emotional woundedness finds healing.

Without having this sanctuary of loving acceptance within our conscious-awareness to flow into, our trapped emotional energy would have nowhere else to go but invade our mind and continue to play out the old scenarios of the past.

Of course, our ability to create this inner-sanctum for ourself is not going to be very skilful at first, but every little bit helps. With persistence, we naturally get better at caring for ourself in this way as our experience grows.

Before we can effectively connect to our human-self however, we must first learn to let go of what prevents this vital connection occurring.

Real healing and awakening comes from opening up to the greater power of my Higher-Self.

LETTING GO

Indulging in condemnation and blame ensures that our ego remains the blind plaything of the distorted and heartless misbeliefs and motivations of an out-of-control human-self driven by primal fight-or-flight emotional reactions. Where there is condemnation and blame, Love is choked out, along with self-awareness. Healing and growth is not possible. We remain at war with our own humanness and the humanness of others and at odds with our Higher-Self.

Our blind, self-righteous ego thinks that judging and blaming protects us and makes us powerful, but in fact the opposite is true. Here the fight-or-flight instinct is using the intellect to try to keep the wounded inner-child safe, but it is doomed to failure. The blind survival-mind is unwittingly possessed by the phantom of past confusions. We have become lost in a storm of fearful emotions, unable to see the real from the unreal. All we end up doing is perpetuating and deepening the confusion.

This confusion is like a play constructed from the things that our inner-child most fears. Whenever our fear and confusion is triggered by something in the present moment, our past drama starts to play itself out again in the present. Unconsciously, we start sucking everyone around us into this play of our imagination. No matter what those, who have been captured by this mental drama, do or say, their words and actions are interpreted in a way that matches the self-condemning plot of the play. Naturally people get frustrated by this delusional behaviour and react negatively, which only serves to feed the flames of the paranoid fight-or-flight instinct. If we could stand back and watch ourself acting out this play yet again, we could see that it is the same old theme repeating itself.

It is therefore essential to let go of the story, which invariably makes you, or somebody else, wrong for being human. We must separate the story from the original pain. The story is perpetuated by our blind and confused ego desperately trying to find a reason and a solution for its pain in what it sees and misinterprets now. This emotional intensity, and the fear and confusion behind it, begins in childhood, which is why it is all so irrational The story keeps building and compounding throughout childhood and into adulthood. It becomes unprocessed trapped emotional energy. The ego doesn't understand that the pain is from the past and that it is being perpetuated by confusion that is imbedded in our own unconscious mind. The ego is trying to make sense of the pain by looking around now for somebody or something to blame.

Even though the story that the ego creates is not real, the original pain that is still trapped within the mind *is* real. The pain *is* our child-self alive in our memories, stuck in the original trauma that caused the confusion.

It is this child, it is this pain, that we must allow into our own heart of compassion, for we are now the guardian of this vulnerable child within us. We are an adult with the capacity for conscious-awareness. We now have the power to heal this trauma within the sanctuary of our own heart, and in so doing, free ourself from the confusion that traps the pain. In contrast, being fooled by the ego's fearful, emotionally driven story, as it tries to play itself out again in the present, keeps us powerless like the child we once were. It is a story that was first created by a powerless child, and therefore, the story can only ever create more powerlessness. We must learn to see the fear and heal the fear rather than keep being the fear. If we truly want to heal and grow, we can no longer justify seeing ourself as a victim.

💝 *My painful emotions point to a trauma within my mind of which my blind ego is unaware. When I drop the blame laden story and focus my open heart on the pain, the original trauma and the confusion that it causes can be revealed and healed.*

To give you a further example of how the ego's drama play takes over our life, let's pretend we are in a relationship. I have levels of trauma still active within my mind from childhood that has been further compounded by a poor first relationship choice, which was a symptom of my negative conditioning. I have learnt some lessons from my previous relationship and assume that I have left it all behind me, unaware of how deep the pain and confusion really is. I am confident that my new relationship with you will give me the security and happiness I am looking for. As a result, my heart is open and vulnerable to you, which unconsciously leaves what remains of my past trauma very open to be triggered also. After the glow of the first year or so of the relationship, my attachment to you, and dependency on you, is much deeper. As a symptom of this growing dependency, my expectations of you, that you have little chance of living up to (and probably don't even know about), start to encroach on the relationship. I may also be under some sort of ongoing stress. This may cause me to unconsciously compensate by emotionally depending even more heavily on my relationship with you in order to feel secure. As a result, the deeper layers of my past trauma start rising to the surface.

Because you are human, sooner or later you do or say something that triggers my trapped emotional energy, and as a result, my mind is suddenly taken over once again by the drama play of my childhood conditioning. As my passed trauma continues to invade my mind, I increasingly see you from the mindset of the powerless and hurt child within me. As a result of falling out of my fragile conscious-awareness, my mind increasingly regards you as being responsible for my pleasure or pain. If I am feeling pain, I will naturally be upset at you for not ensuring that I feel pleasure. As time continues on, and if I am unable to take responsibility for my pain and regain my perspective, my fight-or-flight survival mind begins looking at our whole relationship for reasons why I keep feeling this pain. The process of condemning you for not living up to my expectations deepens. I have lost touch with my fragile conscious-awareness. I have forgotten that as soon as I am feeling fearful emotions, as soon as I start making myself or you wrong, I am getting lost in the confusion of past conditioning.

By perceiving you through the eyes of a powerless and hurt child, I have become dependent on you to change before I can be happy. Worst still, my survival mind now has use of my adult power, so anger and pride in the form of self-righteousness is my safety zone. To feel safe, I must be right and you must be wrong. I may try to solve this situation by lashing out at you and pushing you away, while the whole time it is my ghosts of the past that I am fighting, thinking that these ghosts are you. Unless I am able to wake up out of this bad dream and take back conscious control of my vulnerable mind, my relationship with you may tragically come to an unnecessary end. I would then be in danger of carrying this destructive drama play into my next relationship.

Clarity Box 7:1

TRIGGERING OF TRAPPED EMOTIONAL ENERGY

ACTIVATES THE FEARS FROM NEGATIVE CONDITIONING

THESE FEARS START PLAYING THE DRAMA OF PAST CONDITIONING IN THE PRESENT

THOSE AROUND US ARE DRAWN INTO THE PLAY

THEY REACT NEGATIVELY TO THE CONDEMNATION OF THEM AND OF OURSELF

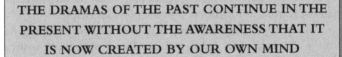

THE DRAMAS OF THE PAST CONTINUE IN THE PRESENT WITHOUT THE AWARENESS THAT IT IS NOW CREATED BY OUR OWN MIND

If I insist on hanging onto this attitude, I have rendered myself forever powerless to take charge of my own emotional life, regardless of what is going on around me. My happiness is always in someone else's hands. This is also called "giving our power away."

Furthermore, we just don't stop at holding other people responsible for our happiness. We blame places and things as well. We blame our job, our living situation, our financial situation and we even blame the weather. We blame the fact that we have children, or don't have children. We blame our health or the government and on and on it goes.

The original story seemed real for the child, but it is not real for the adult, because an adult has the power of consciousness, the power of choice where our own thoughts are concerned.

Some people are so locked into this self-righteous mindset that it becomes their standard approach to life. Using such a mindset can certainly enable us to assert a certain level of control over others. We can certainly force others to do what we want. We may even become very wealthy and powerful in the material world. What we will never be able to control, however, are the hearts of others, their free will in other words. Real, fulfilling relationships with people will always elude us. We might be able to fool people into admiring us or being subservient to us, but real intimacy will always be lacking. As a consequence, real happiness will always be beyond our grasp. Our own heart will be closed off and we will be slowly dying on the inside, despite outward appearances.

This is a fear-based form of power and control that is driven by pride, and within it are always the seeds of its own destruction. Genuine healing and personal development cannot enter a heart in this state until the individual's pride is broken down through his or her own personal crisis, for example, or by the all powerful hand of Karma, as I mentioned in the previous chapter.

In reality, the ego has very little control over anything. It lives a life of delusion and denial. Real control is found within the greater consciousness of the Higher-Self, through living the principles of Unconditional Love and Personal Responsibility. From this grander perspective, we come to realise that gaining command our own human-self is the surest way to gain command of our life in general.

♡ *I gain awareness of my misbeliefs by focusing on how my own mind emotionally reacts to any given situation.*

People who are consistently happy and fulfilled are not simply lucky. Their contentment comes from their willingness to actively take responsibility for their own emotional life. These positive people are usually far better at getting ahead in a healthy and sustainable way. The secret to their success is in the fact that they know that happiness is a choice that they have the power to make, no matter what circumstances they are in. Their positive choices can be unconscious due to simply possessing good conditioning, or they can be conscious choices due to leaned lessons in life.

It is important to note that suspending negative judgment and blame does not negate wise discernment, a positive form of judgment. Discernment is essential for responsible choice-making. Discernment is observing and assessing the reality of a situation as it is. For example, you may have a friend who is often unreliable and unkind. You do your best to talk to her about this but to no avail. You have given her the benefit of the doubt while carefully observing her responses. You still care about this person, but you conclude that you must distance yourself for the sake of your own wellbeing. In the big picture, you are also doing your friend a favour by helping her experience the consequences of her negative behaviour, which is essential for her own evolution, whether your friend can see this at the time or not.

Such choices are based on an assessment of what is for our highest good in line with loving self-responsibility. Even though such choices may not always please everyone, they are never designed to condemn, punish or hurt anyone. In the case of wise discernment, those who are displeased are likely to be hurting themselves with their own misguided thinking. With such skilful self-responsibility, personal affairs can be managed where the long-term, big-picture outcome is beneficial for everyone. This is the secret behind being assertive rather than aggressive.

We don't have to figure out what is good for everyone else. When we make our choices for ourself, based on the Laws of Consciousness (our Higher-Self), we are choosing from a level of consciousness that is in some way connected to all beings.

Your happiness and fulfilment depends on you accepting, knowing, and having faith in the power that is within your Higher-Self to heal, change and grow. If you want to change, the means to do so are right there within you. You don't have to waste time waiting around for someone else to change first.

As adults, we have the power to learn new ways and develop new choices. Life-skills need to be learned just like anything else, but we won't learn anything new if we are not prepared to let go of, or at least question, our old beliefs that keep us down—beliefs that cause us to regard ourselves as powerless victims. In this way we can stop our future being a perpetuation of an unsatisfactory past.

Letting go is therefore about *not* holding other people, places, and things responsible for our pain or for our fulfilment. Our pain is about the powerless child within our mind, who is still stuck in past memories and misbeliefs. To find happiness and fulfilment, we must let go of trying to control others to avoid facing our fears and instead focus our energies on being the compassionate carer of our own mind. By allowing our emotional pain to flow into our heart of consciousness, by staying with the pain and observing it from the position of self-acceptance and self-responsibility, we are awakening our conscious-awareness and connecting to the power of our Higher-Self.

Letting go means no longer judging, blaming and fearfully controlling. An open heart lets in the Light.

Clarity Box 7:2

TRIGGERING OF TRAPPED EMOTIONAL ENERGY

ACTIVATES THE FEARS FROM NEGATIVE CONDITIONING

THESE FEARS START PLAYING THE DRAMA PLAY OF THE PAST CONDITIONING IN THE PRESENT

CONSCIOUS-AWARENESS RECOGNISES THAT BLAME AND CONDEMNATION IS CONFUSION

THE STORY THAT WE ARE AGAIN A VICTIM IS DROPPED AND OUR HEART OF COMPASSION OPENS INSTEAD TO THE PAIN

THIS PAIN OF THE PAST IS HEALED BY THE LIGHT OF COMPASSION FLOWING THROUGH OUR CONSCIOUS-AWARENESS

TUNING IN

Often it is not until we really begin to make an effort to care for our mind in a genuine way that we discover how deeply ingrained our negative conditioning is. Unless we wake up our conscious-awareness, we are doomed to blindly and unconsciously act out these negative programs. When we do set forth a real intention of take responsibility for all that we think, feel, say and do, our efforts in self-care then enable us to see our negative conditioning as if for the first time, even while these old self-defeating habits still have us in their grip. We discover that our heads are full of misbeliefs that create attitudes and perceptions that, in turn, cause us to be out of step with reality and out of tune with our Higher-Self. That is why we hurt. Through emotional pain our body/mind is trying to bring the destructiveness of these misbeliefs to the attention of our conscious-awareness so that we can consciously do something about them.

Instead of paying attention to this vital information, like a wise parent would pay loving attention to a troubled child, as blind egos we have learned to shoot the messenger by judging, rejecting and repressing our emotions and anyone else who might dare to stir them up.

These habitual misbeliefs cause us to be in conflict with ourself and as a result, we continually fall into condemning ourself or others. We have become our own worst enemy. Little wonder we spend our life running away from ourself. To get away from ourself we remain in a constant state of "tuning out". We tune out because we are still stuck in that impossible childhood bind. We think we have to live up to some crazy standard that says we are not allowed to be human while at the same time not being able to be anything else. In order to deny our own humanness, we phase out, and we do it in countless different ways, and in ways that have become so ingrained into our society that we call it normal behaviour. Smoking, drugs, and drinking are just a few ways. There are also many natural human behaviours that are used in a distorted way to hide from ourself, such as unhealthy eating, sex, work, power, entertainment and so on.

Tuning into our emotions and questioning our long-held beliefs is not easy at first. We are shaking up the very beliefs that we thought were our foundations, but if this confusion has been our foundation, then we have been living on very shaky ground. It can be a shock to discover what we have been doing to ourself for so many years—to realise how much we have been contributing to our own suffering. We can easily fall into self-condemnation again, but this would be making another mistake. We are only uncovering what was already there. Awareness is an essential first stage to healing and growing, as with self-acceptance.

Changing the way we react to life's circumstances can still be hard to do, because we can easily lose our way. We need to stay focused on the life-enhancing principles of Steps 1 and 2, acceptance and responsibility. We need to stay motivated to continually care for our vulnerable emotions until this responsible self-care becomes our new habit of living.

It is our feelings/emotions that tell us when our thinking is constructive or destructive by being either pleasant or painful. By tuning into our emotions in the spirit of Unconditional Love and Personal Responsibility, we can discover what our mind is up to. We can become self-aware—conscious in other words.

> *By tuning into myself and contemplating the nature of my thoughts and feelings, the reality of any situation will have a chance to be revealed to my awareness.*

When we tune out from ourself, we are running away from ourself. When we lash out at others and accuse them of abandoning us, for example, in reality, we have abandoned ourself. We have refused to take responsibility for our own human-self. We run away from ourself because we don't like ourself. In the process we cut ourself off from our Higher-Self, our ultimate source of Love and fulfilment. This causes us to feel empty, lonely, afraid, angry, and so on. We try to capture those around us and make them our source of fulfilment, but then hate them if they can't live up to our expectations. We become an out-of-control needy child in an adult's body, lost in aversion and attachment, creating our own suffering.

It's time to wake up out of this bad dream and create something new. It is time to stop holding prisoners instead of having relationships. It is time to let go and open our heart to where Love really comes from, the centre of our own conscious-awareness.

OUR THOUGHTS MAKE US OR BREAK US

I can't emphasise enough that all emotional and physical actions and reactions follow thought, especially in adulthood. The quality of our lives is determined by the quality of our thoughts. Even deeper are the beliefs (thought habits) that we hold about ourself and the world around us. Our thoughts are our creative power. We are creating our life, good or bad, with our thoughts.

We so little realise what we are doing to ourself with our thoughts. For example, we cause so much unhappiness for ourself when we blindly assume that a particular perception that we have about someone is the truth and stubbornly defend it, no matter what it is doing to us. We are often so sure of the motives behind what someone does or says to us. Sometimes we do have a reasonable idea of what someone is thinking, but more often than not we don't. We just think we do. Often the person in question does not even know. We waste so much time and energy analysing and assuming instead of communicating and taking responsibility for our own fears and insecurities. We don't stop to think that many different meanings can be applied to any given experience.

For example; my partner may point out to me that the way I parent one of my children is adding to that child's anxiety. I immediately assume that my partner is criticising me and as a result, I react angrily to what she shares with me. In reality, my partner really Loves me and is simply trying to help me have a better relationship with my child. My misbeliefs cause me to think that my partner is attacking me, when in fact *I* am the one who is making *myself* sad. I am attacking myself by choosing to believe that her words are meant to attack me. I could have chosen any number of interpretations. Why do I choose that thought in particular out of thousands of possible other thoughts?

Why do we fixate on just one particular interpretation and discount all others? The reason for this of course is our own unconscious beliefs or conditioning. It is that habitual story that keeps playing over and over in our mind. So much of Step 3 is about letting go of what we "think" we know and allowing reality to reveal itself as it is.

When our thinking comes under the control of our conscious-awareness and therefore our Higher-Self, it becomes a power of good. With our thoughts, we can create a world in our mind that is positive and constructive that will continually attract positive things to us, while enabling us to move through challenging situations peacefully and skilfully. Our mind is very much our home. If it is controlled by a fearful and confused ego, it will be hell to live in. If our mind is embraced by conscious-awareness, serving the higher Laws of Consciousness, then it can become a sanctuary where we will always find peace.

If you can first consider that no one is intentionally trying to hurt you, and that everyone is really looking to be Loved and wanting to be in harmony with you, you will be right at least ninety-five percent of the time. I kid you not? Most people want this, but often don't know how to achieve it. They are just as afraid of you as you are of them.

All too often, though, our ego assumes that others are out to get us and creates a miserable world for ourself. The ego does this out of its fearful belief that it is powerless and so it can't skilfully manage a difficult situation in a way that is appropriate in that moment. It can't let go of its defences and delusions long enough to even try to learn. As a result of its paranoia, the ego shoots first just to be on the "safe" side.

In reality, most of the time the other person is just confused and doesn't know how to communicate constructively in that moment. There is an inner-child inside them waiting for someone to reach out to them in an effort to try to understand them.

Imagine how good it would feel if other people did this for you. Imagine the joy and harmony this would bring to your life. The same goes for others.

What we do to ourself with our thoughts, largely determines what we do to others. Learning to take care of our mind and therefore ourself, enables us to be more positively open to the moment, where we are able to experience what is really there.

On the rare occasion that we are confronted with real danger, whether emotionally or physically, our conscious-awareness is more able to be aware of it. Furthermore, if you are experiencing an ongoing abusive situation in your life now, the more empowered your conscious-awareness is, the better you will be at protecting yourself and changing your situation for the better (see pages 325 to 326, part D. for more information).

When my thinking is in line with Unconditional Love and Total Responsibility, my mind is in a state of peace and clarity and I can act skilfully for my highest good and for the good of all.

The following set of exercises will help you to get started on that journey, or to get restarted. The first part of the exercise will help you build a powerful awareness of how your mind is tuning out. The second part will help you to implement positive life-enhancing behaviours into your daily routine. The third part of the exercise is about looking for what is good in you, about looking for what you have achieved. Like all the other exercises, you will need to return to them many times as your awareness deepens and your healing progresses. Each time you do, you have an opportunity to go deeper. Read all three exercises through before you start on the first one, which is exercise 7.

EXERCISE 7
TUNING IN TO TUNING OUT

a) Over the space of a few days or a week, list in your journal all the ways you catch yourself "tuning out". In other words, list all the ways you are avoiding paying attention to how you are feeling, whether it is your thoughts, your emotions, or your body you are actively not paying attention to.

b) Remember, whenever you feel prolonged disharmony within your body and particularly your mind, you can be sure that a belief that is not aligned to reality is in control. Your body/mind is trying to communicate this very fact to you with emotional energy and physical symptoms. Your experience of life will not permanently change in any real way until that belief has been identified and turned around.

c) This is not an exercise in beating yourself up. This is an exercise in raising your self-awareness so that you can replace old self-defeating habits with new life-enhancing ones. This exercise will also help you when it comes to deeper processing.

d) **Some of the ways we tune out are:**

- ✗ Comfort eating
- ✗ Alcohol abuse
- ✗ Using mind-altering drugs
- ✗ Criticising others or ourselves
- ✗ Too much TV
- ✗ Too much time on computer games
- ✗ Spending hours on the internet
- ✗ Unhealthy sexual activity
- ✗ Being overly busy in anything
- ✗ Severe dieting
- ✗ Using your will to shut down your emotions
- ✗ Continually making light of things
- ✗ Being overly rational, sceptical or suspicious
- ✗ Being gullible—not thinking for yourself
- ✗ Worry

- ✘ Regret
- ✘ Self-pity
- ✘ Over-working
- ✘ Too many nights out
- ✘ Reading half-a-dozen self-help books at a time
- ✘ Too much reading in general
- ✘ Controlling people or allowing others to control you
- ✘ Being a rigid perfectionist
- ✘ Being dominating and rigidly controlling

Are there any other examples that have occurred to you?

e) Carry a small notebook with you wherever you go and jot down what you observe if you can't get to your journal right then and there. Then when you can, spend some time writing down and further exploring what you have discovered in your journal. This includes spending time just feeling and getting in touch with it.

f) Don't overwhelm yourself while trying to do this. Sometimes we are shocked by what we find and fall into self-condemnation. Remember Step 1, Total Self-Acceptance. Remember that you are only uncovering what is already there. By becoming aware of it, you will be in a position to change for the better. Perhaps just do it every alternate day if that is better for you.

g) What are you doing to yourself when you tune out? For example:

- ✘ Not caring for yourself
- ✘ Neglecting yourself
- ✘ Indulging your fears and insecurities
- ✘ Running on empty
- ✘ Disregarding your own wisdom
- ✘ Harming yourself physically due to carelessness
- ✘ Harming yourself physically due to poor diet
- ✘ Harming yourself physically due to substance abuse
- ✘ Punishing yourself in other ways
- ✘ Repressively controlling yourself

 ✖   Locking up your mind in pride and self-righteousness
 ✖   Denying your feelings
 ✖   Condemning yourself for being human
 ✖   Allowing others to mistreat you
 ✖   Allowing your mind to indulge in stress and worry

What else has occurred to you?

h)   Write down what you have discovered as a first step to turning these self-defeating behaviours around.

EXERCISE 8
MOVING FORWARD

a)   Considering each point that you have written down, spend time now contemplating on positive, life-enhancing approaches to life. Use the table in Appendix 2 on page 359 to help you with ideas. See Appendix 3 on page 363 for a list of misbeliefs and their positive opposites. Write down what comes to mind.

b)   Using these positive ideas as a guide, look at what attitudes and behaviours you can work into your life, such as ongoing gratitude for what you have. Over the coming weeks, do your best to implement those ideas.

c)   Don't expect to stop the old conditioning in its tracks. Old habits die hard. Focus on creating new approaches to life. Create a new self and put your energy into that, learning by trial and error. You are writing a new program straight over the top of the old one. This is the quickest way. The old programs get starved of energy as the new programs grow more complete and robust.

d)   Don't try to do too much at once. Perhaps choose one or two small ideas that may give you a chance to see positive results quickly. For example; tidying up your living space and keeping it that way.

e)   Write your intentions down in your journal and also place them in prominent places at home and at work to keep reminding yourself of your new direction. You could also leave yourself reminders on your mobile phone.

f) **It is essential to keep yourself aware of and faithful to the new programs you have set in place, otherwise the old habits will creep back in. These old habits don't sleep and they don't think. They are blind automations that just keep on going until they are replaced. You have to stay on top of them in order to create enough counter energy to reprogram them.**

g) As well as this you may want to choose something more substantial that will take more long-term effort, such as getting fit, or seeking regular counselling.

h) Keep track of your progress in your journal, knowing that change is often gradual.

i) Be aware that in your attempt to implement positive change in your life, you will encounter difficulties and complications around you and within you that you will have to patiently work your way though. Situations are rarely what the ego expects. Accept what comes as part of the process and work with it.

j) Know also that any attempt to implement positive change in your life will confront and reveal your own negative conditioning that you may not yet be aware of. Do not be discouraged by this. It is normal and useful. It is an opportunity to gain awareness and to heal on a deeper level.

k) Take whatever time you need to work with these external and internal obstacles using the deep processing exercise on page 273 and then gently push forward with the positive behaviours again until more healing is needed.

l) Know that all obstacles, either internal or external, are opportunities that Life is giving you to learn more about yourself.

m) Be aware, therefore, that **you will always be working through continual cycles of pain and confusion, prompting self-acceptance and personal responsibility, leading to awareness, healing, insight, conscious action and growth, which gives us more ability to further step out into life. But then we find ourselves confronted with deeper layers of fear and insecurity. The cycle then starts over again with pain and confusion prompting self-acceptance and personal responsibility and so on. This is the normal process of a growing consciousness.**

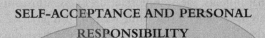

Clarity Box 7:3

VULNERABILITY TRIGGERING PAIN

AND CONFUSION

⬇

SELF-ACCEPTANCE AND PERSONAL

RESPONSIBILITY

⬇

AWARENESS, HEALING, INSIGHT, CONSCIOUS

ACTION, GROWTH

⬇

STEPPING FURTHER OUT INTO LIFE

AND FURTHER INTO HUMAN-SELF

WITH GREATER POWER

⬇

VULNERABILITY TRIGGERING PAIN

AND CONFUSION

⬇

SELF-ACCEPTANCE AND PERSONAL

RESPONSIBILITY and so on...

n) Be aware that on each turn of the cycle, you will be on a point further along your road of personal development, even if it may not always look or feel like it. This is the natural process of trial and error that is expanding your consciousness. These cycles can range from everyday trifles, to major crises or transitions that can last months or years. They are a natural part of life and you can make them work for you.

o) Keep track of your progress in your journal. Be free to adjust your goals to ones that are more appropriate for you, as you learn more about yourself during the ongoing adventure that is the journey of your life.

EXERCISE 9
LOOKING FOR THE GOOD

a) How has the way you care for yourself changed since practicing self-awareness?
b) What insights, ideas, important decisions, affirmations and goals have come to you while working this process?
c) Write down the positive changes that you have discovered about yourself in your journal.
d) In your own heart, be quick to validate your progress. Even if progress is slow, acknowledge the efforts that you are making. BE YOUR OWN BEST FRIEND. BE THE GUARDIAN, THE MENTOR, WHO LOVES TO ENCOURAGE YOU AND EMPOWER YOU.

DEEP EMOTIONAL HEALING

What Lies Beneath

While we are condemning ourself for simply being human, we are always going to want to tune out from ourself, and while we continue to tune out, we will never get beyond our self-defeating behaviour patterns. Our misbeliefs will be free to keep controlling our lives and robbing us of our potentially bright future in the process.

Children are dependent on others because they do not have the necessary degree of consciousness needed to look after themselves. They naturally get lost in their confusions. They have a survival investment in having others take care of them. Being emotionally dependent is necessary for children. Such an approach to life clearly does not work for an adult, however. It keeps us locked into behaviour patterns that bring us unhappiness. We do not truly become adult, where our mind is concerned, until we can consciously take responsibility for our own thoughts and emotions.

To effectively work with and process our deeper, more irrational, emotional vulnerabilities, we need to learn how to *be* with emotions. In other words, we need to open our heart and mind to them and allow them to freely flow through our conscious–awareness.

Often, when we do attempt to work with emotions, we try to "fix" them by suppressing them or analysing them away. This is often a fear-based reaction, which is rooted in self-rejection, or a limited belief about our ability to process emotions. It is about trying to escape from our emotions, to get rid of them, rather than genuinely heal them. Trying to fix deep emotional trauma in this way is just misunderstanding the nature of the problem. The success of this approach to emotional healing is limited, because it reaches the problem only on a shallow level. What needs to be understood is that emotions are meant to be felt. They contain essential information.

Emotions are like energy waves. If allowed to flow freely the way emotional energy is meant to, even the most intense emotional release passes quite quickly, once having delivered its essential message to our consciousness. Emotions themselves don't need fixing, because that is not where the problem lies. The problem lies with our distorted thinking patterns. It is our distorted thinking patterns that cause, accumulate and perpetuate emotional energy unnecessarily. Sometimes though, the distorted thinking pattern that keeps the emotions trapped is beyond our grasp.

Cognitive Behaviour Therapy (CBT)[52] is a very useful therapy tool designed to correct erroneous thought patterns. In fact, there are strong similarities between CBT and the Buddhist approach to self-analysis. It is a basic therapy tool and I use it throughout this book. It involves learning constructive ways of thinking. With this new awareness, it is then easier to identify destructive forms of thinking. We then endeavour to apply these new constructive forms of thinking and associated positive behaviours to our everyday lives. In other words, we construct new programs for our mind and attempt to lay them down straight over the top of the old ones. If we are consistent enough, the old programs give way and the new ones take hold.

Unfortunately though, this often does not work the way it should. This process remains an important tool to have in your

---

[52] http://en.wikipedia.org/wiki/Cognitive_behavioral_therapy

tool box, but it falls short of being able to effectively heal and clear certain deeper emotional pain and confusion that seems to be deeply rooted.

An example of this deeper trapped emotional energy is what is created in early childhood experience. Children's minds are emotional minds, whereas adult minds are more dominated by thinking. This is why trapped emotional energy tends to be driven by irrational thoughts, which were first set in motion when we were children. The thinking, or cognitive, aspect of the memory system of children is not as formed as the emotional memory, particularly before the age of five. Thought processing at this age is very confused, irrational, and jumbled. A young child's memories are mostly made up of magical images that are often very frightening to a small, acutely vulnerable child and these imaginings can produce intense emotional energy. These imaginings are the result of actual events that the child does not know how to process. The child gets frightened of something and this fear sparks the child's imagination and it takes on a life of its own. Much of this memory content simply gets lost along the way to growing up, but certain irrational ways of perceiving ourself and the world remain and continue to influence and distort our future perceptions. This is not new to what I have described before, other than the fact that this trapped mind stuff is very resistant to any form of analysis because it is so irrational and so protected by our fight-or-flight response. This early childhood thought stuff is so lost and obscure that we can't get a rational handle on it, even when we do manage to access it. Because of the intense emotional nature of it, our primal automated mental defence system is too strong and shuts out any attempt to access it.

What this means in regards to healing our mind is that at times we must work with our mind on purely emotional levels. Deep, trapped emotional energy from early childhood tends to keep overriding any healing that is done on more shallow rational thinking levels. The younger you were as a child when the trauma occurred, the less effective CBT is.

Other mental states can also cause this problem, such as active past-life phenomena and repressed memories associated with trauma from any stage in our life.

As strange as it may seem to those not familiar with transpersonal therapy, there is another memory system available to us, and that comes from our Higher—Self. This type of memory is crystal clear. It is not distorted by the child-mind. During deep emotional clearing therapy, I am able to access these higher memories that can reveal real events at an early age (or any age), but access to this information is controlled by the Higher-Self. Only what is useful comes through.

I call this therapy technique that I use, "Multilevel Healing". Through a guided meditation process, I am able to help my clients bypass the primal mind and its interfering defences. This approach is not restricted to early age trauma. I use it for a broad range of issues. Higher states of consciousness can be accessed that in turn enable deeper levels of the unconscious mind to be accurately and safely revealed and healed. This is a common approach in transpersonal psychotherapy and there are a number of different names given to this process. If you say that you need a guided meditation therapy that enables you to clear deep subconscious trauma in a way that helps you learn how to care for your own emotions, an alternative or transpersonal therapist, who has this skill, will know what you are talking about.

I use Multilevel Healing for a wide range of applications such as; processing trauma and loss, anxiety and depression, phobias and compulsive behaviours, helping those who have experienced NDE's better understand and process that experience, including safely reliving it, achieving spiritual awareness and connecting to higher guidance and so on. During this process, spontaneous past life regressions sometimes occur, giving the opportunity to carry out some healing work on this level as well. Indeed, anything that has deep emotional content to it, benefits from this approach.

Before such higher states of consciousness can be access in order to initiate healing and awakening, we need to first get through any deep, intense, trapped emotional energy.

Clearing Intense Emotional Pain

I am going to focus here on the process of clearing intense emotional pain. This will also help you understand how to work with emotions of any intensity. This will reveal to you the process of emotional clearing in its full power. If emotions on this level can be successfully cleared and healed, then emotions on any level can be healed.

On these deeper, more purely emotional layers of the wounded mind, there can be a mass of intense emotional pain that, when triggered, creates a state of extreme vulnerability, despair and even panic in our mind. This reflects the acute vulnerability that a small child feels when he or she is under threat either physically (including sexually) or mentally/emotionally or all of the above. This pain is very difficult to deal with, because this extreme vulnerability triggers off very strong fight-or-flight reactions.

If we are carrying such intense pain in our mind, our ego can do its best to avoid feeling it or having it triggered, but the cost is a significant reduction in our every day functioning in life. We must avoid certain things in life that might trigger the pain, which differs for every individual and can also worsen over time. As a result, we may be prone to phobias, nervousness, paranoia and other irrational fears. When the pain is triggered, the result is a dramatic mood swing. One moment we can appear happy and calm, the next, we can be in a state of suicidal despair, uncontrollable rage, or debilitating fear, just to name a few examples.

To uncover the deeper layers of emotional pain and work with them, we need to literally discount the irrational thoughts that are set off by the pain and hold ourself open and steady to these emotions that are rushing through us. If we can do this with a strong conscious intent to open our heart of compassion to this pain, while not being diverted by the thoughts (to be conscious-awareness observing and embracing our human-self), this intense emotional energy can be effectively and safely dealt with. Easier said than done, of course, but look at it like this. When it is triggered, this intense, trapped emotional energy is like a very small and very traumatised child who needs to be held for a period of time while being allowed to empty out emotionally.

Not surprisingly, the survival mind thinks it is not going to live through this experience, because it still regards itself as the acutely vulnerable and powerless child. Nevertheless, from the position of conscious-awareness, we must hold steady and trust that emotional pain is no different to physical pain. If we are severely injured, the pain can be seemingly unbearable, but its purpose indicates the extent of the injury. It will pass in time. If we can consciously open to physical pain, we can learn to cope with it much more effectively. Giving birth is a good example. The same goes for emotional pain. As I said before, intense waves of emotional pain actually pass through our mind quite quickly if we can open up to it and allow its free flow.

Breathing deeply but slowly is also helpful during this process, just like it is when giving birth. This helps to keep the mind calm and the energy flow open. I will talk more about this in the next chapter.

It is the irrational thoughts that this pain triggers on the way through that are the danger. It is the thoughts that cause us to react in self-destructive ways. Consciously, we must remember that all of this type of emotional pain is from the past. The ego desperately tries to look for a reason for it in the now, but if we can stay consciously above the ego enough, we would see that there is nothing happening in the now that would cause such an intense emotional reaction.

Even when the emotional trauma is the result of a dramatic event in our life now, such as an accident, or suffering an act of violence, the emotions can be worked with in the same way. We can stay calm under pressure by being the detached observer, in other words. This enables us to act skilfully, rather than get lost in the emotional reactions that could be triggering off all sorts of unconscious content from our past.

Obviously, releasing intense emotional pain of this sort is a very difficult process to manage on your own. It is essential that you have a therapist or lay person with you who is experienced in emotional release work. They will provide a safe and accepting environment for you and help you to stay focused on the emotions without getting sidetracked by the irrational thoughts. It is not unusual to momentarily revert back to being like that traumatised child while this intense energy is being released.

The Gain from the Pain
Once the pressure of this trapped emotional energy eases off and if a space of loving compassion has been held open for this trauma to flow through, a heightened state of consciousness can emerge from this pain. This is because the ego has been temporarily disengaged

by us opening up our heart to these intense emotions. The ego has literally been blasted out of the way. This deep state of openness enables our mind to be embraced in the Love/Wisdom/Power of our Higher-Self. As a result, we may experience strong feelings of Unconditional Love and emotional security. We may also receive clear and positive insight into things such as past memories, the fundamental nature of our worthiness as a human being and the importance of loving ourself unconditionally, which all can be quite blissful. This intuitive insight reveals a more positive and empowering perspective on the past or present situation.

Do not underestimate how powerful this process can be. As one who often facilitates such a process, I find the bigger the pain to begin with, the bigger the bliss at the end; such is the power of Unconditional Love. A trauma that may have seemed insurmountable for perhaps many years of our life can be swept away by the mighty hand of Love in just one therapy session, if the conditions are right.

There are many examples I can give from my own psychotherapy practice. One simple example that comes to mind was a session I did with a very macho, rough-around-the-edges male. He wasn't the type to share his feelings, but he was being eaten up with grief around the death of his young child and he could stand it no longer.

As soon as he started sharing his story, his tears started flowing. Before he had too much time to think about it, I directed him to focus on what he was feeling. Instead of avoiding the memories of his daughter, which he had been trying to do for years, I helped him to totally open up to them. While he kept his breath open and flowing, enabling his conscious-awareness to remain open, I helped him to relive in detail his experience of his daughter's life. I suggested to him that his grief-stricken emotions were normal and right in the light of what had happened. I suggested that allowing those emotions to flow freely was a way to honour his love for his child and that their Love will never die and that she is still very much a part of him in his memories.

At first, only the pain and the anger surfaced. "How could such a young life be taken?!" he cried. I encouraged him to courageously face the realities of life and death as his emotions flowed. I gently suggested to him that death was no barrier to Love.

Soon however, other memories began to surface. All the beautiful moments that he shared with his daughter, that had been pushed aside by his overwhelming grief, came to the fore of his mind. The pain and anger was quickly replaced by the rapture of those beautiful moments shared. Excited sharing and laughter filled the room where a moment ago years of pain had dominated. His grief, duly honoured, had now given way to the Love between himself and his daughter that lives on. He walked out of my therapy room a changed man.

Such a process does no harm to the body, but afterwards you may feel very tired. A good, deep sleep usually follows such an emotional releasing session. There is often a feeling of relief and a care-free lightness the following day, along with the same feelings of warmth and Love.

This process for dealing with extreme emotional pain is the same for dealing with any emotional pain that is less intense. It is always important to hold your heart open to the pain first in order to allow the trapped emotional energy to be released and to neutralise any fight-or-flight reaction. This staying open to your emotions, while not getting caught up in the ego drama play, enables your conscious-awareness to take over the process.

It is our distorted thinking that needs fixing, therefore, not our emotions. The emotions are the foliage of the weeds that we see in the garden of our mind, but the distorted thinking is the roots of those weeds. If you do not destroy the roots, the weeds will keep growing back, but if the emotion is intense, this needs to be released first before any clarity can be gained. The dense foliage of emotion needs to be cleared before the roots can be exposed.

My emotions/feelings are giving me vital information about my mind and the world around me.

Working with our Memories

With our new attitude of loving acceptance of our humanness and a firm commitment to care for our emotional reactions, misbeliefs can be safely re-examined and corrected. The ego's self-condemnation is removed enough for us not to be so fooled by it. We can see past these old thoughts to what is really needed. Often healing happens quite automatically, because we are consciously re-entering this vulnerable memory-space with a loving heart, something that was missing when the emotional traumas first occurred.

Emotional healing is very much like entering an emotional time-tunnel that leads into various memories. Sometimes these old memories resurface quite vividly, sometimes we only feel the waves of releasing emotions and are not aware of the rest of the memory, particularly if these emotions come from a very early age. It is as though we, as conscious-awareness, return to the scene where we find our past child, adolescent or adult self stuck in the difficult situation that created the confusion and emotional wounding.

Past-life therapy works in the same way. At times, while guiding someone through an emotional clearing process, expecting to be working with some sort of childhood memory, a past life memory will surface instead that is strongly associated with my client's present life situation. Emotional pain usually has a lot to do with childhood trauma in any given life, which remains until it is eventually cleared.

This confusion and trapped emotion became buried in our subconscious because there was no one there for us at the time with enough skills to help us process the hurt.

When we are not heard as children, particularly on an emotional level, when people don't take time to connect to us for whatever reason, we literally feel like we don't exist. We develop beliefs which conclude that we are not important, that we are unworthy of Love. Now we can validate our own existence, which is the root of self-healing and self-empowerment.

Imagine a time when you were a child, during a moment of real sadness and intense fear. Imagine being this child feeling lost and alone without a friend in the world. Perhaps you were rejected and tormented by bullies at school. May be you remember hiding in your room or under the house after being mistreated by an adult or a sibling. You feel helpless and hopeless as you withdraw into your shell, thinking that this sadness is never going to end.

Suddenly, from out of nowhere, this magical scene opens up before your eyes. It is like a beautiful park, a sanctuary, with this loving guardian reaching out to you, waiting there just for you, like something out of a Disney movie. This loving guardian greets you kindly and then sits down with you. Your guardian quietly talks to you about how special you are and comforts you with gentleness and patience. When you are ready, you are led into this wondrous place that has opened up before you where you are safe, Loved unconditionally, and are free to be yourself. You discover that this is your new home.

This is what this healing process is creating for our human-self, our vulnerable inner-child, whenever we consciously face and open up to our sad and vulnerable emotions with the desire to accept them and care for them with loving kindness. This child in us is going to have such a different experience. Our trapped emotional energy is going to flow into a very different space within our consciousness where healing is going to be a natural process. The safe and loving home for our vulnerable inner-child is our own heart of consciousness.

When appropriately managed, cared for and embraced, my emotions/feelings connect me to the essence of Life in all its beauty and wonder.

By returning to these past memories in your own mind, with an open loving heart and a more enlightened attitude, you can literally be there for your own human-self in a way that enables your inner-child (the emotional needs of your human-self) to be freed from confusion and emotional stuckness. It also helps to imagine your aware, conscious, adult self actually stepping into this scene with your helpless child-self in order to take loving care of this precious child. You have an opportunity to be that special caring person that your child-self had/has always longed for. You can say the things your child-self longs to here from that loving guardian, which is you. You can allow your child to perhaps have a good cry, to get out those pent-up emotions within your own imagination and through your own feelings as you hold your heart open to your child, providing acceptance and safety. You can offer the warmth and intimacy that your child-self didn't receive at the time. After the initial release of emotion, and once you feel comfortable with one another, you may want to create that new sanctuary together and spend time just having fun, doing the things that you always wanted to do as a child.

What you are doing is releasing the emotional pain from the old memory and in the process, creating a whole new positive memory that can now put your mind at rest.

Of course this child is within you and these emotions are going to be felt by you now and released through you now, which is often confronting. Keeping open your compassionate heart to your humanness enables these emotions to be released safely and effectively. You may at first experience such emotions as fear, shame and anger. Your ego-defences may block you out of the process for a time. These are all reflections of past trauma and self-condemnation. As always, self-acceptance and your total commitment to be the loving guardian to your human-self, will eventually break down these barriers, as it would have done when you were that child, who is still alive within your mind. Imagine someone coming to spend time with you all those years ago, just you, and who had all the time in the world for you. Imagine that person not being fazed by your defensiveness and aloofness. This person would just keep showing up, offering you Unconditional Love. This Love would inevitably melt your heart, because that is what real Love does, if given the chance. There is nothing greater than this.

When guiding clients through this process, they are often astounded by the vividness of the memories that come through, as well as the new images that are created. They can literally experience themselves caring for their child-self, who is independently interacting with them within this mind space, this place of healing. People often have their first experience of real Unconditional Love during this process and this Love comes from themselves! A whole new world opens up for them. The process of healing their emotions makes a lot more sense to them after that. It is not so abstract.

The process is usually more intense and vivid when guided by a skilled therapist. Nevertheless, with the use of meditation and your journal and the fact that you have an opportunity to connect with your inner-child / human-self on a daily basis, your own process will have the desired effect. Combining your own process with appropriate therapy will of course empower your process greatly.

It is very important to understand that as an adult, your mind, along with your memories, belongs to *you* now. As conscious-awareness, you are now in charge of this mind space and you now have the power to take control of it and sort it out, no matter how scary the original experiences were. It is all happening on the level of mind, and your mind is within the unlimited power of your conscious-awareness. No one has power over you within your own mind unless, through confusion, you give that power away.

My open compassionate heart is the ultimate sanctuary for my vulnerable human-self

Emotional Healing is not Self-Pity

Be aware also that this process is not about self-pity. That will be a fleeting part of the process at times, but the intention is to take responsibility for the pain, to take care of it, not to wallow in it.

This emotional releasing process is valid for both women and men. In general men like to think they are not afraid or hurt. They have been taught to bury their feelings in order to be warriors and tough workers. Unfortunately this denial of feelings shuts down the heart and also destroys relationship intimacy. Men deny their vulnerability, their fear, by covering it up with anger. However, anger is fear projected outwards, which is covering over a vulnerable human-self in need of Love. This is a boy who has been deprived of emotional intimacy and shamed and bullied if he tries to enter this space. He quickly loses touch with the fact that these feelings even exist and suffers the emptiness and confusion that men so often feel. Men even learn to disrespect and ridicule feeling/emotion. The wider community then suffers the consequences of this confusion as men try to be dominant so as not to feel emotionally vulnerable.

I have noticed that unnecessary anger is also an increasing problem with women, who are trying to regain and assert their power, but in the wrong way. Power must be the servant of Love and Wisdom, otherwise it only adds to the problems in our society rather than being a part of the solution.

Self-pity is about believing we are victims, which means we must be holding someone at fault for the way we feel. There may be issues that need to be addressed concerning another's behaviour, but until we deal with our own confusion, we are likely to approach this issue as an upset inner-child rather than an empowered and mature adult. This process is therefore about self-responsibility, about self-care. You are caring for your human-self, your own mind in other words.

The most effective healing for children is to help them know that they are Loved, that you accept them and Love them no matter what. By giving them permission to safely feel and express their emotions, without abusing others or themselves, they quickly move through this energy. When children are consistently accepted in this way, they feel safe and are able to trust. They are able to accept more readily the appropriate guidance that is offered to them. Then you can give them some positive encouragement and gently nudge them back out into the world again. The wounded memories in your own mind are no different. The feeling of finally coming home to a safe and loving place and to a warm pair of arms to hug you is no different either. You are giving yourself an inner-hug.

Trying to "fix" emotions is like telling emotionally distraught children to "pull their socks up and get on with it", without actually connecting with them on a heart-to-heart level first. It is the ego telling the child to shut up so its comfort zones are not disturbed. This actually buries the emotion, erodes trust and destroys intimacy.

Neither is it good to pander to the child's emotions, or adult emotions for the same reasons. This just creates weakness and selfishness such as self-pity and self-indulgence at the expense of others. It is important to teach our child personal responsibility in ways that are appropriate to their stage of development.

The healing process has a beginning, a middle, and an end. If properly handled, emotions can be effectively and efficiently processed, leading to insight, wisdom and inner-strength. It is essential that your emotional life is respected and properly looked after. Your world will literally come alive (in the right way) as a result.

♡ *I have the opportunity to access my highest potential when I choose to live my life using the principles of Unconditional Love and Total Personal Responsibility as my guide.*

Healing is an Ongoing Process

Our emotional mind is very deep and very complex. There are no quick fixes. Healing one misbelief often opens the door for other deeper confusions to be revealed to our awareness. Healing our confusion is an ongoing journey of self-care. It is a matter of ongoing mind-maintenance.

Peace and happiness is *not* about no longer having issues to deal with. Life will always have its challenges. Peace and happiness is brought about by learning to be skilful and confident in the process of looking after our mind. We are learning to be a skilful parent/guardian of our own human-self.

Stepping into this new way of *being* can take some guidance, because we will run up against our old misbeliefs time and time again. This is not a bad thing though, because each time we do, it is an opportunity to see ourself in a better light. We then have the opportunity to consistently feed into our subconscious mind new positive beliefs that work in our favour. In other words, we naturally get better at spotting these self-defeating beliefs and turning them around. Increasingly, our old habits turn into new ones that work for us rather than against us.

Being an adult means we must learn to effectively parent our own child-self that is still alive within our memories. One of the wonderful spin-offs of building this type of relationship with ourself is that everything we learn that helps us to make a real conscious connection to our own vulnerable self, also helps us connect to our loved ones, particularly our children, which is perfectly logical when you think about it.

For many people, making a real heartfelt connection with themselves, and therefore their Higher-Self, is one of the most special and profound events in their life. This in itself can be life-changing. For those of us who suffer chronic depression, for example, this can be the very thing that breaks the grip of the depression for good, like it did for me.

See Diagram 9 on the next page for a summary of the process of personal growth.

We do not truly become adult, where our mind is concerned, until we can consciously take responsibility for our own thoughts and emotions.

Diagram 9: Learning to Process Emotional Energy

Emotionally Shutdown or Reactive **1**		Rigid fear-based habitual belief systems. These conditioned beliefs keep the mind in a state of fight-or-flight, which keep vulnerable emotions trapped in a state of defensiveness. Perceptions generated from these beliefs tend to be a projection from the past.
		Trapped emotional energy. This energy is created by old emotional wounding as well as continual perceived wounding created by misperceptions. This energy continues to build up over the years like a pressure cooker.
		Pressurized emotional energy forced out through the lower consciousness. This energy is also laced with victim-based perceptions that expect conflict and continue to perpetuate conflict even when it does not exist.
Learning to Process Emotions **2**		Trapped emotional energy is beginning to be released in constructive ways that promote healing and awareness. Less emotional energy is now kept trapped, leading to less negative outbursts.
		The ability is now growing to question rigid fear-based belief systems. New beliefs are now being put into action, allowing greater flexibility. Emotions are now beginning to be processed rather than trapped.
		Due to practicing self-acceptance and personal responsibility, the heart is beginning to open. Trapped emotion is beginning to be healed and transformed with compassion. Compassion then naturally radiates to others.
Mastering Integration Process **3**		Trapped emotional energy has come under the direct influence and care of the heart. Emotions are being processed on a continual basis before too much pressure builds. Genuine integration is now occurring, enabling emotional energy to be used as a valuable tool for consciousness.
		Reprogramming of fear-based belief systems is well in place. New beliefs and perceptions now facilitate inner-healing and personal growth. Cooperation and communication has replaced paranoia and conflict. A strong personal process for working with emotions is now the new habit.
		The heart is now mostly open and radiating compassion easily and strongly. A deep compassionate relationship now exists between conscious-awareness and the inner-child or human-self. As a result, a strong conscious alignment with the Higher-Self is now in place. The higher reasoning of consciousness now dominates thought processes and feelings.

CONNECTING TO OUR HIGHER-SELF

In my experience, confusion sets in when, for whatever reason, we get out of touch with our higher consciousness that is always guiding us forward on our grand journey to enlightenment. When we tune into our emotions and thoughts with a real commitment to self-acceptance and self-care, at first without even knowing it, we are also tuning into our Higher-Self. We are actively shifting our ego identity from mere survival to caring and empowered conscious-awareness. Instead of just acting out our emotional baggage, we are increasingly taking care of it and reaping the benefits of an expanding consciousness in the process.

In my experience, the process of mastering ourself is the most grounded and surest way to walk the spiritual path. Chasing the spiritual by trying to escape the world is missing the point of being here. Trying to find fulfilment in material possessions will only lead to emptiness and disillusionment. Our sacred relationship with our own human self is the doorway to Universal Love, which is the very Life-Force that governs our existence.

We can only be the parent of our human-self by aligning our awareness to a higher level of consciousness. This is where dedicating ourself to the eternal, life-giving principles of the Higher-Self is essential. Our commitment to Unconditional Love and Total Personal Responsibility teaches us how to be that conscious-aware parent—Love's representative to our own human-self and from there, overflowing to the world around us. Acting on behalf of Love aligns us to its source and naturally strengthens this vital connection.

This marvellous process, in its many forms and flavours, is the conqueror of the scourge of humanity, which is fear. Fear is the opposite of Love. Fear is the misbelief that we are separate from Light/Life/Love. Fear is the cause of every thought and act that results in suffering. Love is experiencing our oneness with Light/Life/Love through our open hearted acceptance and embrace of some aspect of life. Our own human-self is the closest and most tangible thing we have that we can Love, and in so doing, we heal our mistaken perception that we are separate from Love. Loving ourself in this way takes nothing from the world. In fact, we become a source of Light to the world. Our growing connection to the Light/Life/Love within us connects us to everything.

This grand journey is not something that is only for the great lights of this world. This journey is not something that is beyond you and I. This journey to enlightenment *is* you and I. It is every little thing we think, feel, say, and do. Its opportunity is in every moment.

If you persistently put in the effort, regardless of misfortune or setback, you will really experience yourself growing in emotional maturity and wisdom. You will experience frequent and increasing feelings of Unconditional Love that seem to come from nowhere. Occasionally we have the opportunity to look back and really see how far we have come, which often surprises us. John Lennon wrote in one of his songs, "Life happens when you are busy doing other things." I would change this around a little and say life works for us while we are busy lovingly caring for ourself, because when we are putting this into practice, we are plugging ourself into the ultimate source of Universal Love, our highest potential.

Despite what many people say, you don't have to be special to experience this personal connection to Unconditional Love. But then again, you are special. You are a child of God. You are the essence of Life itself with its magnificent potential available to you. You can have this opportunity as a normal part of your life. It is as easy as taking the time to lovingly and responsibly care for yourself, and making this a central part of your lifestyle. Your connection with your Higher-Self grows as it simply becomes a natural part of what you would call common sense. Many people have this without even realising it. The rest of us have to make the effort to learn this self-Love, but we gain the added bonus of a deeper conscious-awareness along with it, and this priceless treasure of all treasures, more than compensates for the pain and struggle. With this knowing, with this skill, life is no longer such a mystery. You become the master craftsman of your own beautiful creation.

The next chapter is about putting this healing and self-realisation process into action.

Diagram 10. **Creating Harmony**

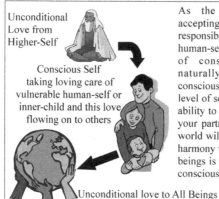

Unconditional Love from Higher-Self

Conscious Self taking loving care of vulnerable human-self or inner-child and this love flowing on to others

Unconditional love to All Beings

As the picture suggests, by accepting and talking personal responsibility for your vulnerable human-self / inner-child, as a being of conscious-awareness, you naturally awaken the higher consciousness within you. As your level of self-mastery increases, your ability to give unconditional love to your partner, your children and the world will also increase. Peace and harmony within oneself and with all beings is the direction an awakened consciousness naturally evolves.

CHAPTER SEVEN SUMMARY

1. Step 3 is learning to process your emotions and undo your mental confusion on an ongoing basis.

2. Step 3 is the most important step when it comes to changing your life on a deeper level, but it is the hardest for the ego to understand.

3. When we are confronted with an emotional challenge, we naturally experience fear, vulnerability, and confusion. This initial rush of emotion often overwhelms the ego.

4. The survival mind of our human-self and its ego is immediately triggered into old habitual ways of coping with these strong emotions in ways that are often self-defeating.

5. Step 3 "Let Go and Tune In", is about building a bridge of healing that enables the human-self to be lifted up into the Higher-Self.

6. Our commitment to face our difficulties, in the spirit of Unconditional Love for our human-self, opens up a sanctuary within our consciousness for our trapped emotional energy to safely flow in to.

7. When indulging in condemnation and blame, we keep ourself trapped in our blind ego and we choke Love out of our heart.

8. Blame and condemnation prevents us from healing and growing.

9. Blame and condemnation keeps us dependent on others to make us happy in a way that never achieves happiness.

10. A fear-based form of power and control that seeks to dominate others has within it the seeds of its own destruction, whether in this life or at the mighty hands of Karma at the end of this life.

11. Ego deludes itself into thinking it has power. True power, that empowers everyone, is found within the Higher-Self.

12. The real power to succeed and be fulfilled rests in the knowing that happiness is a conscious choice no matter what the circumstance.

13. Letting go, therefore, is about no longer holding other people, places, and things responsible for our happiness.

14. Life skills need to be learned just like anything else, but we won't learn anything else if we are not prepared to let go of, or at least question, our old beliefs.

15. Steps 1 and 2 remind us that there is no one to blame, not even ourselves. We are just human beings who are confused.

16. Letting go is choosing to *NOT* focus so much on what is being done to us, but rather to focus on how our mind is reacting to the situation.

17. The fear-based reactions of our survival mind cause our heart to close. This is a warning sign for our growing conscious-awareness. Instead of shutting down, we must tune into and open to our human-self / inner-child, while resisting falling into blame and condemnation.

18. Tuning into our feelings and emotions, with the intention to care for ourself, soon reveals to us the extent to which we have been neglecting ourself.

19. It is our emotions that tell us when our thinking is constructive or destructive by being either pleasant or painful.

20. While we are condemning ourselves for being human, we become our own worst enemy. We are always going to want to tune out from ourselves and so never get beyond our negative conditioning.

21. Using an effective healing process, we can open our hearts of compassion to our vulnerable human-self and work with, in loving kindness, all that flows through our awareness. The strong emotions of our inner-child then flow through us more easily and are healed and released.

22. Attempting to escape from our emotions by trying to "fix" them is driven by fear and will have only limited success.

23. Emotions are meant to be felt and will pass quickly through us if handled in the right way.

24. It is distorted thinking that unnecessarily prolongs painful emotions.

25. Prolonged painful emotions reveal distorted thinking, so by observing the emotions, we uncover the distorted thinking.

26. It is the thinking that needs fixing, not the emotions.

27. Following the "feeling trail" often takes us into old memories where the traumas were initially experienced.

28. By opening our compassionate heart to these old painful memories, we add the Unconditional Love that was missing then, which enables healing to occur naturally.

29. Opening our compassionate heart to these old painful memories is like going back in time to take care of our own vulnerable self, who is still stuck in these memories.

30. Our memories now belong to us. As conscious-aware adults we can re-enter our memories and actively care for our vulnerable human-self / inner-child within this mind-space. Our conscious-awareness therefore, becomes our sanctuary where we can essentially rewrite these memories.

31. We do not truly become adult where our mind is concerned until we can consciously take responsibility for our own thoughts and emotions.

32. This process is not about self-pity, it is self-responsibility, self-care.

33. Some of us may find this process difficult at first, having been taught to deny feelings by using anger, for example, to mask our vulnerability.

34. Anger is fear expressed outwardly. We dominate others to feel safe/powerful.

35. Using the right process to clear the emotional backlog from a memory or present situation creates space for the Higher-Self, in the form of intuitive insight, to enter our awareness.

36. Intuitive insights give us a greater perspective that is more empowering and enables us to deal with issues more skilfully.

37. The mind is very deep and complex. Memories are multi-layered and healing therefore can take time and persistence.

38. The garden of the mind will always need looking after. What brings peace and happiness is learning to be a skilled and confident gardener.

39. With confidence, we come to realise that the challenges of life are not so much a problem, but an opportunity to grow in ever more peace and happiness.

40. Each time we choose to be the representative of Love to our human-self, we connect even deeper to our Higher-Self.

41. As a result of this deepening connection with our Higher-Self, in time we feel ourselves being filled with a deep sense of Unconditional Love that seems to come from nowhere.

✓ **Open your heart to your emotional pain. It is Love's opportunity to help you heal and grow.**

✓ **As conscious-awareness, you are the loving sanctuary for your human-self.**

✓ **With Unconditional Love as your guide, correct your thinking to heal your emotions.**

✓ **As you love your human-self, you merge with Love itself.**

✓ *NEVER GIVE UP. SUCCESS IS INEVITABLE!*

CHAPTER EIGHT

STEP 3
LET GO & TUNE IN
PART TWO

It's Time

I offer you a helping hand, you imagine a closed fist.
I offer you my open heart, you feel a cold grip on yours,
I offer you light and freedom, you see dark walls that hem you in.
Oh my love, it's time to heal the past.

The future lies ahead, clear and bright.
The old days are gone, left far behind in some false reality,
Yet you still bring it with you
and paint those dark colors on all that you see,
Oh my love, it's time to heal the past.

The phantoms of the past only occupy your mind.
Open the door and sweep them out.
The future is yours now.
The key is in your hand, the lock ready to turn.
Oh my love, it's time to heal the past.

You are a bird free to fly high above that turbulent ocean,
Your wings are ready but you deny they're real.
The mud has become too familiar to your feet.

Before you is an open vista, the world calling you forward,
Oh my love, it's time to heal the past.

It's time to open your heart to the Love that is you,
To allow Love to flow into your wounds like a warm healing balm.
You are not what others have made you,
Nor what your mind has become.
Open your door and let the Light of true reality into your Heart.
Oh my love, it's time to heal the past.

HEALING AND CLARITY

REPROGRAMMING YOUR MIND

Your past is there to teach you, not to trap you. If you approach your past and your present difficulties with acceptance, with an open heart, while being totally committed to loving yourself unconditionally, a whole new reality will open to you. Conscious-awareness, devoted to the great life-giving principles of the Higher-Self, transforms the past into opportunities for healing and self-realisation.

This chapter is about putting this healing and self-realisation process into action. Firstly we will focus on some tools that will help you tune in. The rest of the chapter will then explore actively tuning in and taking care of what you find.

This whole book, and particularly this chapter, is about you reprogramming your mind. The most powerful way to do this is to create new programs based on accepting total responsibility for loving yourself unconditionally. The old programs will still be there, still trying to run your life, but you must no longer place any conscious belief in them. Instead, it is essential to place all your faith and energy into the new programs and do your best to live them, to *be* them every day, regardless of how the old programs react to this change. This transition won't be very tidy. The old programs will get the better of you time and time again. Do not be discouraged. You must keep pulling yourself free of this confusion. You must keep stepping back into the process of creating and living the new life-enhancing programs that match your true potential. It does not matter how long it takes. It does not matter how many times the old negative conditioning defeats you. Never give up. Success is inevitable if you are willing to put in the consistent effort. The new programs, your new way of being, will deepen, strengthen, and inevitably gain control of your mind. The power of the Universal Life-Force flowing through your commitment to Unconditional Love and Total Personal Responsibility, as subtle as it may seem at times, is the great transformer. Nothing can stop its positive effect on the mind if the mind is consistently held open to it. Nothing is more powerful than Love and Wisdom, except for your own free will. Your free will is your power of choice. It is the door to Light/Life/Love that you have been given full authority to open or close as you see fit. The guiding hand of Karma will eventually have its way though, because reality is reality, what works, works. We must let go of our futile ego-based illusions if we hope to free ourself from suffering and limitation. We must realise that the Universal Life-Force, our Higher-Self, is our friend, our companion, the treasure of all treasures, our doorway to freedom.

STOPPING THE BLIND REACTION

Instead of being continually controlled by our blind reactions that are driven by trapped emotional energy and underlying misbeliefs, we need to create a diversion, a gap in the reaction, that allows our conscious-awareness to step in and take charge. There are two main tools that can be used to circumvent the fight-or-flight reaction of the ego. They are **slow breathing** and **clarity**.

Controlling the Breath: When the mind is thrown into a state of fight-or-flight, our breath quickens and becomes shallow. Our body tightens up like a wound-up spring. Our mind is reduced to a tunnel-vision-like state. This is not a state of mind that is going to take the time to calmly assess the reality of a situation. It is a state of mind that shoots first and asks questions later, if at all.

By consciously controlling the breath, we can find the off switch to this blind, primal defensive reaction. The logical thing to do here is to breathe deeply and slowly, with an emphasis on slowly, otherwise we can hyper-ventilate and get a little dizzy. Breathing in this way evokes a state of calm within the body and mind. This slow, deeper breath is the sort of breath I recommend my students and clients.

I recommend practising this type of breathing during meditation and throughout each day as a part of the process of mindfulness (see pages 125 to 126). Our breath tends to be too shallow anyway, which may be an indication of the ongoing stress that the average person is generally under. Tune into your inner-being on a regular basis as a part of this deep breathing and take loving care of what you find in the process. This will go a long way to setting up good consciousness-enhancing habits within your mind. Your own treasured sanctuary is then only a conscious breath away. This type of breathing, linked to your conscious-awareness, develops within your awareness the ability to "see" inside your own mind through the pathway of your emotions and feelings. In other words, you develop the power of insight!

To aid in the natural life-giving force of this breath, practice lowering the focus of the breath to your abdomen. This is called "diaphragmatic breathing". Singers are trained in this type of breathing. Physical vitality also comes with this type of breathing. We tend to just focus the breath in the upper chest area, but this does not fully extend the lungs. Don't get too hung up about getting it right. A deep, conscious breath that tunes into your inner-being in the spirit of loving kindness is the key. You will get used to it. I did.

Breathing this way sends a very different signal to the human-self that is something like, "It's okay. Stay calm. Conscious-awareness has arrived on the scene to take care of things." It is a conscious response that indicates that you are awake, ready and willing to allow this trapped emotional energy up into your awareness, your heart, and out of harm's way where it can be effectively processed.

This applies whether we manage to catch the emotional reaction in the moment or process it sometime after the event, which is more often the case at first.

Clarity: The clarity is about increasing your awareness of how this reactive state of mind feels so that you can quickly identify it and make another choice. This awareness comes from your sincere determination to *want* to face up to and gain command of your self-defeating reactions in the spirit of Unconditional Love. The essential factors here are firstly, your *willingness* to be open to your fears and insecurities, which evokes your conscious-awareness and secondly, your *intention* to Love yourself unconditionally, which invokes the power of your Higher-Self (refer to Exercise 4 "Higher-Self Meditation on page 84). Consistently centring yourself in this perspective empowers your conscious-awareness enough to be able to observe the reaction when it comes, or at least do so soon afterwards, rather than be completely swept away by it. With this greater power of observation, your perception of when this reaction is being triggered naturally increases as you gain skill in the process. Eventually you will be able to keep the reaction within your conscious-awareness and dissolve it with clarity and Love before it takes control of you.

This clarity is also strengthened by the realisation that any disturbed emotion is the product of the more primitive fear-based human-self. When such emotions are felt, it is safe to immediately consider that your mind has been thrown into a state of confusion. You must therefore stop and check it out, in the spirit of Total Personal Responsibility, rather than blindly follow it.

The Higher-Self can also send us warning signals, but this feels quite different. This higher signal tends to be more refined, subtle and intuitive and condemns no one, whereas reactions from the lower human-self are blunt, clumsy and heavy, like they're coming from our inner-caveman. Remember the limited process tools that it uses—fleeing, dominating or suppressing.

With this realisation, you can know that when an emotional reaction is triggered, it is a call to your conscious-awareness to take a deep breath and pay attention to your own mind. Just a split second pause can make all the difference between an argument and a constructive discussion, for example.

When I choose to accept myself as I am and commit to taking personal responsibility to take loving care of my mind and body in all that I think, feel, say, and do each day, then the power of my higher-consciousness is initiated into my life.

THE MULTIDIMENSIONAL MIND

During this healing process, an interesting dynamic is set up within the mind. We become very aware of the different levels or dimensions of the mind. On one level, we are consciously choosing to observe and care for our vulnerable human-self in the spirit of loving kindness and compassion. On another level our ego, deluded by misbeliefs, is thinking self-attacking thoughts and making our inner-child/human-self sad and fearful. On yet another level there is our small, vulnerable, powerless inner-child crying out for help, or just huddled in a corner without any hope at all.

We can really experience the healing process when, as the loving guardian (conscious-awareness), we stay above the confused misbeliefs of the self-destructive ego and reach out to our vulnerable child-like human-self, offering it complete acceptance. This power of Unconditional Love causes the attacking ego to fall away, enabling our Higher-Self to embrace our helpless child-self through the open heart of our conscious-awareness.

Two very different mindsets come into contact with one another—a loving guardian holding the heart of Love open to a wounded inner-child and a wounded inner-child having the experience of being in the presence of a loving guardian. Here we are able to experience both positions at once—the emotional release and comfort as the wounded child and the deep satisfaction of providing healing and comfort as the loving guardian. See diagrams 1 to 8.

Remember that you cannot truly Love another in a sustainable way that also truly honours and cares for yourself, until you can truly Love your vulnerable human-self. Furthermore, you cannot truly connect to your Higher-Self until you are willing to Love your human-self. You invoke the Love that is your Higher-Self through your act of compassion toward your own human-self. You invoke the Wisdom of Love through your deep commitment to a process of self-realisation that empowers your loving actions.

FEELING GOOD DEPENDS ON YOUR OWN THOUGHTS AND ACTIONS

Don't expect to always feel this Love. It is hard, at times, to get unstuck from the ego. The bubble of ego that blocks the mind from experiencing the Universal Life-Force of Love can still be strong, even as we are endeavouring to consciously awaken. At times the painful emotions continue on despite our best efforts.

Trust that with your good intentions and associated actions, good things are happening, even though you may not at first be aware of it. It has been my experience that the benefits of emotional healing can be delayed—they may be felt later in the day or the next day perhaps. If you are suffering deep depression, for example, it may take longer—some weeks perhaps, due to the intensity of your negative conditioning. Trust that all sincere efforts make a real difference, even if feelings of comfort don't come straight away.

There is a sequence to the way we, as conscious-awareness, direct the mind toward healing, clarity, and balance and how the process gathers momentum. See the clarity box on the following page and also Table 6 on page 270.

Because of our ego's desperate need to escape from painful emotions, we are afraid to give a mind-healing process a chance. We lack faith in ourself and we easily give up. This is why those of us who are suffering from chronic depression and anxiety, for example, so often conclude that we are not capable of healing and succumb to our fears, and even the belief that we are somehow mentally impaired. We just don't persist with the process long enough to experience the wall of misbelief crumble to reveal the light of day.

Clarity Box 8:1

LOVE-EMPOWERED WILL

TAKES CONTROL OF THE INTELLECT

USES INTELLECT TO LOVINGLY CARE FOR VULNERABLE HUMAN-SELF

THE POWER OF UNCONDITIONAL LOVE AND INTUITIVE INSIGHT ERODES MISBELIEFS

AS MISBELIEFS CRUMBLE, EMOTIONS HEAL AND HIGHER FEELINGS EMERGE THROUGH THE GAPS

RISING HOPE THROUGH EXPERIENCES OF HEALING STRENGTHENS FAITH IN THE PROCESS

Live-in healing retreat centres that offer us the right type of nurturing and therapy would be helpful for working with such chronic conditions. Unfortunately the vast majority of our government subsidised mental health institutions are based on the drug therapy model that tries to stop emotions almost at all cost. The symptom is treated while the cause continues on largely untouched. Unfortunately, orthodox psychiatry still lacks faith in Love and has little comprehension of consciousness. One is doomed to remain at the level of an unconscious and powerless ego.

Armed with the awareness that every human being is in possession of an all-powerful consciousness, the whole process of mind healing can be approached very differently. Even if a Soul is not ready to awaken out of ego, there is much that can be done to empower that person to believe in themselves and to experience their greater potential, even while still evolving on the ego level. It requires the right level of support and the awareness of the potential of human consciousness on the part of those giving the support.

We don't have to enter into a spiritual awakening journey in order to make great improvements to our life. The ego still has to grow and mature to great heights before the mind is ready for the Soul to directly take control of the personality, which at first can be very destabilizing. All personal growth, on any level, serves the Soul and the Higher-Self.

Once you learn to more skilfully master your mind, feelings can be used at will to powerful, positive effect when it comes to consciously creating the life that you want.[53]

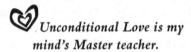 *Unconditional Love is my mind's Master teacher.*

The following "Deep Processing" exercise is designed as a comprehensive tool for emotional healing and achieving clarity. It is important to integrate this exercise into your ongoing self-management strategies. Make regular use of it to keep your life on track.

As a part of this exercise, make good use of the emotion and belief charts at the end of this book. Also, the tables, diagrams, affirmations, clarity boxes and summaries make for good quick reference guides.

---

[53]   http://en.wikipedia.org/wiki/Abraham-Hicks

Table 6: Sequence of Action for Healing

1. **ACTIVATING CONSCIOUS-AWARENESS:** Making the decision, or setting the intent in other words, to accept total responsibility to Love yourself unconditionally and acting on it, evokes your Higher-Self, your power to heal and grow. This aligns your conscious-awareness to your Higher-Self, the will of Supreme Consciousness, or God if you like. This is your ego awakening into conscious-awareness.

2. **ACTIVATING HIGHER INTELLIGENCE:** Your conscious-awareness sets about creating new self-loving programs, even as the old negative programs are still habitually running. You do this by persistently engaging your intellect in a process for healing, clarity and personal growth, such as with the 5 Step Process. Your conscious thinking then is serving your Higher-Self and comes under the greater intelligent power of intuitive insight. I call this "thinking with feeling".

3. **CLEARING YOUR EMOTIONS AND GENERATING HIGHER FEELINGS:** As your misbeliefs are gradually dismantled by your awakening conscious-awareness, painful, trapped emotional energy is released, healed and no longer accumulated. Feelings that reflect the qualities of Unconditional Love that are being generated by your consistent loving actions toward yourself, slowly start emerging through the gaps in the crumbling misbeliefs.

4. **DEEPENING FAITH:** The inevitable, but at first fleeting, emergence of loving feelings gives you longed-for relief from the painful emotions and a new sense of hope arises. From this hope a growing faith in the process emerges, which in turn, strengthens and empowers conscious-awareness.

CHAPTER EIGHT SUMMARY

1. Breathing deeply and slowly enables you to counteract the mind-blurring effects of the fight-or-flight reaction.

2. Essential factors of clarity are your *willingness* to always be open to your human-self with the sincere intention of Unconditional Love, which evokes your conscious-awareness, which, at the same time, invokes the power of your Higher-Self.

3. Slow breathing that is designed to tune into your body/mind with conscious-awareness develops your capacity for insight.

4. Clarity is also strengthened by the realisation that any disturbed emotion is likely to be the product of the more primitive fear-based human-self. You must therefore stop and examine it rather than blindly follow it.

5. When an emotional reaction emerges, it is a call to your conscious-awareness to take a deep breath and pay attention to your own mind.

6. When working with the healing process, good feelings don't always come straight away. The right thoughts and actions create the right conditions, however, for good feelings to inevitably emerge.

7. Intense negative conditioning can delay the onset of good feelings, even though the process is still working.

8. It can sometimes take time for the wall of negative conditioning to break down enough to let the Light in.

9. This delay in positive feelings is a major cause of us giving up on a healing process.

10. The sequence of right thought and action that creates the right conditions for healing are:

    1) **Activating your conscious-awareness** by choosing to accept total responsibility to Love yourself unconditionally.

    2) **Activating your Intuitive Intellect** by creating new life-enhancing programs by persistently learning and practicing a self-healing and self-realisation process—thinking in harmony with your feeling—your connection with your Higher-Self.

3) **Disturbed emotions heal and positive feelings arise** when negative conditioning/misbeliefs are sufficiently overcome due to persistent effort.

4) Greater hope is experienced with the onset of good feelings, which gives us a **deepening faith** in the healing process.

11. Once you learn to more skillfully master your mind, feelings can be used at will to powerful positive effect in your life.

✓ Your breath is the seat of your consciousness.

✓ You are the calm observer of your human-self.

✓ By opening your conscious heart, you can embrace all that you experience with the ultimate power of Love/Wisdom.

✓ Your conscious-awareness has unlimited potential.

✓ *NEVER GIVE UP. SUCCESS IS INEVITABLE!*

EXERCISE 10
DEEP PROCESSING

In order to bring real healing and clarity to your mind, there are five important questions you need to deeply explore. In this section, we will look at the nature of these questions and embark on an exercise that you can work with in your journal and with a mentor/counsellor/therapist. As usual, it is important to read this whole exercise first before you do it. If your trapped emotional energy is intense and has a lot of fear attached to it, then you are strongly advised to seek assistance from a professional or a mentor who is experienced in emotional processing.

The five questions are:

1. **How do I feel?**
2. **What are/were my needs or wants at the time of my difficult situation?**
3. **What can I do to heal, validate and nurture myself now?**
4. **What can I do to empower myself now?**
5. **What can I do to accept full responsibility for my life and care for myself with loving kindness toward myself and all others?**

An effective way to process your emotional reactions and your underlying vulnerabilities is to spend quality time with your emotions and thoughts and ask yourself these questions. It is important to spend plenty of time with each question so that you have a chance to access the depth of your experience and awareness. As I mentioned before, exploring your thoughts and emotions in your journal adds depth and power to your process. Until you do this, real clarity around your fear and confusion and the problems it causes is unlikely to be found. Using your journal for creating new empowering beliefs or programs and then living them is also essential. Without it, your success at reprogramming your mind will be limited.

Sharing your process with a mentor/counsellor/therapist is also very effective, but even then you still have to do the work for it to work. Your mentor can help you in various ways, such as clear up any confusion that arises, give you perspective when you are being hard on yourself, brainstorm ideas with you, and just be a listening ear while you share your story and verbally process things.

The old conditioning has had control over your mind all your life. Just thinking about it is trying to defeat the conditioning on its own ground. It will continue to get the better of you if you limit yourself in this way. It is essential to pull all of this unconscious content out of your mind and into the light of day, into your conscious-awareness in other words. Committing this process to your journal and seeking assistance from someone experienced in this process will give your conscious-awareness the upper hand.

Do not expect yourself to be very skilful in your first attempts at this exercise. Healing the mind is a learned skill, just like parenting is a learned skill. In the process of working with this exercise, you are building within your consciousness what is called emotional intelligence, Wisdom in other words. Every attempt to work with this exercise, as well as the other exercises, will benefit you and expand your awareness, so just do it as best you can with your current level of awareness. Every time you work through this exercise, your growing awareness will enable you to go deeper and to open your heart to your humanness more skilfully.

Be aware that there are no right or wrong answers to the questions that you encounter during this exercise. There is no right or wrong way to lay it out in your journal. Simply try to be thorough and yet spontaneous. Do your best to let your thoughts and emotions/feelings flow freely while accepting yourself as you are. This is your process, a process that you will adapt and evolve over time to suit your own needs.

Before you start, spend a moment in meditation and prayer in order to connect to your Higher-Self and any other source of spiritual guidance being offered to you at this time. Do your best to open your mind and heart to receive this Love and Wisdom. You are a child of God, an essential part of Light/Life/Love. Be free to imagine a loving presence who is with you throughout this process in a way that is most special to you. Spirit Loves to connect to you through your imagination. Imagination is a wonderful tool when used for Love. It can be a wonderful gift that you give to yourself and an open doorway for Love/Universal Life-Force to enter your heart and mind in a very personal way. Refer to Exercise 4, "Higher-Self Meditation" on page 84. You are the one who does the work, but you are never alone on this journey. Remember that your positive intensions and actions invoke your higher consciousness and more. What you are sending out to the higher dimensions of consciousness is; "I accept that I am worthy of assistance from the Universal Life-Force and I am ready to receive this assistance in any form that is appropriate for my highest good."

Questions 1, 2 and 3 are addressed in this section. Questions 4 and 5 are addressed at the end of Chapter 9 on page 322.

1. HOW DO I FEEL?

Accepting the Pain

With an attitude of compassion and caring toward yourself, do your best to stay open to your emotions. Remember, as conscious-awareness, you are the loving guardian of your vulnerable humanness.

Remember to breathe deeply and slowly and do your best to allow the emotional energy to flow freely so it can wash through you. In this way the emotional pressure can be released. Remember that you are not trying to fix or get rid of your emotions. You want to pay attention to them, listen to them and consciously connect to your human-self through them. The pain will heal naturally as it enters the loving compassion that you are invoking within your heart for your vulnerable self, your inner-child. Remember that you are completing a process that you did not have the opportunity to do at the time when you were most vulnerable and upset.

Emotions are simply energy. Releasing them cannot harm you. Only the wrong mental attitude causes potential harm. You harm yourself by condemning yourself. This is what creates the fear. The confused ego then tries to protect itself from its own self-condemnation by condemning others or just shutting down.

The longer an emotional charge remains trapped within your body/mind, the more chance there is of anxiety, depression, and harm to your body.

Remember that an attitude of loving compassion and caring toward your pain will eventually replace this pain with healing and peace. A few moments of release can make a big difference. With deeper issues, this process may need to be done in stages over a longer period of time. It is important to persist, because you can save yourself from years of suffering.

Know that any level of self-condemnation is confusion, as well as any condemnation of others or from others. Don't get caught up in the blind ego's drama play. You have a right to be human. You have a right to make mistakes. Let the story and the people in it go. Love, compassion and forgiveness are waiting for you at the centre of your own heart, your own conscious, open breath.

Don't expect what comes through from your human-self to be rational or tidy. Be aware that much of this trapped emotional energy will be coming from the limited perceptions and emotional memories of yourself as a child. It is important to create a sanctuary within your conscious-awareness for this child to freely enter into, whatever state this energy may be in, so it can be cared for. You may wish to refer back to Exercise 5 on page 97.

You are now ready to take care of your humanness, your inner-child, even as you are experiencing this vulnerability.

Processing and Writing

a) To begin with, focus on the person or event that is triggering your pain in order to access your vulnerability, then shift the bulk of your attention onto the trapped emotional energy within your human-self. Follow your disturbed emotions with your awareness and see where they take you.

b) After spending some time observing and experiencing the situation that is troubling you and your associated emotions, and even as you are still observing them, write about what you are experiencing in your journal. Give your human-self a sanctuary within your self-acceptance and a chance to let out those suppressed thoughts and emotions.

c) As you continue to allow this process to flow spontaneously, it is common for memories to become quite vivid, as though you have gone back in time and are suddenly really there again. Remember that these are memories that you are working with. It is now only happening within your mind and within your power to heal your mind. Do your best to stay open to this and trust the higher-power of your compassionate heart to handle any emotional release. Know that your Higher-Self is your companion and support throughout this process. Know that your Higher-Self is not separate from you—you are literally in your Higher-Self. Remember that your conscious-awareness is always in the here and now, and encompasses your entire memory system. Now is where you really are.

d) Be free to experience these emotions as they pour through you. Give yourself time to cry if you need to. This is not just for the sake of self-pity. This is about allowing the release of genuine emotions so they can be processed. This is important for healing.

e) Anger is okay too. Make sure you don't harm yourself or anyone else with it, however. You can safely express the anger in your journal. Perhaps let it out vocally at a picture of the person in question or bash a pillow. It is important to give your inner-child plenty of room to release these emotions. It was perhaps difficult or unsafe for you let them out at the time of the trauma. For a child, these emotions are natural and understandable. Don't get stuck in the anger though. Keep in mind that the purpose of this exercise is to enable yourself to heal. You are now conscious-awareness. *You* are in charge of your life now. Your child is now safe within you. Don't give others your power by getting stuck in hate and resentment.

f) Look deeply into what is coming through your vulnerable human-self from your new, more aware perspective of loving personal responsibility.

g) Don't get caught up with trying to over analyse others or yourself. This keeps you in the limited ego. Your inner-child does not need to be fixed. Your child needs to be accepted and hugged. You want to *be with* your inner-child/human-self with your heart open so that the higher intuitive Wisdom of your Higher-Self can enter, so your inner-child no longer feels alone. Acceptance, awareness and understanding are what is important here.

h) As you are writing, pay special attention to your emotions so that you can move deeper into them. Do your best not to get side-tracked by the ego with its need to condemn. This process is about learning to Love and heal yourself through your own power of consciousness. It is not about wasting time with thoughts of punishing yourself or others.

i) Make space in your mind and heart for any associated memories that are spontaneously surfacing. Write what comes through in your journal and explore them further. Note how they connect to the issues you first began to focus on.

j) There may be lots to write about. Don't be in a hurry. Finally your human-self has someone who cares and who can just listen. That person is you.

k) Do your best to observe how it was for you then at whatever age you were at the time of that experience. Note how you were simply doing the best that you could with what you had to work with at the time. If it is a memory from your childhood, observe how small, vulnerable and powerless you were.

l) If it is a childhood memory, do not make excuses for the adults that were supposed to be caring for you at the time. The responsibility of care was fully theirs, not yours as the vulnerable child. Children should not be made responsible for their parents. It is not about condemning them either. It is about having a clear feeling/understanding of the dilemma that the small child within you faced and the reality of the trauma that you were experiencing at the time. You must open your heart to the depth of this trauma so the healing will be deep. It is important to be aware of how powerless and vulnerable you were as a child.

m) Also be aware that, as an adult, whenever you feel vulnerable, you are likely to be experiencing these same or similar childhood emotions.

n) Do your best to name the emotions that you are feeling from your human-self and describe them as best you can. Consult

Appendix 1 on page 355 for a list of emotions and their definitions.

o) Spend time writing about your experiences and whatever insights that may come through for you. This is all about consciously connecting to the depths of your humanness with an open, compassionate heart. Do your best to be your own best friend, your own loving guardian, knowing that every little bit helps. The power to heal and grow is within you.

2. WHAT ARE/WERE MY NEEDS OR WANTS AT THE TIME OF MY DIFFICULT SITUATION AND HOW AM I TAKING CARE OF THEM NOW?

Needs and wants can be classed differently, but that difference is not important here, so I am just going to use the word "need" in order to keep it simple. Needs in this context can be seen as essential requirements for survival and fulfilment, as well as our individual desires. Our needs are not good or bad. We are simply trying to get by in our experience of being human.

Particularly when we were children, the way our needs were handled by our carers has great bearing on how we created our identity and self-worth and how our social-conditioning was formed. Our own natural character can have a lot to do with our needs as a child, which could have differed from our siblings.

For example, as a child you may have needed to feel safe and cared for when instead, your environment was chaotic and abusive. Or you may have needed approval from your parents or peers for the things you were interested in, but instead no one paid attention to you or you received rejection and ridicule.

It is important to recognise what you needed in a given situation, whether as a child or an adult, and what happened instead that created pain and disappointment.

Be aware that needing Love in some form is the bottom line in any human desire and that emotional pain is caused by not getting what we need.

Now that we are adults, taking care of our needs is our own personal responsibility. As a result of confusion, however, we are often still handling our needs as if we are still that powerless child we once were. Childhood needs have become adult neediness, and we keep losing our power and compromising ourself in the process.

You must forgive and accept your humanness here, but at the same time seek to become aware of how you are taking care of your needs now. Question 4 will further address this part of your healing and awakening.

Processing and Writing

a) Examine what you were needing in the experiences that came through for you while working with the first question and write about it with an attitude of loving compassion for yourself.

b) Note what was happening instead. Pay attention to the situation that was the reason for your pain. Write more about this in your journal if you need to.

c) Was this a common occurrence? Be aware that repeated experience creates deeper conditioning. Pay attention to how long you lived with these difficult experiences. Note how much they dominated your life and how powerless you were over them at the time. Spend time writing about this in your journal.

d) Try to identify the self-defeating, self-attacking beliefs that you now carry in your conditioning as a result of these experiences. Use the beliefs chart on page 363 to help trigger your awareness. Spend time writing down these misbeliefs in order to raise your awareness of them. In the process, know that all of these misbeliefs are false. We all have a right to be human without being condemned.

e) Spend some time contemplating how these misbeliefs have caused havoc in your life. Try to identify the ways you acted out the recurring drama plays that this confusion created. Be careful. Do not condemn yourself for this confusion. You did your best with the awareness that you had at the time. Now, with your growing awareness, you have the opportunity to do things differently. Refer to "Letting Go" in Chapter 7.

f) As a reinforcement of Exercise 8 "Moving Forward", using the same chart on page 363, write down the positive, empowering beliefs that will help you override the negative ones.

3. WHAT CAN I DO TO HEAL, VALIDATE AND NURTURE MYSELF NOW?

Love is not something that is separate from you. Love is the Universal Life-Force that you are within and of which you are a vital part. This reality of Love provides you with the realisable potential to channel this Love to your own human-self.

Persistently embracing our human-self in the ways that are outlined in this book is the key to healing and awakening. Love/ Wisdom is all powerful and is the only thing that heals the mind. Every process that has a positive effect on the mind, whether it is orthodox psychology or some type of alternative therapy, has that effect because it is in some way initiating the Life-Force of Love/ Wisdom into our consciousness.

As I have stated before; every sincere effort to responsibly care for yourself with loving kindness will have a positive effect, whether you feel it or not. At first, at the very least, as you are attempting to work this process for healing and awakening, you are no longer directing negativity at yourself. That is a good thing in itself. If you persist, you will not only learn to nurture yourself, you will also learn to be your own source of strength and wisdom. This is your journey. It is unique to you. Take your time, but keep on with it. The power is within you, but it won't be realised without your persistent effort. By making this approach to your life your new life-style, healing and awakening is a natural outcome.

Processing and Writing

a) Empowered by the previous stages of this process, within your imagination, spend quality time with your inner-child/human-self. Be the loving parent or mentor to your vulnerable self in a way that you needed then.

b) As the loving guardian or mentor, go back to that time of difficulty and look after your vulnerable self. This is your memory. Take charge of it and re-create it in a way that is nurturing, validating and empowering.

c) When we were children, so often we just needed someone to be there for us and connect to us. We wanted to be seen, heard and felt by someone special, who truly cared. Be there for yourself now and be free to explore the emotions/feelings that arise from this. Take your time with this nurturing part of the process.

d) No one knows how your inner-child/human-self felt more than you. No one knows what you needed then more than you. Your inner-child belongs to you. Your heart of consciousness is that child's new home—his/her sanctuary. Every conscious breath you take can be an open embrace of acceptance and loving kindness to your vulnerable inner-child/human-self.

e) Do not let feelings of inadequacy as the loving guardian/mentor discourage you. Such emotions are a normal part of the experience. We are often not used to turning our Love around toward our own self. Open up to these feelings of inadequacy and get to know them and understand them. Forgive yourself for your humanness. Keep steadily persisting and you will soon get used to being there for yourself.

f) Within the memories that have come to mind, your inner-child/human-self may have needed protecting from abuse. As conscious-awareness, the loving guardian of your vulnerable inner-child/human-self, you now have the opportunity to re-enter that memory and offer that protection to your vulnerable self. Know that you are the power within your own mind. Know that your Higher-Self *is you*. That potential is activated by your faith in yourself, and the loving kindness you give to yourself. Within your mind, you can face those who mistreated you with the understanding that you have the power now in order to create a place of safety for your inner-child/human-self.

g) As a part of this process, within your imagination and in your journal, speak your truth to the people who made things difficult for you. It does not matter if the people in question never listened to you and perhaps still don't. It does not matter if they are no longer in your life or if they have since past away. In this process, you are talking directly to their Soul. Your communication to them will be stored within the consciousness of their Higher-Self and will be fully received by them at some stage of their Soul's journey when they are capable of hearing it. Take it for granted that in this process, you will be heard and the truth of your experience is honoured. Life hears you and knows you! Even though you can't always be in control of situations in this physical world, in the heart of Universal Consciousness, all is heard and all is known. All truth is eventually revealed within the heart of every individual consciousness.

h)   Be vigilant to not fall back into to indulging in victim thinking during this part of the exercise. Do not give others the responsibility for your happiness. Your inner-child was powerless in that experience, but you are not. You are totally responsible for loving yourself unconditionally and you have that power within you. Condemnation does not belong here, only truth. The truth is about facing and taking loving responsibility for your own mistakes. It is also about seeing the reality of your past dilemmas.

i)   This part of the exercise is as much about validating yourself as it is about being heard by others. Your truth is important and deserves to be heard. In your journal, you can write a letter to each person involved (without actually sending it, unless that person is receptive). In your imagination, you can speak directly to each person.

j)   If doing this part of the exercise still brings up too much pain and fear, allow yourself more time to work through this trauma. You must heal and grow at your own pace. When you can constructively face this person within your imagination, know that you have gone a long way to healing this trauma.

k)   You don't have to be eloquent. You don't have to say it all now. Your healing journey takes as long as it needs to.

l)   The same process applies to making amends to those who you may have hurt in the past.

m)   In Part 2 of this exercise, on page 322, you have the opportunity to explore how to approach speaking your truth and making amends to people directly, if and when you are ready to do so.

n) In your imagination, you may also wish to take your vulnerable self away from the place where the painful experience occurred, to a sanctuary within your imagination that you create together with your inner-child/human-self.

o) Together with your inner-child/human-self, explore ways of deepening your relationship, within your imagination and in your journal. As that child, what sort of parent would you love to have? Listen to your feelings. Take time to explore this and then be that parent to your inner-child. This may involve gently helping your child with his/her school work, playing games and creating together, participating in hobbies together or going on holidays together and so on. To your vulnerable human mind, this loving world that you are creating is very real, and so is the Love that is evoked.

p) What can you do to nurture yourself now? Why not bring out the child in you now? Perhaps you can take yourself down to the park and swing on the swings. You can get out that old dolls house or make that model aeroplane that you always intended to make, but never got around to it. You can take a new look at your own children and go be a kid with them for a while. Have fun and be free!

q) Be the Love and receive the Love. Know that this connection to Love and to your human-self is very real.

r) All that comes your way in life, particularly when you actively enter into a healing and awakening journey, has the potential to reveal deeper layers of your past-self for you to heal. Every moment is an opportunity for you to become more conscious. Trust the process. There are higher guiding forces always working with you. You are Loved beyond what you can imagine.

Continue using this process as a matter of routine. Use it particularly each time you find yourself stuck in emotional disharmony. This will enable you to get to the bottom of things and release yourself from unhealthy dependency on others and the inevitable fear and conflict this brings.

This can also be done in an abbreviated form if your time is restricted. Ten minutes a day will still make a difference. Refer to Exercise 12 on page 349.

Write down what you discover from each point in your journal to help your conscious-awareness work with the issues more powerfully and effectively. It will also be there to refer back to so you can gain more insight later on.

Ultimately, this life is one assignment that goes toward your ultimate degree in self-mastery that leads to inevitable enlightenment. If you want to gain this degree in good time, you must put in the same effort that it takes to learn any skill. You are in the University of Life. What you have attained in consciousness is retained by you at the end of each life. That is all you take with you, apart from all the illusions that you still carry in your mind, there to be worked through at some time in a coming life with the benefit of your growing consciousness.

Trust your higher knowing. Your Higher-Self does not require you to reach some standard of perfection in order for you to be in the eternal embrace of Unconditional Love. You are in that ultimate sanctuary always. To awaken to this most wonderful of revelations, you are only required to do the best you can in any given moment—to simply have an honest go. Your Higher-Self is constant and non-discriminating in its Love for you. This greater power is always there for you. Make sure the door to your heart is open to let your Higher-Self in.

NEVER EVER GIVE UP!

CHAPTER NINE

STEP 4
LIVING IN THE NOW

A BRIEF INTRODUCTION TO STEP 4

As human beings, we can only act in the now. We cannot act in the past or the future. Regret and worry, therefore, is confusion that disempowers us. We heal the painful memories of the past in the now. We access our potential in the now. The power of conscious-awareness, aligned to the Life-Force of Unconditional Love, is accessed by accepting and working with all that we experience now. In the now we can learn from the past, make plans and set goals for the future, and then ask the Life-Force, our Higher-Self, to partner us in this creative process via intuitive insight and other forms of guidance. With experience and faith, we come to know this greater power and so consciously draw on its unlimited strength. When we forget and slip back into old self-defeating ways, we can pick the process up again at any time and learn from our human mistakes. Every day is a new day. With this realisation, our life simplifies even more and we find we have a greater ability to make the most of our opportunities every day. It does not matter what directions in life we take, or what obstacles are in our path. By working the steps in the now, and therefore staying connected to the guidance of our Higher-Self, we can rest assured that we will always be moving forward.

BARBARA AND BRYAN'S STORY

Continuing the story with Bryan . . .

As I sat in the study last night and wrote in my journal about how my day unfolded and how I felt about it, I found myself pondering on how I came to have my present job. My ponderings were triggered by my writing about what it was like when my boss, Ted, and I sat down yesterday over lunch and talked about the argument we had earlier in the week. I have never had a boss who was willing to take the time to sit down and talk about personal issues, even when they related to work. Not only is he willing to talk about them, he's always keen to explore his feelings and what he can learn from the encounter. He is the type of person who endeavours to lead by example, and workplace relations is no exception. Not only that, he is always happy to tell you how it took two failed businesses and a failed marriage to get him to begin owning his feelings. He now says he wouldn't have it any other way. Ted explains that the health of the company and his personal life now depends on how well he is in touch with himself.

When I first got the job, I didn't appreciate this quality, this depth in him. In fact I didn't want to know about it in those days, or at least not consciously. I still wonder at times why he employed me. He said he just had a hunch, a feeling I was the man for the job. I don't know how he could tell that, because I wasn't very good at it when I started. I was often distracted and kept making mistakes, forgetting things or missing important details altogether. I was emotionally on edge. It was at that time that my marriage was in jeopardy, although we were at least attempting to work it out by then. On top of that, all the personal issues of my life, which I had avoided facing, broke out of the box I had locked them away in and were mercilessly waging war on my mind.

I kept waiting for Ted to come and tell me I no longer had a job. Instead, whenever he came into my office, he would just sit in one of the spare chairs and talk to me like we had all the time in the world. To my initial discomfort, he would tell me about his personal life and his past. He would tell me things you wouldn't expect your boss to share with you, things a friend would think twice about sharing.

He didn't dump it on me. He just told me what had happened and what was happening in his life in the moment and how he was dealing with it. I was somewhat amazed and a bit bewildered that he would trust me with stuff that was so personal. And yet, in a way, I somehow felt lighter and even inspired by the time he wandered out again. He would often pause at the door before he left and say, "You have all the time in the world Bryan, so don't waste a moment of it." That just confused me at first. I realised later that he was referring to me getting centered within my conscious-awareness and getting out of the stress and struggle of my ego. When I am centered, I am calm and it's like time slows down for me. In order to get to that calm place, I have to make the effort to create my inner-sanctum of conscious-awareness and not waste time with judging and blaming.

He seemed to have his life so well together, and yet his stories often told of disappointment, failure and pain, but always told with good humour. Talking over lunch about our argument the other day was no exception. He just laughed about what a pair of idiots we must have looked like.

I didn't realise in those early days that he knew very well I was a mess, but he could somehow see my potential and was willing to give me a chance. What he was doing, apart from being himself, was giving me an example of "being real" and being okay about it. It took me about six weeks before I was willing to open up in return, and then I didn't even realise I was doing it. I was so emotionally shut down. I didn't know one emotion from another. I didn't know an emotion from a Mack truck, or a financial management package for that matter. That's what I do. I'm a financial manager. I now manage my department. I couldn't even manage myself back then.

So how did I come by the good fortune of getting this job and having such a caring boss like Ted? I have pondered on this question many times and each time I do, I learn something more about how life really works for you if you let it.

I can remember before I got the job. Like I said, emotionally I was a mess. I had been made redundant from my previous employment. My old job was one of my many issues back then— the old story—overworked and underpaid. No matter how much I did, it wasn't enough, and I never got any thanks for it. I thought leaving Barbara and the kids was going to be inevitable, so I needed a pay-rise to help me handle the transition. I finally plucked up the courage to go to the manager, but before I got a word out he handed me a letter and mumbled something about a company takeover and that our section had to be culled. Instead of a pay-rise, I found I had just been made redundant. He hardly even bothered to look up from his computer at me. I think I was numb for about a week, and then very angry. And then I was just plain depressed. I felt completely trapped, hemmed in by hassles on every side.

In this state of mind I spent each day of an entire week sitting in my car looking out over the bay reading my first self-help book, and thinking about my next move. My wife had bought me the book three years earlier but I had never read it. By the end of the week, I had concluded that I had no idea which direction to take, but at least I got in touch with what I wanted—really wanted.

I spent days trying to reach past my ego hurts and pride and feel my heart. I think probably for the first time in my life I actually went out of my way to pay attention to what my heart was saying. My heart told me that I didn't want to leave Barbara and the kids, that I somehow wanted to make a go of it. I wanted to be free of all my past issues that I realised I was spending so much useless time and energy avoiding what I had to face. I also wanted a better job, a job where I could feel good about myself and look forward to being there each day. I also resolved to do whatever it took to make these things happen.

The prospect of this scared me, particularly the thought of opening up to someone and letting them see what a spineless phony I had become. That just made me want to crawl into a hole. But then all this no longer scared me as much as the consequences of spiralling down even further.

The first thing I did to start changing my life was tell Barbara what I wanted. The next was to get counselling. Before that I would just complain to my doctor and all he knew to do was give me anti-depressants. I knew that was getting me nowhere. My counsellor tried to help me gain a deeper awareness of my feelings without much success. I was too stuck on "doing" things to improve my life. I hadn't realised then that my life began with me—what I felt and believed. She told me lots of things but not a lot sunk in. I did want to improve my life though, and I did want to face my

PHIL GOLDING

stuff, even though I was still restricted in my thinking. What I did hear my counsellor say was "go with the flow" and to accept things more at face value. She told me that when an opportunity comes up, I need to just explore it and not talk myself out of it with negative fear-based thinking. I had to push through my fears of failure and rejection and just do it.

So I did, and I kind of blindly took the first job that came up. Normally I wouldn't have considered such a job. It was a bit out of my field and only casual hours and it looked like a pretty shonky operation. However, they were all so laid-back in that place, it gave me a good change of pace. It helped me get my confidence back. The work didn't impinge on my life and I had time to read and to work on myself. Things started to improve at home. Barbara and I began seeing the counsellor together and we were able to spend time doing more things we enjoyed, on our own and with the kids. We slowly began to work through some issues.

After a year and a half, I felt strong enough to want to do more at work, but found my employers were too apathetic and too disorganised. There was no get-up-and-go in the place. My efforts to improve things there were constantly undermined by their lack of discipline. Around that time I was talking to a sales representative from one of the companies we were dealing with. He told me about a job going there. It was a company I had been admiring for a long time. It was so innovative and seemed to be very well managed. Those working there seemed to have a real pride in the place—they felt they really belonged there. The company seemed to have a real integrity about it and people had a lot of good things to say about the general manager. I was excited about the possibility of working there, but I was scared as well. The company was such a good performer in the marketplace. I was afraid that I wouldn't make the standard. I vacillated for two weeks, sort of half hoping that the job would be taken and I wouldn't have to make a decision, but for some mysterious reason the general manager couldn't find the right person.

Finally after a pep-talk from my counsellor and then from my wife, I put in my application and the rest is history. It was like the job was mine all along and some strange force was holding it open for me. I'm sure there would have been plenty of financial

290

managers better qualified than me out there, but it seems the job was meant for me.

Looking back, I can see I was doing my best at the time to live in the moment and take personal responsibility. Even though I was still unsteady on my feet, I was trying hard, and because of this, doors were opening for me. Life obviously knew how to accept me as I was. It was teaching me an important lesson. I was making my own luck by doing my best in the moment. By this I mean I was doing my best to own my fears, stay positive and just have a go. Sometimes I was lousy at it, but consistency won out in the end.

I have a much better feel for this process now. Life is always giving me opportunities that, if taken, will help me to grow. I can even see how the hassles are opportunities to grow, a least after I stop banging my head against them. By staying in tune with myself, and paying attention to the now moment, I can stay in the flow, even when I am barely aware of where it is taking me much of the time. And I can see how one connection leads to another, which leads to yet another. I do my part and my Higher-Self, in conjunction with all Souls, which amounts to what I regard as "Life", never fails to do its part. I have since learned that this is called synchronicity.

NOW IS WHERE THE ACTION IS

You can only live your life in the here and now. You cannot act yesterday or tomorrow. You may set an important goal for the future, but you can only make your way toward achieving that goal by what you do now, and the now in every day until you get there. What you are experiencing now, therefore, was created by you, by what you thought and did in the past, including the people you have drawn to you. The future does not actually exist. It is just a set of possibilities based on your potential and what you envision and then put into action on a daily basis. Your actions on a daily basis, and the outcomes of those actions, create your future. Your future, therefore, is within your control. With the positive use of the power of your mind, matched with consistent action, you can proactively create your future, even though there are still aspects of life that are beyond your control. If you face, accept, and positively do your best to work with whatever life presents to you in each moment, including your own humanness, a fulfilling future is assured.

You cannot change the past. The past is gone. You can only know the past because it resides in your memory now. When trapped emotional energy is triggered, for example, it may have come from a trauma from years past, but it is flowing through your consciousness in the now from your memory system that is in your mind now.

The unawakened ego, however, does not understand this. Our ego thinks about something that might happen in the future, or something that may have occurred in the past. We have an emotional reaction to that thought and because of this reaction, our ego thinks that something real just occurred. But it is no more real than watching a movie or reading a novel. Because of this misunderstanding about the nature of the mind, the ego gets lost in its own self-created dramas and becomes largely disconnected from the reality of what is in the now moment. Our ego does not know how to make use of what the mind has to offer, such as its powerful ability to imagine, for example. Our imagination can become driven by fear and we can lose touch with what is real. For the average person, most of what the mind is thinking is not about anything that is actually real now. The mind is full of imaginary stories about what we are afraid might happen, or what we wish would happen and we are continually acting as though these stories are real. There is that aversion and attachment mesmerising the ego again. On the level of conscious-awareness is where we are able to harness the mind's power.

Our emotions and feelings are telling our conscious-awareness vital information that we need to know in each moment. Emotions and feelings are there to prompt our conscious-awareness to pay attention, to observe and assess the reality of the situation, rather than blindly react from old fearful imaginings like our ego does.

As we put steps 1 to 3 into practice, we can *feel* what is going on within us and know, or at least discover, what these feelings and emotions mean in regards to caring for our vulnerable humanness and also honouring our potential. Whether it is emotional healing or achieving your goals, skilfully managing what you are experiencing in the now will determine your future success.

When we accept that our life is a journey of continual learning, growing and awakening, we can then harmoniously work with what comes our way. We are no longer in conflict with, or emotionally dependent on, the circumstances and conditions of our life. We can see that every moment is an opportunity to accept our humanness, to know ourself better and to gain a greater mastery of ourself. We can gather more awareness of what our human mind is doing with that moment and how it gets itself all tangled up and lost. We can relax into the moment we are in and see it for its benefits. We can step forward with our conscious-awareness, our open heart, and be the skilful manager of our life in every now moment.

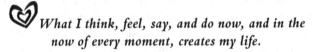 *What I think, feel, say, and do now, and in the now of every moment, creates my life.*

GUILT, RESENTMENT AND WORRY RUINS YOUR FUTURE

One of the things we discover while we are learning to care for our minds is how much time we devote to not accepting the past and worrying about the future. Be certain that guilt, resentment and worry (or anxiety, a more acute form of worry) are a complete waste of time. Not only that, they are the destroyer of a positive future.

Accepting the past does not mean accepting unacceptable behaviour. The same goes for forgiving others. An essential factor when learning from the past is learning how to honour and care for yourself now.

Forgiveness arises from the awareness that carrying hate and resentment within your mind is self-destructive and keeps us dependent on, and vulnerable to, those we have bad feelings for. We can still say no to someone we have forgiven. It is still important to hold them accountable for their actions if we can, but be very aware that seeking justice is not necessarily going to bring healing and a bright future.

Guilt is about *not* forgiving yourself. It comes from not claiming full authority over your own life, from not acknowledging your human right to make mistakes. Take charge of your life, learn from your mistakes and move on. That is how to grow and mature. If you have harmed another through your mistakes, then making amends may be important to your moving forward, but mentally thrashing yourself is violence and should play no part in this process. Self-condemnation is the biggest mistake we ever make. Be aware that acceptance is another word for forgiveness. Forgiving yourself and others therefore, is essential for your healing and wellbeing. You are learning to act as an empowered adult, rather than continuing to react as an oppressed, helpless and angry child.

Paradoxically, by accepting the past and learning from it, we can transform the way we feel about it. In a way it does change the past because we are healing our memories. A difficult past can become a benefit rather than be a burden, because it can enable us to become stronger and more mature, wise in other words.

Worry is taking all the fear and confusion that your human-self has accumulated from the past and creating an imaginary future with it, and a scary one at that. In reality, the ego knows nothing about the possibilities of the future. It only knows its own confused perceptions of the past.

To justify this confused way of thinking, the ego looks into the past and says, "considering what the past has been for me, I am just being realistic." The ego is unaware that its perceptions of the past are often not accurate, and that its worrying is simply perpetuating confusion.

Worrying is also the result of a lack faith in our ability to take care of each moment and in particular, our ability to take care of our own self in each moment. Putting this process to work in our life everyday resolves such fears.

The ego even thinks that worrying is being responsible. Our ego thinks it is doing something tangible by worrying. If we don't worry about a loved one then we think that it means we don't care. Of course it is important to have concern for a loved one, who is in need of help, and to do all we can for them, but worrying is not an action, it is indulging in futile thinking that does nothing other than harm ourself. In reality, worrying does not help our loved ones in the slightest. In fact, it will probably stress them out even more. Instead of being a benefit to them, we become another burden.

Worry disempowers us. It prevents us from clearly seeing what we can positively do now that will take care of our future. It makes us a slave to fear and negative conditioning. What the ego does not stop to realise is that because of its worrying, it has been continually making poor decisions that keep attracting to it the same old unhappy experiences. The ego is the unhappy author of its own drama.

Instead of being lost in our own self-created scary movie, we can look squarely at the reality in front of us and work with it as positively as we can. A large part of the work is sorting out our own human confusion by paying attention to, and taking compassionate responsibility for, what we are feeling. This inner-work is absolutely essential to gaining the clarity to see life with the right perspective.

It would be a safe prediction to say that our future won't be bright if we spend our time worrying and resenting and beating ourself up with guilt and so on. Our future depends on how we take care of ourself today, everyday.

I am in charge of my life. With the laws of Consciousness as my guide, I will create peace, fulfillment and abundance.

HUMAN BEINGS LEARN BY TRIAL AND ERROR

Having gained a few insights into the nature of our troubles, our ego has a tendency to think that it has got it all figured out and becomes attached to this belief. We don't truly know if we have genuinely learned something, however, until we have attempted to put it into action. In doing so, our ego discovers that there is a lot more to learn. Our ego's pride tends to get upset at this and falls into thinking that it is all too hard and that life is unfair. The ego just makes it hard for itself by trying to grasp at the reward without doing the real work.

In relation to this, unrealistic expectations placed on children to get things right first time is a very sad and common theme. Children often impose these expectations on themselves as well. As a therapist, this is one of the most common stories my clients share with me about their dysfunctional childhood experiences. Once their awareness is awakened to the destructiveness of this type of thinking, it is often a shock to my clients to realise how much their lives have been affected by it.

In reality, one of the most joyful and satisfying experiences a child can have is the freedom and encouragement to explore new things. There is a certain thrill about approaching a new project in various different ways, suffering a bit of frustration at times, but with some gentle guidance and encouragement, finally mastering a new skill. If the parental guidance is appropriate, what the child will remember the most is the excitement of the achievement. All the mistakes and frustrations along the way will not be regarded as a problem, rather, they will be regarded as the natural stepping-stones to success. As a result of this positive mentoring, the child grows up confident in his/her natural abilities and creative power. Disappointments are taken in one's stride without a sense of reduced self-worth.

How different it is when a child is expected to get a task right the first time. When this does not happen, the child may be criticised and ridiculed when he/she naturally lacks understanding or stumbles over new challenges of coordination and problem solving. Fear and shame quickly invades the experience, and trying new things soon becomes a source of anxiety. A lack of self-confidence and creativity is the inevitable result, along with a limited ability to effectively face life's challenges.

It is vital to understand that trial and error is a natural and essential mode of learning for any human being. Denying this fact is a fast-track to suffering. Everything takes time to learn, no matter how academically clever we are, no matter how naturally adept we may be in something.

Playing golf is a good analogy for this. You can digest a library full of golf books and DVDs but it is a very different matter when it comes to placing that little white ball onto the tee and slogging it straight and high down the fairway, especially if there is a group of onlookers. If you think learning to play golf is hard, try changing an old ingrained habit, such as regret or worry. It can be done, but it takes time, persistence and a lot of trial and error.

It is impossible to grasp the nuances of such complex tasks in a short time. Repeated experience is required to simply gain awareness of what there is to grasp.

How long did it take you to learn your trade, or to gain your diploma or degree? How much effort did you put into that? Do you think mastering your human mind is going to be any easier? Think again. It is your life's work, and be sure that everything else depends on it. Being skilful at caring for your mind is the foundation of all your happiness and wellbeing in every area of your life.

Be very aware, therefore, of when you are being hard on yourself for not getting things "right". Fully mastering some deep issues may not even be possible in your lifetime, but learning to skilfully manage these issues certainly is possible. Other issues go less deep, and with persistence can be completely overcome.

I am routinely helping people manage and even overcome self-defeating behaviours, just as I have overcome the chronic depression of my past. Often more orthodox therapists have given up on these people. My clients are often told that medication is their only solution. I have had the pleasure of showing them otherwise.

To achieve this success, each of these people has learned to accept and care for their human-self, using their own adapted variations of this powerful process. Their success was assured, because they did not give up. They have learned to open their hearts to what is in front of them in each moment and make the most of it.

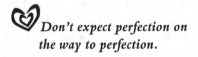

Don't expect perfection on the way to perfection.

DISCIPLINE, ONE DAY AT A TIME.

Putting this process into action requires discipline. Discipline in the form of persistence, determination, and structure is essential for facing life's challenges and creating the life you want. Discipline brings with it freedom to be who you want to be, but only if this discipline serves the heart, the greater principles of your Higher-Self.

Unfortunately, for many people, the word *discipline* brings up bad memories of being dominated by unskilful parents or other authority figures. When a child is disciplined with unrealistic expectations and harsh judgment, necessary guidance becomes oppressive and Soul-destroying. The child either gives up, rebels, or becomes an unthinking conformist, or an unfeeling perfectionist on the road to a heart attack before the age of fifty. Depression, anger and anxiety are common consequences.

When the discipline is erratic and contradictory, the child becomes confused, scattered, angry and fearful. There can be a lack of consistency in adult life, leading to many disappointments. The individual's personality can often lack sincerity, trust and trustworthiness, due to not having someone to rely on as a child.

When the child gets too little discipline and is left alone too often without positive mentoring, there develops a shallowness and a lack of commitment. Depression and various habits of trying to escape life may develop, because the child didn't learn how to push through with difficult tasks.

When discipline is rightly employed, our conscious-awareness develops a great strength of will that serves our highest good. Setting up and persisting with daily routines such as reading, journaling, and meditating as a process of caring for our human-self, develops within us an ability to stay above our old negative conditioning. With persistence, new life-sustaining habits are built into our mind, over-writing our old self-defeating habits. As I mentioned in the previous chapter, it can be hard work at first, but it gets increasingly easier as time goes by.

Discipline is also much easier when you divide it into small chunks. Life is lived in small moments, which go together to make a bigger moment like a day or a week. Conserve your energy by focusing on NOW. Do the best you can in the moment you have. Every small effort is taking you forward. Only giving up or beating yourself up is taking you nowhere. Tomorrow is a new day. There is always a new opportunity to put into practice what you have learned from the previous moment.

Focusing on and making the most of this moment sets you up in the best possible way for the next moment. Even if you make a complete mess of one moment, you always have the next moment to try again, armed with what you have learned. There is no tomorrow to worry about. There is only now. When tomorrow comes, it will be a new set of now moments to apply your ongoing process to. If you want to climb a mountain, start with the rock in front of you, and then the next one and so on. If you continue to look up at the peak and allow yourself to keep being daunted by it, you are likely to give up. It is how we do the journey, including taking care of our human-self along the way, that makes all the difference. Reaching the peak is then an inevitable reality.

When discipline serves my heart, my Higher-Self, it sets me free to be who I want to be. Wise discipline is strength of will aligned to conscious-awareness.

Goal Setting

Discipline is about setting goals and creating routines and then sticking by them. It is about your commitment to your life. This brings forth the power of your potential and an opportunity to gain more awareness of how to care for your vulnerable human-self.

When we set a goal, we are focusing ourself on a definite course of action. In the course of trying to create this particular outcome, we inevitably run into obstacles in the form of other people, physical and environmental limitations and, in particular, our own negative conditioning. This unpredictability must be accepted as part of the journey.

Whilst we are working toward accomplishing a chosen goal, we are learning, healing and growing along the way. To our unaware ego, this can be a source of frustration and inevitable conflict. The ego thinks events should unfold precisely the way that it wants. Our ego, however, is just being grandiose. Our ego often thinks it has some sort of godly powers over life, the universe and everything. But then in the next moment, it thinks it has no power at all, because it starts blaming others when things go wrong. We don't like accepting that we are human and therefore often confused and unaware, just like the other human beings we are relying on to help us achieve our goals. This is reality and therefore an inevitable and natural part of the journey. The more we accept what comes to us in every moment and positively work with it, the more efficient our journey to our goal will be.

Setting goals is essential for giving your life conscious direction. Goals can be short, medium or long term. If you don't take responsibility for your direction in life, you risk being taken over by your negative conditioning and also by other people's agendas. You risk not paying attention to what feels right for you.

Regularly keeping track of your goals and your progress in your journal is essential to success. If you don't, it is very easy to get distracted and forget your intensions. Six months later, you may suddenly remember the goal that you set and wonder how you lost track of it.

Using your journal in this way is like managing a business, your life business. A manager is lost without his/her work dairy and frequent staff meetings that keep track of progress and problems. Your mind is the staff, who you have been given the responsibility to manage.

In every moment I have the power of choice, and the opportunity to learn from the experience of every choice.

Creating Routines

Routines are essential for ensuring that your journey toward your goal stays on track. For instance; getting up earlier than normal may help you achieve your goals. Your human body/mind may not agree with this routine, but your conscious-awareness, utilizing your will, must override this. To carry this extra load, you may also need to improve your diet and get to bed earlier.

You create this new routine and keep it consistent by using your conscious-awareness.

The old habits will naturally resist. The primal body/mind is a habit bound creature. Habit forming is important for survival and efficiency. It gives our conscious-awareness less to do, so we can get on with more important things. When it comes to changing a habit, it is you as conscious-awareness who must make this happen. The new habit must be burnt into the brain's synaptic pathways while the old habits are erased. Erasing these old habits means going against them, driving through them, with the new program. To use the previous example, getting out of bed earlier than usual might feel like pushing against a heavy object. We may literally need to let out a roar of galvanized strength and determination to push our human-self out of bed. In order to achieve our goals, that are envisaged and created by our conscious-awareness so that we can express our potential, we must not let ourself be controlled by our old blind habit-bound mind that clings to the same old ways. Our conscious-awareness is the guardian and facilitator of our potential.

Your body/mind is your vehicle in this life. You, as conscious-awareness, are the driver. It is like riding a horse. You train the horse and guide the horse, not the other way around. A well trained horse knows what to do in a way that is in harmony with the rider, but the rider must ultimately be in control. It is not the horse's fault if it does not know where it is going. In order to achieve your goal, you must take full responsibility for what is required. You must implement self-empowering behaviours and persist with them until they become the new habit. Routines are essential therefore, for creating new life-enhancing habits. After all, that is how most of your conditioning was created in the first place.

Of course, in the process of galvanizing our will and pushing through with the new routine, it is important not to abuse ourself. There must be a balance between nurturing our human-self and expanding it. When we push ourself, we often trigger old emotional wounds that can start to undermine our progress. This is one of the challenges of discipline. This must be accepted. Time out needs to be taken to process and heal these old wounds in order to gain the strength to push forward once again. Slow and steady wins the race when dealing with our humanness, otherwise we are likely to give up, or if we keep driving through regardless, we could burn out.

Reading, journaling and meditating, for example, needs to be set to a routine to ensure that time is created for it.

Of course routines, as well as goals, may need to be adjusted as we gain more awareness of what is best for us along the way.

Creating constructive routines in my life is a part of setting in place in my mind the life-enhancing programs that will create the life that I want.

PREDICTING THE FUTURE: THE QUESTION OF CLAIRVOYANCE

In an attempt to gain some insight about what is happening in our life, many of us seek the assistance of a clairvoyant.[54] Many of my clients and students seek advice from me about this. I find there is much confusion about the usefulness of clairvoyance and whether it is real or not.

Clairvoyants have a particular natural ability that enables them to consciously tap into a wider spectrum of consciousness that is loosely termed the spirit world, or the quantum field, if you are a physicist. We all have this ability, but for most of us it lies deeper within our subconscious. We can all use this ability by listening to our intuition, or gut feeling, as it is often called. I will talk more about this shortly. For the clairvoyant, the channel to the spirit world (I am talking here about the collective human mind and consciousness and certain guiding forces. I am not meaning that clairvoyants are closer to God than you or I as such) is more open in a certain way to their conscious-awareness.

In order to make constructive use of this information, like any professional, a clairvoyant must be skilled in many areas, including psychology and counselling and also in their own personal development and integrity. A skilled clairvoyant can provide a very important service to humanity as a sort of go

---

[54] http://www.parapsych.org/index.html

between, bridging the consciousness gap between the human mind and the higher dimensions of the spirit world.

Clairvoyants can tell us about our potential future and offer deeper insights about our past. They can also connect us with discarnate Souls or Spirit Guides that are intimately involved in helping us along in life.

Without such professional knowledge and personal development, an unskilled clairvoyant may be prone to distorting the message with their own ego neediness, bias and confusion. There is also the likelihood of attracting discarnate Souls of a low consciousness that may seek to cause mischief rather than be helpful.

In speaking about this I might seem like I am contradicting myself. Before I was saying that there *is no* future. Now I am saying that our future can be predicted. Let me explain how it works. Even when a clairvoyant tells us about our future, they are still describing possible outcomes that are dependent on how you and I may act in every now moment. In the ultimate knowing of the Universal Life-Force, all possibilities are known, because all beings and their potential, according to their level of consciousness, are a part of the Universal Life-Force. The ultimate knowing of Karma would not be possible otherwise.

Predicting our future is made more possible by the fact that human beings are creatures of habit. We are deeply bound to our particular character and our social conditioning, as well as to the intentions that our Soul has set for a particular life. We are therefore, in many ways, very predictable. When we seek the counsel of a clairvoyant, that person is picking up from universal consciousness the potential outcomes of who we are now. The actual outcome of our life path can turn out to be better or worse, depending on whether we take daily responsibility for caring for our mind or not. In other words, we are not ultimately bound by that prediction, but we are unlikely to veer so off course, or become so suddenly enlightened, that information forwarded to us by a skilled clairvoyant would be rendered meaningless.

A consultation with a skilled clairvoyant is simply another form of counselling that is there to give us insights about ourself and life. Its higher purpose is to help us take responsibility for our life. A skilled clairvoyant approaches their interaction with us with this in mind. They are helping us to help ourself.

On the other hand, a clairvoyant who is unskilled and perhaps lacking in integrity may play on our ego's fears. As a part of worrying, our ego may take us to a clairvoyant to find out about our future in order to somehow feel more in control. The ego wants to hear something positive in order give it some relief from its worrying. Instead of wanting to face our fears and insecurities, our ego is actually trying to avoid them. The ego is foolishly trying to outsmart Life. In this instance, we are not taking conscious responsibility for our mind. We are instead indulging our fears. When this is the case, we are at risk of attracting to us unhelpful forms of guidance.

When I was thirty, I sort the counsel of a clairvoyant for the first time. I was doing my best to take responsibility for my life and so I attracted to myself a practitioner who was skilled and honest. Through her, my Spirit Guides / Higher-Self laid out for me important aspects of my path in this life. In so doing, they helped me better understand my potential as a writer in the field of Transpersonal Psychology. At that time, I was writing science fiction, but my stories always had a deep psycho-spiritual nature to them. Also, even though I had at that time set an intention to study psychology at university as a mature age student, the information that the clairvoyant provided for me helped me understand the significance of this and helped me have a deeper faith in that decision.

Being made more aware of my potential did not help me achieve my goals as such. My goals in life were not handed to me on a silver platter. To ensure that I make the most of my potential, I have to take responsibility for my life every day.

Therefore, clairvoyance is NOT a substitute for personal responsibility. Having a knowing of the potential of your future will do you no good unless you are accepting full responsibility to Love yourself unconditionally every day. Everything in your life is there to teach you how to be Love.

To some of you, the notion of clairvoyance may all seem a bit fanciful, but the phenomenon of clairvoyance is there for anyone to openly and honestly investigate. Many have done just that, using sound scientific principles, which have revealed significant results supporting this phenomenon. To reject clairvoyance and other extra-sensory-perceptions out of hand is not science; it is bias that comes from the fear of the unknown. The most that we can honestly say is that we don't know whether it is real or not and keep an open and observant mind. The ego is being grandiose again when it thinks that it has Life all figured out. At most, we perceive only a small fraction what there is to life. We are all still babes lost in the woods.

We are all connected to this higher dimension of knowing in one way or another, whether it is the Universal Consciousness of the Life-Force or our own Soul's accumulated experience within that Universal Consciousness.

The power in me to take charge of my life is the Universal Life-Force that can also reach me through those around me, in spirit or in physical form.

FOLLOWING THE GUIDANCE OF YOUR HIGHER-SELF

When I heard someone tell me to "let go let God", (have faith in the guidance of my Higher-Self, in other words) my first impression was, "that is all very well, but what is God? How do I know things are going to work out?" The answer of course was, "you don't!", and that was scary. Some buried ancient part of me always sensed God's presence (or at least some form of Higher Power) but I didn't know God and I couldn't really feel God, apart from my belief in doing good and frequent feelings of guilt that I blamed on God. I wanted something tangible—a face, an image. I envied those who had some form of religion, but upon reflection, I realised that believing in God doesn't mean having faith in God or being empowered by this belief.

Through the teachings I was following, I realised that what was more important were the principles of Unconditional Love and Total Personal Responsibility. It was made clear to me that by doing my best to live by these ultimate principles each day, I would come to experience the presence of God, my own Higher-Self, within my own heart. I had to *put my faith to work* through my own efforts and trust in the transformational power of those divine principles.

A profound spiritual experience, be it subtle and gradual over time, or a sudden intense experience, is self-initiated through our own efforts. I have experienced variations of both since embarking on this journey of conscious-awareness.

What I have also learned is that experiencing spiritual phenomena is not necessarily an indication of a higher state of consciousness. If it is, that expansion is often only subtle, and the phenomena are just an indication that you are going the right way. It won't necessarily keep occurring.

This is another area where the ego gets carried away. All too often we get distracted by chasing spiritual experiences for all the wrong reasons, such as trying to escape from the realities of life, or to prop up a low self-esteem. I have observed that even when someone has had a profound spiritual experience, this in itself is rarely enough to make a real sustainable difference to that person's life. Such an event is more often a wakeup call. To sustain such a personal transformation, we must also be willing to put in consistent effort to live the insights that come to us. If not, the real potential benefits that this wakeup call can give may not be realised. What we are here for is to master our human mind and to literally become Love. That is done through our own efforts, and a part of that effort is the divine power that we are that becomes evident through our own efforts. This statement requires contemplation.

Expanding our consciousness is a slow increment by increment process. Big jumps of consciousness only occur because an accumulation of previous experience finally falls into place. Sometimes I have clients who have a lot of potential that is waiting to be accessed, but they were simply not aware of how to put it all together. As a result, one or two sessions with me were enough to enable them to turn their life around.

We usually need a big push before we are ready to rely on something beyond our ego. I had my push in the form of fear, anxiety and chronic depression. Finally after much hesitation, due to an old belief that I was somehow unworthy because I didn't know all there was to know, I accepted that I didn't really know the answers to my problems. I got humble enough to seek out those answers and to listen.

In some ways, I was one of those people who had a lot of potential ready to fall into place. This was the case where understanding the process was concerned. I soon discovered it was second nature to me. In other ways though, it was hard step-by-step work, such as learning to Love myself unconditionally enough to break free of depression for good.

With my new and still somewhat crude understanding, I tentatively put one foot in front of the other, asking this unseen Higher Power to come with me like a guiding friend. What did I have to lose? With a bit of newly found courage (which came with self-acceptance) and persistence, it didn't take long before I saw this guidance taking shape.

My fear-based assumptions about the everyday events of my life were diminishing. I was choosing to question them and look beyond them. It was my higher Feelings, guided by the principles of Steps 1 and 2, that I was doing my best to listen to now. When I decided to defy my negative beliefs and assumptions and follow my higher Feelings / intuition / Higher-Self, these fear-based fantasies were repeatedly proven to be false, such as when I would assume other people were judging me. I had to refuse to see myself as a victim and instead realise that every situation could be worked with and overcome, so long as I didn't give up. This meant changing the way I thought and therefore perceived things. I had to realise that in order for my circumstances to change, I had to change first. Faith was accepting that Life was ultimately good and was working on my behalf. I was learning how to give it a chance to do just that. I was finding the still, silent gap between aversion and attachment. I was getting more centred in my conscious-awareness.

Faith has much to do with the willingness to endure our anxious and confused mind when it tells us that we have been abandoned or forgotten or that nobody cares. Faith is holding onto the empowering, life-giving belief that we count, that the very fact that we exist means we are essentially one with the Universal Life-Force—we simply can't be separate from Universal Love.

It was indeed a struggle at first. I literally had to "fake it until I could make it", as the saying goes. In other words, my old self-defeating habits seemed more natural because that was what my mind was used to. I still felt clumsy trying to be the loving guardian to my human-self. With persistence though, I was able to experience this strange, mysterious force of Universal Love and guidance working in my life. This gave me great hope. Knowing that Life was on my side opened up for me many possibilities.

With this new-found faith, I was more willing to stop fighting reality and work with the circumstances of my life with acceptance. I was able to look more positively at the circumstances I encountered in each moment. This led me to do things that, by using my own limited reasoning alone, I would not normally have done. Normally I would talk myself out of taking a chance. To my surprise I discovered that when I gave opportunities more of a chance, I found myself in places that were precisely where I needed to be. Once there, I would find another link to a further opportunity. Then I would perhaps meet someone who gave me an experience that would help me to grow, which then led me to some other place, and so it went. As a result of these ongoing seemingly mysterious coincidences, I increasingly became aware of the phenomenon known as "synchronicity".[55] I could to see how Life was working for me. With my new positive approach to life, I was "going with the flow", as they say.

That was many years ago. I had to make my way through much rough terrain, and even a few more dark nights of the Soul, but the Light has never abandoned me, even though I frequently lost sight of it. As a result of facing those challenges and not giving up, I have experienced many marvellous things.

Along the way I made another important discovery. My Higher-Self didn't expect me to do the impossible. I was only required to do the best that I was capable of doing on that day and my Higher-Self did the rest. The important thing was my sincere effort. When I needed it, help seemed to mysteriously appear out of nowhere. After all, I was letting guidance give me a hand. Later on though, I was capable of more, so naturally I had to do more for myself. Isn't that just wise parenting?

---

[55] http://en.wikipedia.org/wiki/Synchronicity

♡ *Faith is trusting the reality of Unconditional Love and Total Personal Responsibility and persistently acting on that faith. Truth then speaks for itself through the inevitable positive outcomes.*

PUTTING FAITH TO WORK

It is a childish notion to think that the Universal Life-Force, or God if you like, can abandon us, like a petulant father withdrawing his love from a child that he has foolishly condemned. If we consider that God is the very ocean of consciousness that we all have our being within, then God is a constant. To me it is Universal Love—Unconditional Love. It is our own feeble consciousness, harassed by our limited fear-based perceptions, that is the only variable. The notion of a petulant God is simply a childish projection of our own ego fears and insecurities. Such misguided thinking is quickly dispelled in one who has their heart and mind open to the Universal Laws of Consciousness, and who is seriously endeavouring to live these principles. Experience has shown me that my Higher-Self is an unconditionally loving, guiding and enlightening force that is grand and cosmic, but also extremely personal—touching and caressing the very depths of my being.

As I have mentioned previously, our conscious connection with the Universal Life-Force is dependent on whether we are willing to open up to it. Our free will is the deciding factor. Guidance cannot occur if one is not willing to be guided.

Some of us foolishly think that depending on the guidance of a higher-power is taking a risk or just being weak. We don't realise that the Universal Life-Force, in the form of our Higher-Self, is who we really are! All we are letting go to is our greater Self—our ultimate potential.

Some of us go to the other extreme and give ourself unthinkingly to a version of a god that is dictated to us by other human beings. We don't think we are worthy enough to have a direct relationship with God and so we ignore our own intuition.

We are told by a self-proclaimed chosen few that we are not even capable of it, which can never be true.

The intuitive guidance given to us by our Higher-Self is like our homing device. Enlightenment is fully realising that we *are* the Higher-Self. It is like our own ultimate potential is calling us to it. The evolution of our consciousness appears to be the ultimate purpose of this spirit—human connection. A genuine desire to grow and to live our potential is an essential factor in this opening up and connecting process. Just waiting around like a helpless or spoilt child expecting to be carried, does not seem to work any more than fighting for survival in the ego chook yard. All we seem to experience from this is more suffering of our own making. Let me now give you a common example of how guidance from our Higher-Self works.

Just as in Brian's ongoing story, you may genuinely need a better paid job. You ask your Higher Power for help in this matter earnestly and sincerely. To your surprise and disappointment, instead of a better job coming your way, you lose the job you have. Your reaction can be a growing disillusionment. However, this is where you need to stop and concentrate on your self-awareness process. For one thing, Life knows you better than your limited ego-centered personality does, for the Universal Consciousness of Life is one with your whole being. Let's just say Life knew very well that you would not yet be brave or confident enough to risk leaving your comfort zones in order to put in the serious effort to find something better. Not only that, what you don't realise is that to find something better, you need new training, and that doesn't mean just academic or professional qualifications. You may also need some lessons in life to build the right amount of personal growth that will enable you to take on a more responsible job, and thus more pay. In other words, you have some growing up to do. All these various factors are beyond the awareness of your limited ego and even your growing conscious-awareness. But then, for your Higher-Self, being one with Life, this level of awareness is its natural state.

The level of our being that is conscious-awareness is always looking for opportunities to grow in our present physical life. This is the *"bring it on!"* factor within us. When we ask for help to improve our situation, our Higher-Self doesn't stand around hesitating before it gets on with the job. On the Spiritual plane, the energy is activated immediately. All possibilities are weighed up, including all the possible connections with those who will be involved in helping us achieve our goals. Whether these possibilities come to anything depends on our attitude and actions in each moment.

These possibilities and connections are like a potential outcome based on your present ability, but this is all very flexible and fluid. If you are willing to accept what life brings, and deal with each moment as it comes, with your best attempt at personal responsibility each day, then you will arrive at these loosely predetermined connections and achieve your goal. You may even do better than originally planned. Free-will always has a degree of unpredictability. This is what makes it all very interesting—a big adventure. However, if you choose to regard yourself as a victim and not accept what comes as ultimately good, then those connections may be lost, along with the opportunities they would have provided. They are not callously taken away by some punishing god. You, yourself are in fact responsible for the loss of the favourable connections.

However, this does not mean there is no room for error. We all make mistakes and have our rough periods. The Universal Life-Force in which we "live and move and have our being"[56] is always there to help us. As soon as we turn around and get centered again, an adjusted set of connections are made. This is going on all the time. We are just not conscious of it. I do not believe that we only get one chance at things. I would be in trouble if that were the case, because I would run out of fingers and toes counting the amount of times I have stuffed up!

Instead of seeing yourself as a victim therefore, you stay focused on your self-awareness process and assess what you can do for yourself each day as you are negotiating your way through your new situation. Each day you do your best to make positive decisions based on the best that you can understand at that moment. That is your responsibility as conscious-awareness. Your Higher-Self takes care of the *big* picture. Your Higher-Self knows the most efficient path to achieving your goals and arranging what

---

[56] The Bible, King James Version. Cambridge Edition. Acts 17.28.

you need to learn in the process. This is just different dimensions of yourself working in harmony together to make the most of your present life on this earth. This is you operating closer to full power.

It is no good worrying about things such as; will you get a job before you run out of money? Such thinking is not going to achieve anything other than clutter your mind and bring you down. Instead, you enrol in a course that will help you boost your qualifications. You talk to prospective employers about the sort of job you want and what they would want from you. You do your best to build a relationship with the people you are talking to. You ask if there is somewhere you can start in a job where you can work toward your goal. There are many ideas and possibilities, depending on the situation. You don't know where any of this is going to lead you. You let go of trying to figure that out. What you are doing is putting yourself out in the flow of life where you can learn and grow. While you remain in this flow, your Higher-Self can guide you by utilizing the opportunities that you are creating for yourself. There are people out there whose hearts are unconsciously switched on to your presence but you won't connect to them if you are moping around at home thinking negative thoughts.

In order to stay positive, you spend plenty of time working with your humanness by reading, journaling, meditating and attending self-help groups etc. Some days you lose hope and don't get much done, but then the next day is a new day. Once again you face your fear and process your pain and get yourself back on track. In this way, the experience of being out of work, however challenging it might be, is helping you heal and grow. It costs you little to nothing to read, write and meditate, but the rewards are immeasurable.

Due to your positive approach to life, you evoke positive responses from those you meet and with guidance from your Higher-Self, you inevitably find yourself at the right place at the right time.

Even if we don't see it from a spiritual perspective, Life still works for us in just the same way. The right attitude is what is important. The Universal Life-Force is there for everyone, whether we are conscious of it or not.

If you have some difficult self-defeating programming plaguing your mind, you need to be very conscious of what you are doing and of how the healing and awakening process works in order to empower your conscious-awareness enough to push through. You will need ongoing help with this if you hope to succeed.

Becoming consciously aware, or Soul-conscious, is getting a feel for our whole Self on all dimensions (see Diagram 7 on page 80). The conscious forces of Life are infinitely bigger than what our puffed-up little ego can comprehend at any one time. It is worth repeating that as conscious-awareness, we do our best in this linear physical existence to responsibly care for our human-self and daily circumstances, while at the same time having faith that our Higher-Self is doing its part, even though we are rarely conscious of these normal higher-dimensional events. It is all a part of accepting that we are not just a limited hunk of flesh and bone in a big bad world. We can relax after taking responsibility for our part each day and know that by doing so, we are taking care of our future. There is always a way. It may not be what we expect.

Your circumstances may force you to look at life very differently. Who you thought you were may require a radical change, but know that contentment and fulfilment is yours if you work with Life the right way.

If we give faith and guidance a chance to work itself out, this new relationship with our greater Self, this new way of being, becomes very special. This is when life and the world begin to look a lot friendlier. We are not forgotten. We are never forgotten. We have the opportunity every day to experience the power of Love that is our own ultimate potential.

When we put this faith to work in our lives, seeing ourself as a "child of the Universe" or a "Child of God" becomes a meaningful concept, and our everyday reality begins to take on a certain beauty, a certain sacredness that reaches out to us as we reach out to Life. It is like the Michael Angelo painting on the roof of the Sistine Chapel, where Adam is reaching out to God, while God is reaching out to Adam.

My understandings, concepts and the higher knowledge that my life challenges have opened up to me have allowed me to travel far beyond where I started in this life. Despite all that however, I still have to keep it just as simple as I did in the beginning, and Life has continually reminded me of that. I still have to put that faith to work! I still have to let go of my futile fear-based ego controlling each day. I still get the choice, even though it is a choice I gladly make in my Higher-Self's favour today. My Higher-Self is who I am. I am in the process of waking up to this fact by throwing off, layer by layer, many lifetimes of confusion. I am a spiritual being, a living Light expanding myself through this physical experience. I am actually deluding myself to think I am anything less, and that also applies to every other human being on the face of this planet.

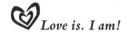 *Love is. I am!*

JOY AND SERENITY IS NOW

Despite what our ego thinks, true joy and serenity is not found by getting what we want in the material world. This may satisfy us for a while, but then the mind soon takes its gains for granted and starts looking for something else. This also includes relationships. True joy and serenity, and even fulfilment, is found by transcending the mind's propensity for attachment and aversion. This treasure of treasures is found in the stillness of being present in the now while accepting everything as it is. The stillness and its accompanying peace arises to the degree that we stop fighting reality as it is. Even as our human mind continues to react, we can consciously stop, rest in our open, flowing breath and observe, while allowing all this reaction to flow through us, knowing that this disturbance is not our true self. We can even get to the point of having a bit of a laugh at our silly human-self as it gets itself all tangled up, like a parent lovingly laughing at the antics of a beloved child, without, of course, shaming the child.

There are those who are just naturally happy due to good conditioning and an easy character. That is just the present cycle they are on in their Soul's journey. We all get a turn at living some lives with such a state of mind, such as at the end of a cycle of learning where we are simply living what we have learned. If being joyful and serene is difficult for you to maintain in this life, then you are in this physical world to learn how to achieve this state of mind with a greater conscious-awareness. You are here to deepen your level of self-mastery (refer to pages 236 to 237).

Our vulnerable human mind suffers anxiety because it thinks that it can't bare this or it can't live without that. When we consciously step back and look within ourself in the spirit of self-acceptance and personal responsibility, when we can stay still and observe the anxiety that is flowing through us without falling into it, we have a chance of seeing that the anxiety has no real foundation.

Without the guiding principles of Unconditional Love and Total Personal Responsibility, consciousness has no real power and descends into being mere ego. Without the power of this greater knowing, the ego is held captive and under the control of the confusion and primal instincts of the human-self. The human-self only displays the pseudo power of fight-or-flight. This lower level of being is reflected in all the misguided behaviour that causes suffering in this world.

When we empower our detached and observing conscious-awareness by identifying with the qualities of our Higher-Self, by seeing ourself as the loving guardian of our vulnerable humanness, a new level of inner-strength is available to us. A key aspect of the power of conscious-awareness, or the "power of now" as Eckhart Tolle[57] described it, comes from the fact that our Higher-Self, our ultimate potential, rests eternally on a higher plane of consciousness, above and beyond all past conditioning and human limitations. This power, therefore, is always available. Within this aware consciousness is the knowing that no matter what comes and goes in the turbulent mind, consciousness can remain still and tranquil, ready to act. From consciousness comes our ability to observe our life from a higher perspective.

This level of our being does not pass away when our body dies. It cannot be harmed or even threatened. It cannot be reduced in anyway. On the contrary, every experience, no matter what that experience, only makes our conscious-awareness stronger and grander. To consciously identify with this greater self enables

---

[57] http://en.wikipedia.org/wiki/Eckhart_Tolle

us to observe our own mind and the world around us through the eyes of our Higher-Self. Even if our perception shifts just a few degrees into the awareness of our Higher-Self, a profound awakening is assured.

If this greater self was not a true reality, then of course we would just be deluding ourself. Any attempt to live this process, no matter how dedicated we may be, would have little or no benefit. This is not the case, however. Naturally, every individual is going to have a different experience when it comes to embarking on and travelling this journey. This difference in experience has to do with our particular character, the degree of confusion that we carry in our mind, the level of maturity of our Soul's experience and so on. The Universal Life-Force, our Higher-Self is there constantly for our growing awareness to tap into. It never wavers.

When we identify ourself with our Higher-Self and do our best to be the loving guardian for our humanness on a daily basis, we are actively creating a sanctuary of loving kindness, forgiveness, acceptance, clarity, commitment and so on for our vulnerable human mind to flow through. In effect, we have created a controlled environment within our conscious-awareness that insulates us from the negativity of the world around us, and even the negativity of our own conditioning. This is transcendence. Contemplate this. It is very important to understand.

Joy is a natural result of being centered in conscious-awareness. Joy, flowing from the heart of consciousness, does not depend on the conditions and circumstances of our everyday changing human affairs. When centered in conscious-awareness, even when we are in the midst of a difficult challenge, joy can be found. It is the deep intuitive knowing that we are eternal consciousness, free in the embrace of Light/Life/Love, not ego that is dependent on the material world.

This does not cut us off from the world—the opposite in fact. We are in the world, interacting with it, but less likely to be thrown off centre by it. We are not building our house (emotional security) on the shifting sand of this impermanent material world. We are building our house on the rock of our Higher-Self that is always there and is always dependable. As a result, we see the reality of things more clearly and can respond to the world around us more effectively. We have taken command of our own mind. We are now creating our own reality, a reality that is in tune with the higher laws of consciousness, regardless of how out of tune everyone else is.

Our conscious-awareness has a greater power to Love. This is the power to Love Unconditionally. This is the ultimate power. This true Love is difficult for the ego to grasp. Ego is created out of conditioned love. Unconditional Love can even scare the ego because true Love can see straight through the ego's facade. In contrast, the hearts of those who are humble (which is a deep, quiet inner-strength) and wise know this Love as their foundation in life.

Mahatma Gandhi[58] (2-10-1869-30-1-1948) provided us with a great example of this power of conscious-awareness. His faith in Unconditional Love and Total Personal Responsibility was unwavering. This one skinny little man was able to unshackle India from its unjust subjugation by the British Empire without the use of brute force. He also managed to calm and constructively direct the volatile passions of the Indian people. No matter how many times he was thrown into prison. No matter what the challenge or hardship, Gandhi was always able to return to a state of joy and serenity. His greatest weapon was his own self-awareness process.

His final act of passive resistance that broke the back of Britain's control over India was achieved through weeks of meditation. While Indian statesmen were waiting impatiently for their leader, Gandhi, to offer them insights as to what to do next, Gandhi simply continued to meditate and contemplate. Finally he came up with a strategy that was so simple and yet so powerful that only a supreme consciousness could have known of the potential of the act. I encourage you to study the life of Mahatma Gandhi. You will learn much from his example. A quick way to do this is to watch the Academy Award winning movie, "Gandhi",[59] that was made about his life. I recommend this to all my students.

---

[58] http://en.wikipedia.org/wiki/Mohandas_Karamchand_Gandhi
[59] Gandhi (1982) Director: Richard Attenborough. Studio: Sony Pictures.

Joy and serenity is within your power to create here and now, regardless of your circumstances in life. It is the very core of your being, your true home and refuge from the confusion of this world and your own human mind.

> *My conscious-awareness is my sanctuary, where I am one with Life itself, where my natural state is joy and serenity can be found, even in the midst of the storms of life.*

After the Step 4 summary, Exercise 11 "Deep Processing: Part 2" continues with questions 4 and 5. This exercise reinforces and deepens the awareness and empowerment gained by working with Exercises 7, 8 and 9 on pages 233, 235 and 238 respectively.

CHAPTER NINE SUMMARY

1. We don't truly know if we have genuinely learned something until we have attempted to put it into action.

2. The ego's pride tends to get upset and falls into self-condemnation, blame, or denial when things don't live up to its expectations. This makes our path of personal growth unnecessarily hard.

3. When we accept that our life is a journey of continual learning, growing, and awakening, we can then work harmoniously with what comes our way, rather than be in conflict with it.

4. You can only manage your life in the now. You cannot act yesterday or tomorrow.

5. Whether it is emotional healing, or achieving your goals, skilfully managing what you are experiencing in every moment will determine your success.

6. Guilt, resentment, and worry are a complete waste of time. Not only that, they are the destroyer of a positive future.

7. An essential factor in learning from the past is learning how to honour yourself and care for yourself now.

8. Accepting the past does not mean accepting unacceptable behaviour.

9. We can still say no to someone we have forgiven.

10. You can still hold people accountable for their actions if you can, but be very aware that seeking justice is not necessarily going to bring you healing and a bright future.

11. Carrying hate and resentment within your mind is self-destructive and keeps you dependent on and vulnerable to those you have resentment toward.

12. Guilt is about not forgiving yourself. Acceptance is another word for forgiveness.

13. A difficult past can become a benefit rather than be a burden because, when faced, it can enable us to become stronger and more mature.

14. Worry is taking all the fear and confusion that your human-self has accumulated from the past and creating an imaginary future with it.

15. In reality, the ego knows nothing about the possibilities of the future. The ego is the unhappy author of its own drama.

16. The inner-work of sorting out our own human confusion, by paying attention to and taking compassionate responsibility for what we are feeling, enables us to have the clarity to see the reality of what is in front of us.

17. Our future depends on how we take care of today, everyday.

18. Unrealistic expectations placed on children to get things right first time can have a deep negative impact on the rest of their lives.

19. Suffering under the pressure of such unrealistic expectations means fear and shame quickly invades the experience of learning, and trying new things soon becomes a source of anxiety.

20. In reality, one of the most joyful and satisfying experiences a child can have is the freedom and encouragement to explore new things.

21. If the parental guidance is appropriate, what the child will remember the most is the excitement of the achievement. The child grows up confident in his/her natural abilities and creative power. Disappointments are taken in one's stride without a sense of reduced self-worth.

22. Everything takes time to learn, no matter how academically clever we are, no matter how naturally adept we may be at something.

23. Being skilful at caring for your mind is the foundation for all your happiness and wellbeing.

24. Discipline in the form of persistence, determination, and structure is essential for facing life's challenges and creating the life that you want.

25. Discipline brings with it freedom to be who you want to be, but only if this discipline serves the heart, the greater principles of your Higher-Self.

26. Unfortunately, for many people, the word discipline brings up bad memories of being dominated by unskilful parents or other authority figures.

27. When discipline is rightly employed, our conscious-awareness develops a great strength of will that serves our highest good.

28. Setting up and persisting with daily routines such as reading, journaling, and meditating as a process of caring for our

human-self develops an ability to stay above the old confusions and creates new life-sustaining habits.

29. Turning our life around can be hard at first, but as our life-sustaining habits become stronger and begin to overtake our old negative habits, life gets increasingly easier.

30. Discipline is much easier when you divide your time up into small chunks. Life is lived in small moments, which go together to make a bigger moment like a day or a week.

31. Conserve your energy by focusing on NOW. Every small effort is taking you forward. Only giving up or beating yourself up is taking you nowhere.

32. The power of conscious-awareness comes from the fact that our Higher-Self rests eternally on a higher plane, above and beyond all past conditioning.

33. Aware consciousness is the knowing that no matter what comes and goes in the turbulent mind, consciousness can remain still and tranquil, ready to act.

34. Joy flows naturally from the heart of conscious-awareness, even in the midst of a difficult challenge.

35. When our consciousness aligns with the super-consciousness of the Higher-Self, it is able to discern the truth of reality, the natural eternal laws of Supreme Consciousness.

36. Consciousness is like a higher will. In order for it to be a powerful force in our lives, it must be activated. We must actively exercise our power of choice and parent our human-self.

37. If we don't face our fears, we don't access the power that enables us to transform our lives.

38. Those who are humble (which is a deep, quiet inner-strength) and wise know Unconditional Love as their foundation in life.

✓ **You can only act NOW.**
✓ **Conscious-awareness is always NOW.**
✓ **Heal your past by embracing it NOW.**
✓ **Consciously create a great future by embracing NOW.**
✓ *NEVER GIVE UP! SUCCESS IS INEVITABLE*

EXERCISE 11
DEEP PROCESSING PART 2

4. WHAT CAN I DO TO EMPOWER MYSELF NOW?

The Issue of Personal Responsibility

Children do not have the ability, nor the opportunity, to take charge of their lives due to being limited developmentally. Children are dependent and vulnerable. Others have the power over their lives and children are genuinely the victims of the abuse of this power.

Adults, however, are in a different position. Adults have full access to the *potential* of consciousness. Adults have the power to take charge of their own lives. Adults can physically remove themselves from unhealthy situations through the power and authority of their own choice. Even when adults do not have that option, due to situations beyond their physical control, they can still have command over their minds and choose not to be emotionally disturbed by a difficult situation. At the very least, an adult potentially has full power in this regard.

Of course not every adult has developed the ability to access that potential of consciousness. It is nevertheless there to be accessed, and that is why adults are deemed to be responsible, whereas children are not. Adults can learn. Children have to wait until they are old enough to have the potential to be able to learn. A sufficient enough degree of consciousness is not available until at least the age of sixteen to eighteen and even then it is not until the mid twenties that a full foundation of conscious-awareness can be achieved (speaking in terms of the average person).

Because we are still learning as adults, our lack of awareness can cause us to feel vulnerable in difficult situations, leading to confusion. Emotional wounding can happen at any time and our adult-self needs healing also.

Often, as adults, we mistake our confused left-over childhood *neediness* for genuine needs and wants. We are indulging in neediness when we are acting like a powerless child, rather than an empowered adult.

Question 4 is therefore identifying how, as an adult, you are giving your power away *now,* by holding other people, places, and things responsible for your happiness and wellbeing. To use a previous example, due to growing up in an environment that was chaotic and abusive, you may now be timid and submissive or angry and argumentative or dishonest and manipulative, depending on your personality and conditioning. If you lacked approval and encouragement as a child, you may still be looking for approval from others instead of taking responsibility for your own choices.

When you were a child, you were helpless and exposed. Even as an adult, you can only do the best you can with what you know at any given time. Now you have an opportunity and the power to learn a healthier way to approach your life. Healing is for your vulnerable self in your past, which may also be very recent. Learning from the past and making new choices now is your opportunity to move ahead in your life. Personal responsibility is the key to self-empowerment.

Be aware always that there are no definitive answers to the questions below. The purpose is to raise your awareness and help you to move forward. If you do this exercise in six months time, your answers may be quite different, due to your different level of awareness then. Remember that you are on an ongoing journey of healing and awakening.

As with the other exercises, if you have a mentor/counsellor/therapist, it may benefit you to ask for their assistance. Also, read through the whole exercise before you start to get a good feel for it.

Processing and Writing

A) Based on what you have already written in response to questions 1, 2 and 3 in Part One of this exercise (particularly question 2, points d), e) and f), write down the ways you are still falling into seeing yourself as a victim in your adult life. Don't judge yourself for this. Accept your humanness while at the same time be honest with yourself so you can uncover how you are giving away the power of your life. It may help to consult appendix 3 on page 363 concerning misbeliefs.

B) Are you holding others to blame for your unhappiness? List those you can identify. Note how you are placing your self-worth in their hands instead of being your own source of authority.

C) Now consider each person (can also be a group of people such as an organisation) that you listed in point B). In regards to each person listed, ask yourself the following questions and consider the associated information. Write what comes to mind in your journal.

1. Is this person really trying to hurt you, or are you just angry at them because they are not doing what your ego wants?

2. Are you taking genuine responsibility for your own fears and insecurities?

3. Are you expecting the other person to alter his/her behaviour so that you can continue to avoid addressing your own fears and insecurities?

4. If this is the case, examine how you can take more responsibility for your vulnerabilities, and also your genuine needs/wants.

5. Examine more constructive ways to communicate your needs to this person, while seeking to understand what their needs are.

6. Explore how you can improve your communication skills, such as reading self-help books, attending a workshop on communication, consulting a relationship counsellor etc.

7. Are you expecting others to take responsibility for your life instead of standing on your own two feet? Write down what comes to mind as you review all areas of your life.

8. Examine if you have placed yourself in a position of dependency, where you regard someone as more powerful, intelligent, skilful and basically worthy than you. This is different to being in equal partnership with someone, where you are working together as a team, sharing different roles based on different abilities.

9. Are you are devaluing your own ability and potential by placing yourself in this dependent position?

10. Are you lashing out at others because they are not doing what you think they should? Write the ways in which you may be acting inappropriately.

11. Can you see how this anger is the result of expecting others to take responsibility for your happiness, for your own mind? Have you behaved in this way in the past? Did you observe others behave this way during your childhood? Write about this in your journal.

12. Are you putting yourself down and giving up on yourself when you should be caring for yourself and working toward a better future? Explore in your journal what comes to mind. Use Table 3 on page 43 as a reference.

13. Pay close, ongoing attention to any negative self-talk that may occupy your mind. Remember that you are the loving guardian of your human-self. You are worthy of Unconditional Love, no matter what. Any unloving thought is basically false.

D) If you still believe this person is deliberately trying to harm you, list what you consider to be the warning signs. Consider the questions and information below to help identify these warning signs. Write your answers down in your journal.

1. Does this person frequently put you down and/or frequently attack you with false accusations?

2. Do you experience this person deliberately lying to you on a frequent basis?

3. Does this person cause you physical harm?

4. Is this person asserting unreasonable control over your movements, your physical appearance, who you see or have as friends, or your financial affairs?

5. Is this person annoyed when you spend time with your family?

6. Is this person trying to isolate you from your family?

7. When you show kindness and cooperation to this person, do you experience this person taking unfair advantage of this, such as using it to gain more power over you?

8. When you try to address your concerns with this person, do you experience this person continually making

you wrong, belittling you and denying their personal responsibility in the matter?

9. Are you compromising your values and wellbeing, perhaps even putting yourself and others in danger, because you are afraid to say no to someone who is dominating and/or abusing you?

10. What are you afraid of happening if you say no? List the fears and examine each one carefully. Assess whether it is only your insecure ego that is being threatened, or whether you or your loved ones, such as your children, could actually be in emotional and/or physical danger.

11. Note that your freedom is paramount to a happy and healthy future.

12. Note that by allowing this dynamic to continue only reinforces the controlling behaviour of the dominating person.

13. Be aware of being very concerned about "upsetting" this dominating person's feelings when you are only standing up for your basic rights. In your over-concern for the other person, are you disregarding the importance of your own feelings, your own personal wellbeing?

14. Examine the longer-term consequences of continuing to put up with this type of domination, to your own health and wellbeing, and to those who are dependent on you, such as your children.

15. IMPORTANT NOTE. If you are in a domestic violence situation, investigate your legal rights before taking action. In many societies today there is a lot of help and protection for victims of domestic violence, providing you act wisely, such as reporting any violence that occurs to the police and thus gaining documented and photographic proof of that violence committed against you or your dependents. Authorities cannot act without proof. This may go a long way to protecting your physical safety as well as your financial wellbeing. You may then be able to have this person removed from your home rather than you having to leave.

Contemplate what can be learned from all these experiences. Every experience, good, bad or in between will serve your healing and personal growth so long as you open up your awareness to the experience, take responsibility for yourself and let the process do its work.

5. WHAT CAN I DO TO ACCEPT FULL RESPONSIBILITY FOR MY LIFE AND CARE FOR MYSELF WITH LOVING KINDNESS TOWARD MYSELF AND ALL OTHERS?

Question five is about putting your commitment to care for yourself into action. Remember, it is not about having to be so self-reliant that you can't reach out for help. Finding the right help is a part of accepting responsibility for your life, just like taking your child to the doctor when necessary.

When you open your heart of loving acceptance to your humanness, it is much easier to face your faults and mistakes. You can forgive yourself for your humanness. Instead of condemning yourself, you can learn from these experiences and make new and better choices in your life now. It usually takes a lot of trial and error, along with the occasional backward step, but with heart and persistence, success is inevitable. *Never give up.*

You must do your best to dedicate yourself to the highest principles when making these new choices. Unconditional Love and Total Personal Responsibility must always be your guiding Light if you expect your life to be happy and fulfilled and to be of benefit to others.

To your human–self, that may often seem like the harder way. It seems easier to take short cuts, to aim lower, to give way to your fears, or to not be so honest in your dealings with others. That higher choice feels right at first, but then the ego's fears rush in and try to snuff it out. Even so, every time you centre yourself and open your heart again, that higher choice will still be there, shining in its purity, calling you forward. Are you going to run away from your higher knowing or are you going to step up and believe in your greater power to make a difference in your life? If you look back over your life with real honesty, when you have let your ego's fear rule your decisions, the way you have treated yourself and others has meant your life has become harder and harder.

Even though the way of your Higher-Self may seem harder, more confronting at first, in time it gets easier and easier as your pain and confusion dissipates and your relationships with others improve. Your potential blossoms and your life becomes more straight forward, due to making wiser choices.

In this part of the exercise, you let go of what others have done to you and concentrate on what you can do for yourself. Your life, and in particular, your mind, is in your hands and no one else's.

If you have compromised yourself for a long time, then you may have created a complicated situation that will take time to undo. One day at a time, one step at a time, continue to work your self-healing and self-empowering process. Brighter days will come, because you are taking responsibility to slowly dismantle your present situation.

If you have tended to compromise yourself and were used and mistreated as a result, then you need to focus more on being responsible, kind, and caring to yourself. If you have tended to dominate others to feel safe and secure, then you need to be more responsible, kind, and caring toward others. You need to allow others to be themselves and to learn to find joy in other people's freedom and happiness.

We must all find the centre of Unconditional Love and Wisdom within the heart of our own growing conscious-awareness. This is our foundation for a happy and fulfilling life

Your deep heartfelt commitment to yourself invokes the power and guidance of your Higher-Self, which is the consciousness of Life itself. With such a commitment, you are going the right way, the way of the evolution of your consciousness, which is what Life is all about. Life will work for you in many interesting and marvellous ways, such as perhaps the way you came by this book.

As a result of your persistent, positive efforts, your Higher-Self will be able to will attract all sorts of people into your life. They are emissaries of Love, often without them or you knowing it. They will just get the feeling to play a positive part in your life somehow.

You may also receive some strange impulses. For example, a notion may pop into your head to go somewhere to further your self-awareness perhaps, that you wouldn't have considered before. You push it away, but it keeps popping back into your mind. Instead of ignoring it, it may be a good idea to follow this urge; it may be the wise, silent voice of your Higher-Self speaking to you.

Don't waste your time waiting for miracles. Such things can never be predicted. Would you know what to do with a miracle even if it did come your way? Many people, who have won large sums of money for example, have lost control of their life because of underlying immaturities in their character being exposed by the unexpected abundance. Responsible self-Love and consistent, positive effort is the key, the guarantee, to a happy and fulfilled life, no matter what comes your way.

I have divided this part of the exercise into short, medium, and long term to make it easier for you. Here is where you reclaim your personal power by taking charge of how you create your life.

Processing and Writing

Short Term

Nurturing Yourself

a) In the spirit of loving kindness, what simple things can you do for yourself today that will enhance your life? It can be as simple as preparing some good food to eat, doing some gardening, going for a walk in the park, reading a good book, tidying up that messy desk, room or cupboard, or relaxing in a nice hot bath. Write down some ideas in your journal.

b) When you have decided on what you want to do, write this down on a separate piece of paper with which to remind yourself and then do your best to do these things for yourself today and during the following weeks. Pay attention to the love that you are giving to yourself by doing these simple things for your own benefit.

c) Pay attention to any resistance to caring for yourself that may be triggered in your mind during the day. Spend some time deepening your awareness of this resistance. Try to track back to where it originates by closing your eyes and following your emotions. Write about your past experiences in your journal (refer to Part One of this exercise on page 273). With this greater awareness in place, do your best to push through this resistance, knowing that what it is saying can't be true.

d) Also be aware of any resistance coming from others, who have become dependent on you being too much of a caretaker for them while neglecting yourself. Know that this self-destructive dynamic must change for your highest good and for theirs. Caring for yourself is self-responsibility, which is a Law of Consciousness. It is truth in action. Don't argue with the other person or try to convince them of your new way. Perhaps just offer a brief statement of your intention and the importance of taking appropriate care of yourself and then get on with it. You must care for yourself whether others like it or not. All those who truly do care about you will come to respect you for it.

Seeking Help from Others

e) What are some ways that you can seek help in order to improve your life? Spend time doing some research on this and make a list of people or agencies that you can reach out to for help.

f) Over the next week or so, make contact with those on your help list and set up relevant appointments. Continue to follow through with this and keep track of your progress and associated thoughts and feelings in your journal.

g) Reaching out for help can be daunting for many. Go back to questions 1, 2 and 3 in Part One of this exercise if you need to. Be aware that you are reaching out to human beings. Some people you reach out to may not be helpful.

That does not mean that there is no help available. Keep trying while doing your best to care for yourself and maintaining the right attitude. You will connect to the right people sooner or later. Keep an open mind. Help can come from unexpected sources.

h) Be aware also that sometimes we expect help from others when we should be helping ourself. Our own self-care is our greatest asset. A thorough and honest examination of the issue in your journal can clarify this for you. A commitment to self-acceptance and personal responsibility is always a key to self-awareness. Refer to question 4 in this exercise.

Making Amends to Others

i) Are there people you need to make amends to? Bear in mind that your own healing needs to always be a priority. Often you yourself need to be on top of your amends list. We often harm ourself more than anyone else.

j) It is important to understand how to effectively make amends to others. You also need to be emotionally strong enough to make such an approach. Therefore, be careful about embarking on this aspect of healing and empowering your life.

k) Make a list of those you know or suspect you have harmed.

l) If you have tended to hurt others, what can you do to show kindness to these people over the coming days, weeks or months?

m) Explore in your journal how best to do this. Each situation may need a different approach.

n) When considering making amends, bear in mind your own safety and wellbeing and the privacy of others. Sometimes making amends anonymously is the better way to go.

o) Be aware of feeling overly responsible for people and feeling unnecessarily guilty for things. Sometimes we think we have harmed someone, when in reality it is in our own imagination. If in doubt, it may help to check with the person in question. Sometimes, due to the immaturity of the person in question, they may have hurt themselves through their own lack of personal responsibility—their pain may not be due to your actions at all. Perhaps you were simply trying to be honest with them, or something similar.

p) Sometimes a person you have harmed has passed away. In such cases you can make the amends on a Soul level, such as I described in Question 3, points f) to j). In some cases, it may be appropriate to make amends indirectly, such as supporting a charity that does good work in your community or out in the world at large. Do this with that person in mind.

q) In most cases, a sincere apology may be enough. A simple gesture of flowers or a small gift or card may be all that is needed. You may also wish to do someone a favour that will help them out.

r) If you have caused significant harm to someone, your amends may need to reflect this. You may wish to offer long term assistance to this person in some way.

s) Also bear in mind that these offerings of amends are unconditional. You are not expecting anything in return other than the satisfaction of healing relationships and freeing yourself from the burden of past mistakes. This is about your own self-respect and personal growth. Whether the person in question is grateful or forgiving or not should not influence you when it comes to making amends. Matters of safety and privacy, as was mentioned before, are what should be genuinely considered.

t) Again, use the first three questions in Part One to help you process any emotions and fears around the prospect of making amends.

u) Explore a plan of action as to how to make amends and then follow through with it. Keep track of your progress and process in your journal whatever emotional difficulties that may arise. You are on your journey to setting yourself free by taking responsibility for your life.

Speaking Your Truth Directly to Others

u) Speaking your truth directly to others, who may have harmed you in the past, can further heal past emotional wounds and also give you the opportunity to heal relationships. A number of factors, however, first need to be considered.

v) Entering into such a process must feel right for you, even though it may also feel daunting. It must be your choice, not just because someone else says you should.

w) For it to be a positive, healing experience, your approach needs to be compassionate, skilfully handled, and as free as possible from attachment to outcomes. You have no control over how your sharing will be received by the other person other than the way you approach it.

x) Unless you are approaching a very understanding and emotionally mature person, who is able to skilfully listen to and work with your sharing, your own personal healing and growth would first need to be well established before making such an approach.

y) As I have mentioned in other sections of this book, your motivations must never be about punishing another person. The focus must always be about taking loving care of yourself.

z) It is unwise to attempt to approach someone who you know has no intention of listening to you and respecting what you may have to say. Such an attempt is likely to provoke conflict and cause further harm to yourself and perhaps the person you are approaching. Always avoid forcing this process onto others. It is better to approach such matters via journaling and meditation (see pages 281 to 284). An example of a situation where an unwelcomed approach would be appropriate is when the process is facilitated as part of a court proceeding, where the victim of a crime is given the opportunity to speak their truth directly to the perpetrator of that crime.

aa) Most situations, however, would involve talking to family members or friends, where there is strong motivation to facilitate healing in that relationship.

bb) If you are unsure how the other person will react to your sharing, then take it slowly. In fact, it is best not to take any situation for granted. Inform them first of what you wish to talk about and let them know that you are looking for a positive outcome. Make a time to talk that suits you both. Be patient with any defensive reactions on their part. Guilt is often felt by the one who has harmed you and this is a difficult emotion to work with—the ego can easily get in the way. Your patience, compassion, and respect for the other are more likely to encourage a positive response.

cc) The person you are approaching may have been very wounded themselves at the time, and discussion around this topic may trigger associated unprocessed pain in them. If skilfully handled, this can be an opportunity for healing for both of you. Remember, you are a representative of Unconditional Love, for your own human-self, and for humanity in general.

Medium Term

a) Here you can look at the bigger goals and issues in your life over the coming year or two. What are the things that are occupying your mind? For example, you may want to improve your health and fitness. You may have debts you want to clear. You might want to buy a new car or travel over sees. You might want to find a partner to share your life with. Perhaps you want to start your own business. You may want to embark on a program of personal development in order to deepen and expand your conscious-awareness. This may also involve speaking your truth to others or making amends to those you may have harmed in the past. You may also want to improve your relationships with your loved ones. Randomly, write down in your journal what comes to mind.

b) Sort each point out in order of priority. For example, what are the more immediate things you need to take care of and what are more long term? Write down in your journal what comes to mind and map it out clearly—don't be a perfectionist; just get it done and gain awareness from the experience. This is an ongoing process.

c) **When it comes to working with unresolved issues**, take some time to consider different ways of seeing each situation with the awareness you have now. Remember that your human-self may be confused from time to time, but totally worthy of Love always. See the others in the situation the same way.

d) How can you change the way you approach these issues by taking responsibility for what you are thinking and feeling?

e) What can you do about these matters today, this week or over the coming months?

f) Explore ways of strengthening your goodwill and cooperation with others by gently, patiently and lovingly caring for yourself and those around you?

g) Don't try to please others by trying to second guess what they want and neglect yourself in the process. Don't be a mind reader, be a communicator. Ask all those concerned what they think and feel on the matter so that you are informed. Having sincerely considered what others have to say, you must then ultimately make your own decisions. Therefore, no matter what needs others may have, when it comes to making that final decision, focus on what feels right for you from the highest choices in your heart. Trust that this will also be best for everyone else. You can't live someone else's life for them. You can only live your life.

h) Making choices in this way leads to good decision making and most importantly, self-respect. Self-respect attracts respect, even from those who don't initially agree with your decisions.

i) There is not necessarily a right or wrong decision. It is important to not be afraid to pick a particular direction and go for it. If you play it too safe, your life will lack valuable experience. If you stay open and willing to learn from your experiences every day, you will have plenty of opportunities for more insight with which you can use to alter your direction. Such insights would not have come otherwise.

j) If your goal is a joint decision with your partner or other associate, then of course ongoing communication is essential, so as to stay aware of, and coordinate, each others needs and ideas.

k) If you need to say no to someone in the process of pursuing your goals, or in regards to dealing with unresolved matters, can you think of a way to be assertive but compassionate at the same time, *without compromising your core values and wellbeing*?

l) Focus on doing what is right for you, not on punishing others. This smoothes your way ahead, because you are not creating more problems for yourself in the future. Create peace, not unnecessary conflict.

m) When you talk things over with others, who may be involved in these decisions, do your best *not* to let other's fears or aggression cloud your heart-felt clarity. You must do what you know is right for you regardless of how other people may react.

n) If you have tended to dominate others, then putting yourself out for someone or some good cause may be the right thing for you.

o) Humbly and selflessly serving the community is often something that provides great opportunities for personal growth.

p) Even if a decision is not the best one you could have made, even if your ego did get in the way, if you keep working the 5 Step Process into your life, you will only learn and therefore benefit from these experiences.

q) Be careful to not over-load yourself or fall into worrying about things. You cannot act in the future. You can plan for the future but you must live life today. Be realistic about what you can do today. Take positive care of today, everyday and the future will already be taken care of.

r) Plan things out in a manageable way. Don't be a blind fear-base ego rushing around going nowhere. Instead, be a calm, conscious-aware guardian who trusts that Life is on your side, no matter how things may look in the short term.

s) Aim toward simplifying your life as much as you can. Give yourself plenty of room to look after your humanness. You must accept that healing your mind is an ongoing process that must be factored into your life. You must heal in order to expand your consciousness. You must expand your consciousness in order to find solutions to problems that have baffled you in the past. Your ongoing connection to your human-self and Higher-Self is the foundation of your life and must be given top priority.

t) Contemplate deeper now about what you can do for yourself over the coming months. Choose approaches to these matters that will be the most honouring to you. List your ideas in your journal and prioritise them.

u) You are designing new life-enhancing programs for your mind. It is important to do your best to live them, to be them, straight over the top of the old programs, even as the old programs keep trying to reassert themselves.

v) Now find ways to put what you have learned from your higher wisdom into practice. Remember that there is no perfection on the way to perfection. You have a right to be human. It is okay to learn as you go.

Long Term

a) Look at the longer term goals and issues, say 2, 5, 10 years ahead. Again, list what comes to mind and prioritise as best you can. Some examples of long-term goals could be buying a house, embarking on a course of education, changing your career, having children and so on.

b) Is there anything that you can do now about these matters, such as gaining more clarity or any preliminary planning?

c) Realise that worrying and regretting is not doing. It is futile thinking that wastes your time and energy. When you have done all you can, let it go until you can do more. When the time comes to do more, you will then be in the right frame of mind to effectively take care of things because you have kept track of these issues using this process.

d) Is there any research that you need to do on these matters to better inform yourself?

e) Is there any education that you need in order to successfully achieve these goals?

f) What fears, insecurities, emotions/feelings arise when you contemplate these bigger goals?

g) As you endeavour to put these new ideas into practice, expect to run up against the old self-defeating programs that are still active in your lower mind. You are bound to be confronted by your old fears and insecurities on a regular basis. This is normal. When this occurs, it is a matter of sitting down with these emotions and misbeliefs and working through them with this process. You can only grow as fast as you can heal, regardless of what the ego might want.

h) Keep up this process on a daily to weekly basis in order to stay above the old programs, the old negative conditioning that will drag you under before you even know it.

i) Slow and steady always wins this race because the healing of your mind will be more thorough and your growing awareness will be deeper. You will not have to back track as often to pick up what you have missed. Where Wisdom is concerned, there are no shortcuts. There is no fooling the teacher, who is Life itself, who knows your heart better than you do. Enlightenment on any level is achieved by your own honest efforts. Know, however, that every ounce of effort, every bit of pain and struggle, is worth your growing conscious-awareness, the treasure of all treasures.

NEVER EVER GIVE UP!

CHAPTER TEN

STEP 5
LIVE THE PROCESS AS
A WAY OF LIFE

A BRIEF INTRODUCTION TO STEP 5

There is no moment in life that does not contain a lesson. Without an effective process for healing, wisdom, and self-empowerment, we are travelling blind in a world of confusion. Having a solid process to guide us ensures that we grow in awareness of these lessons and learn from them effectively. Being totally committed to such a process means that it becomes our normal way of life. Every experience in life then becomes an opportunity to expand our consciousness and overcome suffering. We do this by facing life directly while keeping our heart open to the way our vulnerable humanness reacts to life's circumstances. In this way, our humanness is continually being lifted into the Light of our awakening consciousness, enabling our life to be an ongoing journey of self-realisation. As we gain a deeper understanding of this new way of being, we soon realise that we have the ability to face anything that crosses our path. We then have something to give to others because, through experience after experience, the Light of Love and Wisdom is awakening and transforming our consciousness as we gradually become one with the source of Life itself.

BARBARA AND BRYAN'S STORY

Continuing the story with Barbara . . .

There was a time when conflict between Bryan and I would mean another nail in the coffin of our marriage. Now it does the opposite—it brings us closer together. The conflict as such doesn't bring us closer, but what we learn from it and the way we can now share our humanness with each other instead of dumping it on one another, does.

The next night after our argument, after we had both processed our fears and insecurities, we were able to be so open, so vulnerable to one another. I am sure this is because we had learned to open our hearts to our own human-selves a little bit more. To think of what we used to do to each other and ourselves makes me feel sad for the time we had lost, but then I have to remember what we have now and be grateful for that. I have to remember what these experiences have taught us.

It is easy now to have confidence about our relationship and my own personal life. Problems are now just stepping stones to more inner-healing, more clarity, and more empowerment. Even when I don't have the answers, I am better able to trust and just stay with the process. Sooner or later the way through is revealed. I can take care of my life because I know how to take care of myself.

I used to dread new situations or being put under pressure in any way. I would get irritable and start lashing out at those around me. When people reacted back, I would then make a big deal of how badly I was being treated. My ego would use the drama this lashing out would create as an excuse to give up. It was always someone else's fault.

Now when I am confronted with the same sort of situation, the old feelings are there, but much smaller. Now I take a deep breath and let my fear up into my heart where I can look after it. I then get on with what I have to do. It is like I am carrying my inner-child in a way that enables her to feel safe and cared for in the face of confronting situations. Most of the time now I can tell the difference between the insecure child in me and the real issues in front of me. In the old days I was the child walking around in an adult body.

The child in me comes out in good ways as well. The free, joyful, spontaneous inner-child is much more a part of me now. I don't take myself so seriously. I can have fun and be silly in a good way. I have a real sense of humour now, which can also be a bit wicked at times, which my friends really enjoy. Bryan is not quite sure what to make of it. He is used to joking around like that with his mates, but in the past I used to take everything the wrong way. Now I catch him by surprise in a fun way.

My growing confidence has also given me the courage to let go of full-time work. I never used to know how to slow down before. When Bryan took a part-time job for a while, it freaked me out at first. My emotional security was so tied up in having a big house and all the material trappings. There was no time to live.

We now live more simply, with more emphasis on what is important. When Bryan got his promotion, he suggested I take the opportunity to spend more time with the kids and just create a better lifestyle for us in general. Now instead of a new car or a home theatre system, we have regular holidays and loads of fun filled family time. Our house is filled with love now, not useless stuff.

This is all because I have learned to put me first in the right way. Now that my human-self is happy and looked after, I can be there properly for others and take better care of my future.

THE ROAD RULES OF LIFE

Human beings have a tragic habit of refusing to take responsibility for the content of their own minds. Our human–self is all too often like a car that is being driven by a confused driver, who has not learnt how to drive that car and who refuses to accept the reality of the road rules. As the ego driving the car, we keep crashing into things, but we blame everybody else for the problem. When we are not blaming others for our poor driving skills, we are condemning ourself as unworthy, but do nothing or very little to learn better driving skills. This behaviour is in conflict with the rules of the road, the rules of Life.

Adult human beings are meant to emotionally stand on their own two feet. Instead we judge and blame to avoid facing the pain and confusion that has accumulated in our minds, and punish ourself and others when we can't avoid this pain. The result, of course, is just more pain. Worse still, we keep passing this pain and confusion down the line from generation to generation. Continuing on in this way ensures that we stay blind to reality and thus never discover the natural laws of life that enable us to create peace, harmony, Love, and fulfilment in our life.

To make it as clear as I can, starting on this page, I have listed an extended summary of these laws of life. Myself and countless others around the world, and also throughout the ages, have spent years researching these natural laws, this perennial wisdom. We have put this wisdom into practice in our own lives and have reaped the benefits.

Table 7: Essential Laws of Life

✓ All decisions you choose to make, make them for positive heart-felt reasons that genuinely feel right for you. Such decisions are more likely to benefit yourself and all others in the long run. Avoid making decisions that are designed to punish others for your emotional hurts–this is the source of so much pain and destruction in the world.

✓ You have the right to look after yourself and to say no when necessary. Saying no does not cancel out Unconditional Love. You do not have to judge/hate someone in order to choose not to agree with them or to even no longer associate with them.

✓ When you fall out of Unconditional Love, know that you are confused. It is your adult responsibility to honestly face this confusion and heal it.

✓ Staying in a state of Unconditional Love depends on no one but yourself. As a being of consciousness, you have total power over your mind. Accessing that power depends on your self-initiated growing awareness and your willingness to act on that awareness.

✓ Love and respect Mother Earth and her abundant nature, for you are a vital cell in her living body, and under the Law of Karma, responsible for her care.

✓ All decisions you choose to make, make them for positive heart-felt reasons that genuinely feel right for you. Such decisions are more likely to benefit yourself and all others in the long run. Avoid making decisions that are designed to punish others for your emotional hurts—this is the source of so much pain and destruction in the world.

✓ You have the right to look after yourself and to say no when necessary. Saying no does not cancel out Unconditional Love. You do not have to judge/hate someone in order to choose not to agree with them or to even no longer associate with them.

✓ When you fall out of Unconditional Love, know that you are confused. It is your adult responsibility to honestly face this confusion and heal it.

✓ Staying in a state of Unconditional Love depends on no one but yourself. As a being of consciousness, you have total power over your mind. Accessing that power depends on your self-initiated growing awareness and your willingness to act on that awareness.

✓ Love and respect Mother Earth and her abundant nature, for you are a vital cell in her living body, and under the Law of Karma, responsible for her care.

There are a thousand ways these laws can be written. So long as their foundation is Unconditional Love and Total Personal Responsibility, they will be of benefit to you.

Their fundamental nature inevitably confronts our ego and throws up a thousand questions in our mind. The reason for this is that these laws cannot be understood by our ego dominated human-self, because this lower level of mind bases its existence on fear-reaction and dependency on this material world. Like a child, our human-self needs a guardian to look after it.

Only conscious-awareness, aligned to the Higher-Self, comprehends these principles. Actively taking loving care of our own humanness is the way to effectively awaken our consciousness to this higher reality, simply because Love is the only thing that heals. It is the *only* reality. Everything else is confusion. By consciously caring for our own mind, we get a direct experience of what works in all relationship dynamics.

There is no compromising of the ideal of these highest principles if real healing and awakening is our goal.

Even so, it is not about having to be perfect. We are human beings on a journey toward fully realising these life-giving ideals. What is important is accepting the validity of these ideals and being willing to have a go at being these ideals every day for the rest of our lives. Any step along this path brings benefit to our life. If we persist, despite the confusions of our human-self, we soon discover how incredibly beautiful life can be, even with the occasional pain and struggle. Getting it right is a matter of a naturally growing self-mastery born out of trial and error and a commitment to never give up on ourself.

Loving others with wise discernment is the natural impulse of a healed mind.

If your life is not working for you for some reason or another, it is essential to stop condemning yourself or other people or circumstances for your predicament. Instead, directly, but compassionately, face up to your own fear and self-defeating beliefs. In this way, you will develop self-mastery, instead of remaining a victim of the ever changing circumstances of life. Changing yourself is the quickest way to changing your world.

As we put our new insights into practice, we soon discover there is much more to learn. When, with new found confidence, we step further out into life beyond our comfort zones, we inevitably find ourself once again exposed and vulnerable in this new environment. We may discover other levels of our wounded/confused human-self that were previously hidden to us. We must

345

conscientiously apply the 5 Step Process when and wherever it is required. Discovering more layers of vulnerability is simply an opportunity to achieve a deeper, more resilient healing and awakening.

The steps of healing and awakening are inseparably linked, flowing in never ending interdependent cycles of vulnerability, acceptance, personal commitment to care for oneself, healing and clarity, and then stepping out further with this clarity, ready to do it all again. Practicing Steps 1, 2, 3, and 4 is living and learning a true balance of thinking, feeling, and acting by staying focused in conscious-awareness (see Clarity Boxes 7.3 and 10:1).

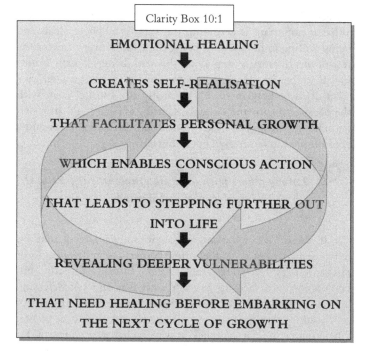

Clarity Box 10:1

EMOTIONAL HEALING

CREATES SELF-REALISATION

THAT FACILITATES PERSONAL GROWTH

WHICH ENABLES CONSCIOUS ACTION

THAT LEADS TO STEPPING FURTHER OUT INTO LIFE

REVEALING DEEPER VULNERABILITIES

THAT NEED HEALING BEFORE EMBARKING ON THE NEXT CYCLE OF GROWTH

As we learn to connect to ourself and be "tuned in" rather than "tuned out", we can act more effectively on our own behalf, because we are giving ourself a chance to see through our confusion. We increasingly gain a feel for the right choices to make in each moment of our life that reflect the guidance of our

Higher-Self. As a natural result, we achieve more as we grow in wisdom and maturity. Our personal power and discipline naturally increases. Of course I am talking about genuine discipline—the sort of discipline that comes from Love, which brings us freedom, not restriction.

The more we work the steps, the more we can act wisely in the moment and the more access we have to our joy and creative intelligence. Our ability to find solutions to problems that once baffled us increases, and we become amazed at the choices that are available to us in life. The most powerful choice we have is how we respond to any given situation. If we respond differently often enough and persistently enough in accordance to the higher laws of consciousness, our whole experience of life transforms.

Step 5 is about recognizing and accepting that life is a journey of continual growth in wisdom and maturity. When we accept this level of responsibility for our life, the key to taking command of our life is in our hand.

It is our stuck ego that says we should be magically happy without actually making the effort to learn how to create happiness in our life. Our ego is still waiting for a mum and dad to finish the job, but this is not going to happen. Our current loved ones can't do the job for us either. It is too much for one human being to take on that job for another. The power for healing and awakening is within our own self.

Life is on my side, regardless of what my ego might think. Life provides me with all that I need to succeed in a way that is for my highest good. It is up to me to understand how Life works for me and work with it.

Because of our lack of knowledge and faith in the Laws of Consciousness, and a lack of belief in ourself, we also have trouble trusting others. We only tend to give self-improvement programs half an effort at the most, and then say, "See, I told you it wasn't going to work." Step 5 urges us to confront this confused thinking and finally see that it is this type of thinking that robs us of the happy and fulfilling life we long for.

We are freer to get serious and take responsibility for our lives when we accept that it is okay to be human. Accepting ourself also means accepting that we have naturally got what it takes to overcome our problems, even though we don't at first know how to access our unlimited potential. If we never give up, and refuse to see so called failure as defeat, but instead just another opportunity to grow, we will find the personal power to manage anything that life can throw at us. In fact, feeling such personal power becomes exciting, and personal growth becomes a natural and desired way of life.

Suffering is a state of mind. Freedom from suffering is a matter of changing your mind. You can be restricted physically beyond your control, but your mind is totally your own. The way you take care of your mind has enormous influence in every aspect of your life. The relationship between your consciousness-awareness and the rest of your being, higher and lower, is your life's foundation. From this perspective, life is definitely what you make it. Therefore, from this moment on, take your mind into your own hands as best you can and step into the positive flow of Life and start living. If you persist no matter what, you will be amazed by the results.

 *Wisdom is intelligent Love in action*

On the following page is a final exercise that utilises all the previous tools to help you maintain your conscious-awareness on an ongoing basis.

EXERCISE 12
EMBRACING THE DAY

ONGOING SELF-MAINTENANCE

Establishing and maintaining the right attitude toward each new day, regardless of what challenges may lay ahead, is essential for continued growth, for increasing inner-harmony, and for successfully achieving your goals.

What this means is that you will be using the skills that you have learned so far in this book in a summarised daily process. At times though, the challenges that you face in your life may be such that they take up much of your attention, and much of your process work will be focused on these issues. You may be in the process of trying to survive each day as you battle through these major challenges.

There is a tendency however, to drop our personal growth work when the crisis is over, which leaves us unprepared for the next major challenge. As a result, we tend to lurch from one crisis to the next. This rollercoaster ride can be reduced, or even avoided, by maintaining a daily self-awareness process, such as I am going to lay out here.

This process of embracing each day is usually done in the evening or sometime in the morning before you start your day. This will of course require discipline. For example, if processing in the morning, getting to bed earlier, and setting the alarm to get up earlier may be required. Such discipline may be tough at first, but the energy saving benefits of consistently sticking to this process will soon compensate.

Of course not everyone's circumstances and schedules will allow for this. Doing the work at some other time in the day or evening will still work, providing that it is consistent.

This constructive approach to your daily affairs covers four main areas, which are: **Acceptance and Responsibility, Gratitude and Connection, Focus** and **Ongoing Awareness**.

Acceptance and Responsibility

a)   If you are in conflict with what is going on in your life, in other words, if you see yourself as a victim, you are not in the optimal position to successfully work through whatever challenges you may have or may think you have. I say "may think you have" as a reminder that most issues are really created imaginings, that we project onto life, that are not real at all. When you believe you are a victim, you are actually denying your potential as an empowered being of conscious-awareness. You cut yourself off from the power and knowing of your Higher-Self.

b)   Know that everything that comes your way today is an opportunity for you to grow. See all things as ultimately beneficial to you and not as a problem, or as unfair. Your Higher-Self is already prepared for them and already knows their benefit to you in regards to your path of enlightenment.

c)   To work with life you must accept it as it is. You must be willing to step up and face it squarely.

Gratitude and Connection

a)   Before the practical part of this exercise begins, spend some time raising your awareness of what you have to be grateful for. Looking for the good in your life lifts your consciousness. It will remind you that just a shift in focus can make all the difference when it comes to having a positive frame of mind.

b)   Open up your journal and make a list of what you have to be grateful for and spend some minutes contemplating this. Don't just look for big or special things. Have a more aware look at the everyday mundane things that you may take for granted. An "attitude of gratitude" is a good step up to connecting to your Higher-Power.

c)   Other ways of lifting your consciousness are achieved by reading some inspirational literature, meditation and music or whatever helps you to connect to (identify with) the Life-Force of Unconditional Love and ultimate Wisdom that is your Higher-Self, your own inner-sanctum—the ultimate you that you are awakening to.

d) This will help to empower your consciousness so that you can see/feel the reality of things more clearly.

Refer to Exercise 4, "Higher-Self Meditation" on page 84.

Focus

a) To begin the practical part of this process, make a spontaneous list of what is ahead of you this day.

b) When this is done, examine each point and separate fact from fiction. The facts are the things that you actually know, such as a bill you need to pay, or a job interview you need to attend. Fiction is all the worry that your ego's imagination may add to the mix, such as convincing yourself that the person who is to interview you for the job is bound to reject you.

c) Create two separate lists—one for the facts and one for the fiction. Separating the content of what you have previously written in this way will help you to process it.

d) Re-examine your fact and fiction lists and expand and refine them if you need to.

e) Using the "fiction" list, under the Heading of "Vulnerabilities", spend some time writing about any fear or concern that you may have about what lies ahead of you this day.

f) Knowing that you are conscious-awareness, the representative of Unconditional Love to your human-self, spend some time processing these thoughts and emotions with an open, compassionate heart. This will help you to redirect this vulnerability through your conscious-awareness to your Higher-Self throughout the day, while at the same time being able to stay above it enough to act consciously and constructively.

g) Don't forget to keep your breath open and flowing as an essential part of the process of channelling and welcoming your human-self into your heart of consciousness.

h) Refer to Exercise 5 "Opening Your Heart to Your Human-Self" on page 97 and Exercise 10, "Deep Processing" on page 273.

i) Now revisit your fact list and get in touch with how you are going to plan out your day. Draw yourself up a quick schedule and a list of things you need to remember. Bear in mind that this will just be a working plan, which will no doubt need altering as the day unfolds.

j) Often, what you thought would be a straight forward task ends up taking far longer than expected. Sometimes something unforeseen occurs that demands a greater priority over what you had previously planned. It is therefore essential to be flexible.

k) This plan, nonetheless, will give you some good direction and allow you to be much more aware than you would normally be.

Ongoing awareness

a) Throughout the day, frequently refer to what you have written in regards to your schedule and other reminders, as well as any fear and insecurity that you were able to identify from within your vulnerable humanness.

b) Throughout the day, use your open, conscious breath as a way to stay in tune with your whole self. Stop, consciously breathe deeply and slowly, and open your awareness. Pay attention to what you are feeling so that you can stay in touch with your human-self and your Higher-Self.

c) Now you have raised your conscious-awareness to what your day may have in store. You have also set your conscious-awareness up to be in tune with the needs of your vulnerable human-self. You will be in a better position to deal with the unexpected, and also your own negative conditioning that can threaten your balance.

d) As conscious-awareness, you have the power to take charge of your day and to embrace it as a most precious gift from life.

HEART OF CONSCIOUSNESS

Step directly into the river of life
with your breath flowing and your heart open.
Yes, even into the raging torrent of the mind.
Your heart is like a vast and tranquil ocean.
The mind is but a mere trickle compared to
the limitless power of the heart.

Let all things flow through you.
Resist them not. Watch, feel and learn.
To the ocean of the heart all is equal and beautiful,
even as the ego judges and complains.
Like a loving and wise parent,
the heart watches over the ego,
this little child of mind
and guides this lost child back to the safety
and bliss of her bosom.

So you think you are this mind?
Watch it come and go with its
endless petty fears and squabbles.
Let it die in the face of its fears,
Behold you still remain!
What you thought you needed
are but trinkets compared to the treasure of the heart.
All will be provided to those who seek the treasure.

So you think you are this body?
Does it not grow old and die?
Watch how it comes and goes as well.
It is a temple they say.
Do not waste time endlessly adorning it.
Spirit dwells stronger in simple dwellings
that are sturdy and well kept.
But the dwelling will inevitably crumble
while spirit remains blazing in the heart of conscious awakening.

So who are you then if not this heart?
Who are you then if not the watcher of things coming and going?
Note how the raging torrent strengthens
and expands your open heart.
The challenges of life are but food for the spirit of awakening.
Your breath of consciousness is the doorway to Life.
Let all enter through this door and be embraced by the heart.
Limitless expansion is your natural way.

As mind and body fade, yet this awakened heart still remains,
alive and vital in its eternity.
Be this heart, this loving guardian of the little body/mind.
Be the embracer of life in all its sounds and colours.
Know the limitlessness of your foundation
and the power of the Love that you are.
Fear is but a doorway to your destiny.
Enter it gladly and feel the Life surging within you and
see how you soar above these turbulent waters.

As this flaming heart, this ocean of Spirit,
pour yourself into life and light the way for others to follow.
Claim your destiny in every mundane step.
There is no perfection on this path of awakening,
only the strivings of those who won't give up.
Perfection is the reward of persistence
and for those who forget the reward.
To lead the way is to be the way,
to shine in your very humanness,
in the beauty of your imperfection.

The heart is an ocean of compassion pouring out to all,
and yet allowing all to find their own way.
Wisdom is the fruit of right action
forged on the anvil of trial and error.
Make your mistakes gladly,
for they are your steppingstones to greatness.

APPENDIX ONE

EMOTION (or state of mind)	DEFINITION
Fear	Feeling in danger from something that may be real or imagined. Thinking that you are separated from Universal Love. The root of all negative thought and emotion.
Anger	Aggressively reacting over loss of control of someone or something.
Anxiety	Fear of not knowing what is going to happen next.
Panic	Acute anxiety.
Hurt	Thinking that someone has deliberately wronged you.
Confusion	Not understanding what is going on.
Frustration	Reacting over loss of control of someone or something.
Depression	Feeling trapped, powerless, unworthy—internally and externally.
Self-pity	Feeling victimised by life.
Loneliness	Feeling empty and isolated.
Guilt	Feeling responsible for another's pain or imagined pain.
Grief	Unwilling to accept losing something I am attached to.
Worry	Dwelling on imaginary negative scenarios that cause fear.
Hate	Acute aversion toward others for perceived wrongs.

EMOTION (or state of mind)	DEFINITION
Resentment	An ongoing aversion toward others for perceived wrongs.
Embarrassment	Feeling like a fool.
Shame	Feeling that I am fundamentally no good as a person.
Sadness	Feeling loss of fulfilment and disconnected from the joys of life.
Numbness	Unable to feel due to being overwhelmed. Sensory overload.
Shock	Acute sensory and emotional overload.
Boredom	Lacking inspiration.
Apathy	An uncaring disconnection from a situation.
Rejection	Feeling unsupported by those important to you.
Abandonment	Feeling deserted by those important to you.
Longing	Feeling separated from an important source of fulfilment.
Jealousy	Wanting what someone else has.
Betrayed	Feeling that someone important to you has deliberately broken your trust in them.
Self-condemnation	Concluding that you don't measure up, that you are unworthy of love.
Regret	Wishing something that did happen, didn't happen.
Self-righteousness	Feeling that you are right and others are wrong and in need of correcting by you—thinking you are superior—playing God.
Shyness	Feeling that you are not good enough to stand out.

EMOTION (or state of mind)	DEFINITION
Stubbornness	Unwilling to see beyond your narrow point of view.
Rebelliousness	Wanting to react against someone you perceive as doing wrong.
Over -rationalisation	Perceiving from a narrow intellectual perspective that is disconnected from higher intuition.

APPENDIX TWO

EMOTION (or state of mind)	MOVING FROM VICTIM TO EMPOWERMENT
Fear	I have faith in life's higher purpose—my Higher-Self. I am one with Universal Love.
Anger	I take responsibility for my own happiness.
Anxiety	I accept that every moment is an opportunity to grow.
Panic	I breathe deeply and slowly and stay aware in the moment and trust that I can work with my circumstances one day at a time.
Hurt	I accept Total Personal Responsibility to Love myself Unconditionally.
Confusion	I honour my own needs by compassionately caring for my human-self.
Frustration	I solve my problems by practicing cooperation and negotiation with clear, open, and patient communication.
Depression	I take loving care of myself by acting on the truth that I am totally worthy.
Self-pity	I accept compassionate responsibility for my needs.
Loneliness	I accept Total Personal Responsibility to Love myself Unconditionally, trusting that Love attracts Love.
Guilt	I willingly make amends when appropriate and set myself free in the process. I follow my own heart, knowing that it is for the highest good of all, even when others don't agree.

EMOTION (or state of mind)	MOVING FROM VICTIM TO EMPOWERMENT
Grief	I take responsibility for my future happiness, and trust life's higher purpose.
Worry	I create a positive future by taking responsibility for my life now and give to my Higher-Self what I have no control over now.
Hate	I take responsibility for my own emotional pain and accept that everyone is an essential part of Light/Life/Love like me.
Resentment	I am responsible for my own happiness and wellbeing.
Embarrassment	I accept my right to be human and Love myself as I am.
Shame	I accept my right to be human and Love myself as I am.
Sad	I accept Total Personal Responsibility to Love myself Unconditionally.
Numb	I breathe, stay open, and allow all that I experience to freely flow through me. As conscious-awareness, I have what it takes to care for my human-self.
Shock	I stay open and flexible to sudden changes in life, knowing that by caring for myself, I am capable of working through anything.
Boredom	I accept full responsibility to create my life according to my heart's highest choices and I am willing to learn what it takes to do this.
Apathetic	I find opportunities to give selfless service knowing that I am a gift of Life/Light/Love being offered to this world.

EMOTION (or state of mind)	MOVING FROM VICTIM TO EMPOWERMENT
Rejection	I accept loving responsibility for my own self-worth and happiness.
Abandoned	I look within for the source of my personal security. I accept Total Personal Responsibility to Love myself Unconditionally.
Longing	I accept my present circumstances as ultimately perfect for my personal growth. I accept Total Personal Responsibility to Love myself Unconditionally.
Jealous	I take responsibility for my own fears and insecurities. I am embraced in Universal Love always.
Betrayed	I stay humble enough to see that other people have needs and fears just like I do, and I take responsibility for my own needs.
Self-condemnation	I accept that my mistakes are simply opportunities to grow, and therefore a natural part of my journey. My worthiness is absolute.
Regret	I accept past difficulties as opportunities to grow and therefore learn from the lessons of my past for the sake of my future.
Self-righteousness	I take responsibility for my own emotional pain and accept that everyone is an essential and equal part of Light/Life/Love like me.
Shyness	I take responsibility for my own potential to shine.
Stubborn	I face my fears so I can step outside my comfort zones and into freedom, into a world and universe beyond my limited imagination.

EMOTION (or state of mind)	MOVING FROM VICTIM TO EMPOWERMENT
Rebellious	I realise that I am a reflection of the very thing I am rebelling against. I accept responsibility for my anger and create change through loving kindness and cooperation.
Over—rationalisation	I choose to not look for quick answers, knowing Life is far greater than I can imagine. I open my mind, observe and feel and let Life be my teacher. Intuitive feeling is the doorway to higher perception.

APPENDIX THREE

MISBELIEF	*MOVING TO EMPOWERMENT*
I must be in control to feel safe.	I change my focus to loving and healing myself.
I must be in control to be loved.	The more I love myself, the more I can give love, and the more I attract love.
I am unworthy.	I exist, therefore I am an essential part of Light/Life/Love. My worthiness is absolute.
I am a failure.	I am worthy even when I make mistakes.
I am out of control.	I can stop, breathe, and embrace myself with my conscious–awareness.
I must control people so they will love me.	I Love myself and free myself by setting my loved ones free.
I am not loved.	The more I love myself, the more I can give love, and the more I attract love.
I can't do anything right.	I am worthy even when I make mistakes.
When you don't do what I want you to do, that means you don't love me.	I am loved even when others do their own thing.
I should know better.	I am worthy even when I make mistakes.
I am powerless.	By actively, responsibly taking care of myself, I will always find a way. I will never give up on myself.

MISBELIEF	*MOVING TO EMPOWERMENT*
I can't be trusted.	I am worthy even when I make mistakes. I accept full responsibility for my fears and insecurities and lovingly care for myself.
I am useless.	I am worthy even when I make mistakes.
I am flawed.	I am worthy even when I make mistakes.
I am crazy.	I am worthy even when I make mistakes. I accept full responsibility for my fears and insecurities and lovingly care for myself.
I don't deserve love.	I exist, therefore I am an essential part of Light/Life/Love. My worthiness is absolute.
I should be punished.	I am worthy even when I make mistakes. I have a right to loving guidance.
I am not heard.	I hear myself. I honour myself by taking loving care of my own human-self.
I am not considered.	I open my heart to myself. I honour myself by taking loving care of my own human-self.
I am not good enough.	I am a child of the Universal Life-Force, therefore I am worthy just as I am.
I am persecuted.	The more I love and take care of myself, the more I attract love, and the more I can give love.
I must always be right.	I am worthy even when I make mistakes.
I am always wrong.	I am worthy even when I make mistakes.
I am ugly.	Beauty is what radiates from my open heart. Beauty sees beauty.
I must look beautiful to be loved.	I am love, and I am beautiful just as I am.

MISBELIEF	MOVING TO EMPOWERMENT
I must have sex to be loved.	I am love, and I am beautiful just as I am.
I must have money to be loved.	I am loved and worthy just as I am.
I must be perfect to be loved.	I am loved and worthy just as I am.
I am stupid.	I am worthy even when I make mistakes.
I am a fool.	I am perfect in every moment, just being myself.
I am a mistake.	I am perfect in every moment, just being myself.
I am unlovable.	I am one with Universal Love. I Love myself as I am.
Life is cold and uncaring.	Life provides me with lessons to help me grow beyond suffering. I look for the good in my life.
When others are in pain, it is my fault.	I must allow others to learn from their own pain, just as I must learn from mine.
I am always to blame.	All adults are responsible for their own needs, thoughts, emotions, and actions, not just me.
I am bad.	I choose to treat myself with love and compassion at all times.
I am nothing without someone to love me.	The more I love myself, the more I can give love, and the more I attract love.
I don't count.	I am a child of Universal Love and therefore an essential part of Life.

MISBELIEF	*MOVING TO EMPOWERMENT*
I am a fraud.	I learn by doing my best and accepting my mistakes as a part of normal learning.
I am insignificant.	I exist, therefore I am an essential part of Light/Life/Love. My worthiness is absolute.
I am a burden.	I accept the limitations that are beyond my control. I allow others to help me and to serve me. I stand in my own power of self-responsibility, no matter what my circumstance, and from there I empower others.
I must struggle to get ahead.	I am the creator of my own reality. With the power of acceptance, gratitude, discipline and above all, Love, I attract joy and abundance into my life.
I must do it alone or be a failure.	I deserve love and support, because I am human.
I am unwanted.	The more I love myself, the more I can give love, and the more I attract love.
I am taken for granted.	I can only take responsibility for my own thoughts and actions. All adults must be self-responsible.
I am not supported.	I stand in my own power of self-responsibility, and from there I empower others.
I must get you before you get me.	I accept Total Personal Responsibility to Love myself Unconditionally with the knowing that this is how to address my fears and insecurities. This is the foundation of accepting and trusting others without compromising myself.

MISBELIEF	*MOVING TO EMPOWERMENT*
The world is unsafe.	Through the power of my conscious-awareness, every experience is an opportunity to grow.
The world is in chaos.	Through the power of my conscious-awareness, every experience is an opportunity to grow.
Because the future is uncertain, it is dangerous.	Through the power of my conscious-awareness, every experience is an opportunity to grow.
The world is out to get me.	Through the power of my conscious-awareness, every experience is an opportunity to grow.
Life is meaningless.	By accepting Total Personal Responsibility to Love myself Unconditionally, I enter into and experience the living essence of Light/Life/Love.
Life is hard.	I am the creator of my own reality. With the power of acceptance, gratitude, discipline and above all, Love, I attract joy and abundance into my life.

APPENDIX FOUR

QUALITIES OF LOVE	DESCRIPTION
1. Compassion	Feels for those who are suffering and does what is possible to help them whilst preserving their dignity. Knowing that ultimately everyone must learn to stand on their own two feet. Knowing when to help and when to stand back and let an individual learn from their own mistakes. Compassion is different to pity, which is ego-based and ineffectual.
2. Humility	A profound acceptance of one's own humanness. A quiet awareness off one's refined abilities, which are usually considerable. Lives simply and humbly, even in the midst of success and greatness. Has minimal needs due to being fulfilled within the inner-sanctum of the Higher-Self.
3. Kindness	This kindness is offered to all because, deep in one's heart of consciousness, all beings are seen as a part of oneself. All are of the one family of the Universal Life-Force or God.
4. Generosity / Charity	Simplicity of lifestyle, a sense of oneness, an ability to tap into the abundance of the Universal Life-Force, knowing how to look after oneself, all this contributes to the joy of selfless giving.
5. Gentleness	The knowing that all beings are children of God and a part of oneself. The knowing that no one is a threat to one's self-esteem.

QUALITIES OF LOVE	*DESCRIPTION*
6. Calm	Not caught up in aversion or attachment. Centred within one's heart of conscious-awareness where true fulfilment and security is found.
7. Honesty / Integrity	Self-responsible. Does not need rules to act for the highest good of all. Intuitively feels the natural Laws of Life and knows how much simpler and more effective it is to live by these Laws.
8. Fortitude / Commitment	The ability to never give up, due to a deep faith and knowing in one's own worth and potential. Acceptance of life as it is and the ability to work confidently with it.
9. Courage	Knowing that one is pure conscious-awareness or Soul—eternal, indestructible, all powerful and not the limited body/mind/ego.
10. Optimism	Knowing that everything, when accepted and embraced, will aid in the expansion of one's conscious-awareness and inevitable success where peace, fulfilment and abundance are concerned.
11. Joy	The natural state of mind of one who is resting in the heart of conscious-awareness and therefore above the suffering of the ego mind.
12. Wisdom	A profound and quiet knowing of the way things are and therefore knowing how to act for the highest good in each moment according to what is right for that particular moment. A deep connection with the Universal Life-Force, the Higher-Self, which is Supreme Consciousness. Intelligent Love in Action.

QUALITIES OF LOVE	DESCRIPTION
13. Gratitude	Is grateful for all that life has to offer. Sees good and beauty in the smallest, simplest things. A deep acceptance and gratitude for every lesson in life, no matter how painful, and therefore commanding a great ability to further grow in maturity and self-mastery.

About the Author

Phil began his own journey of personal and spiritual development in 1984, motivated by his need to overcome chronic depression and a search for a deeper meaning to his life. Having succeeded in his goal of overcoming depression, Phil continued to explore the path of self-awareness and as a result he experienced a series of spiritual awakenings. With this new awareness, Phil soon found that he had a natural aptitude for helping others with their healing and personal development, with one to one counselling and group work.

Over the years, Phil privately studied Existential Psychology, Theosophy, Buddhism, Metaphysics, and Hands-on Healing. He also completed a degree on the subject of Human Consciousness at the University of Queensland, which included Transpersonal, Jungian and General Psychology. Phil now works as a psychotherapist at his own counselling and complimentary therapies center in Brisbane. He teaches and writes on the subject of personal and spiritual development using, amongst other frameworks, the 5 Step Process, which he developed himself.

The 5 Step Process is closely aligned to the school of Psychosynthesis, developed by Dr Robert Assigioli. Phil is also teaches self-awareness and meditation using contemporary Buddhist and Theosophical frameworks as well as the 5 Step Process.

He is a dedicated practitioner of his own spiritual and personal healing, integration and development, which he regards as his most important source of training as a therapist and personal development teacher. He regards his life as a living meditation, seeking harmony with life on every level, allowing all life's experiences to be his teacher. Phil lives in Brisbane, Australia, with his wife and two step daughters.